Dear Nancy...

Other books by Nancy Van Pelt:

The Compleat Marriage
The Compleat Parent
The Compleat Tween
Creative Hospitality
From This Day Forward
Get Organized!
We've Only Just Begun: A Guide to Successful Dating
To Have and to Hold: A Guide to Successful Marriage
Train Up a Child: A Guide to Successful Parenting
Highly Effective Marriage
How to Communicate With Your Mate
Smart Listening for Couples
Smart Love: Straight Talk to Young Adults About Dating, Love, and Sex
Smart Love: A Field Guide for Single Adults

Dear Nancy . . .

A trusted advisor gives
straight answers to
questions about marriage,
sex, and parenting

Nancy L. Van Pelt
with
Madlyn Lewis Hamblin

PACIFIC PRESS® PUBLISHING ASSOCIATION
Nampa, Idaho
Oshawa, Ontario, Canada
www.pacificpress.com

Book design by Eucaris L. Galicia
Cover photo/art copyright © by FotoSearch.com

Copyright 2005 by Nancy L. Van Pelt and Madlyn L. Hamblin
Printed in the United States of America

Additional copies of this book are available by calling toll free 1-800-765-6955
or by visiting http://www.adventistbookcenter.com.

LIBRARY OF CONGRESS CATALOGING-IN-PUBLICATION DATA

ISBN: 0-8163-2046-2

05 06 07 08 09 • 5 4 3 2 1

Dedication

I dedicate this book with special thanks to all who have read my books and attended my seminars and shared with me their . . .
> emotional confusion,
> shattered dreams,
> heartbreaking problems,
> and tragic pasts,

and their . . .
> unexpected healing,
> restored harmony,
> and unprecedented opportunities!

It is also dedicated to all who still believe that creating a family can be exciting and fulfilling—and especially to those who wish they could believe. May these stories be as meaningful to you as they have been to me.

Acknowledgments

I am particularly indebted to the following specialists, who made certain I was on target before this book went to press:

Gina Beckman, M.S., a marriage and family counselor currently practicing in Fresno, California.

Freda M. Delgardo-Putz, a board-certified diplomat who specialized in mental health and marriage and family counseling. Freda, who retired recently, was in private practice in Fresno, California, for twenty years.

Dan Fawcett, a singles pastor and biblical counselor at Northwest Church in Fresno, California, for eighteen years. Dan is a doctoral candidate in church growth at Fuller Seminary.

Dr. Ardyce M. Morgan, school psychologist in Lewis County, West Virginia. Ardyce is responsible for testing students and for counseling and consulting with students, parents, and teachers regarding all problems affecting academics.

Bob Phillips, M.A. and Ph.D. in counseling. Bob has written more than eighty books with total sales of more than seven million copies. He is a licensed marriage, family, and child counselor who is currently director of Hume Lake Christian Camps.

Susan Pizante, B.A. in psychology from Fresno Pacific University. Susan is director of women's ministries at New Creation Ministries, a ministry dedicated to healing sexual brokenness and addiction.

Bruce R. Wright, Ed.D., a licensed psychologist who specializes in the treatment of assaultive and sexual offenders in correctional settings and in private practice.

Special thanks to Harry Van Pelt, my husband, who has spent hours providing technical assistance on the computer, along with formatting and editing the manuscript. And special thanks to Nikki Brys, a technical assistant at the Hamblin Company, for her work on the appendix.

Table of Contents

Foreword

Nancy and I have traveled extensively around the world together. I've watched her in action and many times thought to myself that the counsel she freely offered to so many should be available to more people.

After one particularly grueling day, we set up appointments for many individuals seeking help for their personal problems. One couple in particular stands out in my memory. They shared a history of affairs, abuse, and alienation. They were convinced they should divorce.

Even though Nancy was dead tired after hours of teaching, she spent much time in the evening counseling this young couple. At night, after coming to our room, she would pray for divine guidance regarding how to advise them. Praise God, before we left that place, the couple had experienced a remarkable turnaround. The Holy Spirit obviously touched their hearts, and they rededicated themselves to Christ and their marriage.

In this book you will read Nancy's answers to many different types of problems. The questions are taken from real life; they reflect some of the tensions and traumas of living in today's topsy-turvy world.

Nancy writes from professional knowledge—but she also understands and speaks from personal experience. Her heart is tender toward the marriage relationship, and she has the ability to diagnose problem areas quickly. She never whitewashes obvious wrongs but helps couples work out solutions.

Many counselors today, although professionally trained, are not attuned to God. Nancy's love of her church and its principles adds an extra dimension to her innate counseling ability. She is a serious and deep Bible student and relies on God to give her wisdom beyond her professional knowledge. That spiritual dimension is essential. Simply put, people may know the appropriate psychological principles, but without the rejuvenating power of the Holy Spirit, without the indwelling Christ performing miracles in their tattered lives, they'll lack the power to change their behavior.

It is my prayer that by reading the answers to questions that real people ask, you too will be inspired to build a more solid foundation in your life—whatever the problem.

Madlyn Lewis Hamblin

Before You Begin

I wrote my first book on family relationships some twenty-five years ago. Since then I've received a deluge of mail from readers around the world. Some just wanted to thank me for a book that helped guide them through a difficult event in their lives. Others asked for further help regarding dilemmas they faced.

I attempted to respond to each situation individually. And I filed each letter—all of them real-life dramas collected from real people, who ranged from average folks to well-known personalities. Those letters, and my answers, make up this book. (Of course, I've changed the names and circumstances to protect anonymity.) You may find that reading it is almost like eavesdropping—like listening in on a private conversation in which these people pour out their hearts to me.

In each chapter you'll find a collection of intimate stories about family relationships—the joy and pain of trying to make things work in a tragically sinful world. Through *Dear Nancy . . .* , you can receive answers and insights into your most intimate questions as well as inspiration to love more and to continue to reach out to those you love.

Many people today have not had positive role models while growing up—adults who pointed the way to highly effective relationships. They've grown up in homes mired in major dysfunction—and they carry their wounds from the past to each new relationship. Since we all tend to be a bit dysfunctional in a world saturated with sin (we differ only in the degree of dysfunction that we suffer), you'll find you can pull something insightful or helpful to your life from many situations discussed in this book.

For a long time I've thought about sharing these letters anonymously in a book to show people that they are not as alone as they might think they are. But I kept putting it off. Then, a couple years ago, Madlyn Hamblin and I began to sift through cartons of special letters I'd saved over the years, wondering whether I could share them without breaking confidences.

Whenever a friend or colleague asked what new project I was working on, I would tell them about *Dear Nancy . . . .* They would listen intently, nod, and say, "Oh, letters from deeply troubled people." I would reply that, yes, some of the letters were from deeply troubled people, but most were from ordinary people who loved their spouses and their families. People like you and me. People who faced a problem or crisis and sought insight.

Let me assure you I don't have all the answers to these difficult questions. It's easy to sound wise when a person isn't emotionally involved, when it's someone else's family problems. And you must understand that I'm not offering blanket advice for everyone faced with a similar problem to the one written up. In fact, you may not always agree with the response I've provided. That's OK. Give a problem to ten different people, and you'll likely come up with ten different responses. But it's entirely possible that when I was responding, I had more information at my disposal than what appears in this book—which permitted me to hone in on something you missed. All the letters have been edited for brevity and clarity.

Sometimes my responses may sound like I'm talking off the top of my head. But let me assure you that I've shied away from dishing out pop psychology and quick fixes. I've often referred to the large resource library that I have in my home. I've also consulted with family therapists and other professionals. Obtaining the advice of others when you fail to see a situation clearly is biblical. Proverbs 20:18 encourages us to "make plans by seeking advice," and Proverbs 19:20 says, "Listen to advice and accept instruction, and in the end you will be wise." And precisely why should we listen to advice? Because, as Proverbs 12:15 points out, "The way of a fool seems right to him, but a wise man listens to advice." I want to clarify that I didn't depend on human wisdom alone; I also leaned heavily on the Holy Spirit for guidance.

The advice offered within the pages of this book may differ from the advice offered by a counselor in an office setting. When working with people face to face, counselors can ask questions, clarify an issue, get the spouse's viewpoint, and continue to guide them as they return for multiple visits. Attempting to guide a troubled person through a one-time written response is infinitely more difficult, because that's likely the only shot one has at dealing with the problem. Furthermore, since the communication is not face to face, one cannot hear the tone of voice (38 percent of communication) nor see the nonverbals (55 percent). In other words, 93 percent of the message is missing. My assessment of the problem needs to be keener, more direct and to the point.

You'll find some redundancy in the problems raised and the answers given. I've retained this overlapping material because none of it is *exactly* the same, and the differing angles presented offer additional helpful insights.

One of the main purposes of *Dear Nancy* . . . is to let people know about resources available to help people in crisis—to direct people to specific types of assistance. Because I couldn't answer people fully in my letters, I often referred them to books I've written that contain more information on the topic. I've retained these references as they appeared in the letters. You'll also see that I often refer people to books written by other people and to certain organizations and other services. An extensive appendix in the back of the book contains a complete listing of these resources. Pastors, teachers, and other professionals who are in a position to direct people to helpful resources will find this appendix valuable.

In what follows, there are letters that tear me apart, and they will you too—the anguish is just too real. Other letters are hilarious. But whether sad or amusing, all are intensely interesting. Stick with me as we look at how holy wedlock becomes unholy deadlock!

Nancy L. Van Pelt

CHAPTER ONE

When Holy Wedlock Becomes Unholy Deadlock

Talk to any couple who have been married thirty or forty years. If they're honest, you'll hear about bad times as well as good times. Ask any couple married this length of time if they ever thought of abandoning ship. Ask about the crisis periods—the big stuff, like career changes, business failures, bankruptcy, the death of a child or another close family member, loss of mental or physical health, an affair, financial stress, lawsuits, an out-of-wedlock teen pregnancy. Romantic feelings fail during the tough times. Sex doesn't seem very important, either. Material possessions may not mean much. Now it's the two of them against the world—toughing it out, testing all their resources. Will they make it?

Dear Nancy: *My husband and I fell madly in love as soon as we met. For three months, we spent every spare minute together. We were so in love that we could hardly keep our hands off each other—the physical attraction was that powerful! Then we began to argue a lot and to get on each other's nerves. We concluded this was due to the sexual tension of our going only so far but no further. We thought the arguments would stop if we got married.*

So, we married. For two months after the wedding, everything was perfect. Then we began having more fights than ever, and now we're miserable. We've been married four years and have two children. We're so angry at one another that currently we're separated. What went wrong?

Dear Angry Wife: Your situation isn't unique. Because you married only three months after you met, you soon discovered that the initial rush of feeling and sexual excitement doesn't continue forever. You married before you rode out the wave of red-hot romantic feelings. When you awoke from your dream, you found yourself in the middle of a nightmare, married to someone unsuited to you.

You rushed into marriage without first establishing a stable base for this relationship. Three months provides woefully little information on which to base a decision as important as choosing a life partner—one who will meet your needs and parent your children. There's no such thing as instant love. Strong, lasting relationships must be paced over a long period of getting to know one another and building friendship. The passion that wells up early in a relationship is too intense to last. No one can maintain that fierce passion for long, although both spouses often vow they will. If all they have going for them is passion, the relationship will likely end in three to six months. Couples who marry based on this initial rush find that when the passion dies, nothing remains to hold them together.

The relationship would likely have died a natural death had you continued to date and test your compatibility for the two years that I recommend. You would have discovered on your own that your arguments and getting on each other's nerves arose from something other than sexual tension. They were a major symptom of discrepancy in values—a symptom you shouldn't have ignored.

Your major task now is to put yourselves in the hands of a capable counselor to see if you and your husband can learn the skills necessary to salvage your disintegrating marriage. (See appendix for specific recommendations.) You must do now what you didn't take time to do while dating. While working to rebuild your relationship, remember that divorce is, as someone has said, "emotional surgery given without anesthesia." Excruciating pain usually accompanies the breaking of a relationship as intimate as marriage, and the pain is more intense and complicated when children are involved, as in your case. You owe your best attempts to save this relationship for the sake of your children.

In our next letter, the writer seems to be concentrating more on the problem than on the solution.

Dear Nancy: *All I ever wanted since I was a little girl was to meet a great guy, get married, be a wife and mother, and have a perfect marriage. But my marriage is terrible. We fight all the time. We just can't seem to show each other love. Most of the time we can't stand each other. We've both threatened divorce* *and now bring it up at least once a day, but I don't really want a divorce, and I hope that my husband doesn't either.*

Dear Unrealistic: You don't need a divorce. What you need is a plan to reduce the anger and conflict between you. You're likely locked into a power struggle, and rather than processing your anger constructively, you're each attempting to "win." The closer you move to the boiling point, the less rational you become. Many couples are caught in this kind of unproductive web of anger and arguing.

You can avoid this trap by reducing your feelings of anger before you respond. Don't yell, throw things, cry, or use any other inappropriate and unsuccessful methods of acting out. Instead, find a way to vent safely: go for a walk, swim, bicycle, do aerobic dance, knead bread, or wash windows.

Next, assume responsibility for your anger. You may be saying to your husband, "You make me so angry when you . . ." His actions may precipitate your feelings, but you're the only one who's responsible for how you respond. So, share the fact that you're angry in an acceptable manner. Rather than communicating a "you message"—"You make me angry"— try an "I message." Say, "I really become angry when you give the children permission without checking with me first, because it undermines their respect for my authority."

When your husband becomes angry with you, accept his anger as a valid expression of emotion. His outburst may be offensive and unreasonable, but he has the right to be angry. But make him responsible for his anger. While staying reasonable, state your concerns in a logical, quiet, caring manner through I-messages. Should your husband threaten you physically or become verbally abusive, state that you will be happy to discuss the matter further when he gets his anger under control. Then leave for safer territory.

You would benefit from reading the chapter "Anger Workout: Coping With Conflict" in *Smart Listening for Couples*. There you'll find the Share-Care Plan for Conflict Resolution. If you master the four steps outlined there, you'll be well on the road to reducing your conflicts.

I believe you and your husband are so busy trying to prove who is right and who is wrong that you're not hearing what the other is saying. When you neglect to uncover the real problem, you can go on for years as adversaries. Leave this destructive behavior behind and learn how to resolve problems constructively.

In addition to these suggestions, the two of you desperately need some playtime together. Playing with your partner is always important, but even more so when your relationship is stressed. This will help you plow through the rough times because it relieves tension and helps keep a sense of proportion when you're struggling with problems. When you get irritated over something, a game, laughter, or some form of play will help you like each other again. One suggestion is to turn the television off one night a week and play games with your husband. Instead of trying to win, enjoy the game—banter back and forth, tease, flirt, converse, and laugh as you did when you were dating.

Although this next couple worked and prayed together, they need to learn how to stay together.

Dear Nancy: *My husband and I have been married for almost twenty-five years. We've made some significant contributions to our community through the business we own and operate together and through our church. We've been blessed with three wonderful children who are now grown. But our marriage is definitely not what either of us wants it to be. We're desperately holding on but tired of the struggle. We're ready to try almost anything to get in touch with some positive feelings about each other. Is there a second chance for happiness at this stage of life?*

Dear Struggling Couple: Someone has said, "Everything left unattended will tend toward disorder." Living in the same house, practicing the same faith, parenting the same children, and sharing the same bed just aren't enough anymore. You stand perched on the brink of "marital burnout," which I define as a state of complete physical, emotional, and mental exhaustion in marriage. It afflicts those who expect marriage to give meaning to life and finally realize that their marriage isn't providing what they want.

What you need most is to schedule time for romantic attention and special activities together. The quality of your marriage will reflect the amount of time you spend on this. Fifteen hours a week of undivided attention is enough to sustain a romantic marriage when the marriage is healthy. But when the marriage is in trouble, as in your case, you need to spend twenty to thirty hours a week to restore the love you once had for each other.

To salvage your marriage, you might consider going on a vacation where you can spend the entire time restoring lost intimacy. Two to three weeks of giving each other undivided attention usually brings a couple to the point where they can make an intelligent decision regarding their future. When I recommend this, couples sometimes say they don't have this kind of time. But if either of you were carrying on a clandestine affair, you would make the time. It is simply a matter of priorities. When endeavoring to restore intimacy, you must re-create the type of romantic occasions you enjoyed while dating.

During your time together, you must give each other focused attention while agreeing not to discuss upcoming dental procedures, strange rashes, transmission problems, or aging parents. And time spent watching television doesn't count. Remember to dress up a little. Spend as much time attempting to be appealing for each other as you did while you were dating. Flirt with each other all over again. A whisper in the ear, a playful hug, a note tucked into a suitcase, or a kiss for no reason will help rekindle romance. Pleasing compliments, intimate lingering glances, a teasing smile, a hand laid lightly on your partner's arm when laughing at a remark, a little footsie under the table show affection. When you have dinner together, regard it as foreplay. Smiling eye contact, suggestive touches, and intimate conversation go a long way.

Once you've restored intimacy, continue to date each other in this manner once a week. And plan similar getaways—an overnight stay in a hotel or motel—every three months. If you want to go the extra mile, I suggest you read Dr. Phil's book *Relationship Rescue* (see appendix).

Remember, relationships do not renew themselves. It is up to you to renew them constantly. The challenge of marriage is learning to keep a relationship romantic, interesting, and alive through all the changing years of marriage.

The following marriage is about to end unless something gives.

Dear Nancy: *I've been married for twenty years, but I am literally starved for love, attention, and affection from my husband. I tolerate our life the way it is for the sake of our two teenage boys. My husband has a demanding job in the health-care profession and is always too tired to talk to me or pay attention to me. I've tried to be loving, kind, and gracious and wouldn't think of confronting him about this because he is so stressed out on his job. And I don't feel like I can talk about this with anyone else because it might jeopardize my husband's career.*

I'm suffering so inside that sometimes I even want to die. At other times I get so angry at some stupid little thing my husband does that I have a terrible temper tantrum, which drives him even further away. I don't want a divorce, but what about a trial separation to wake up my negligent husband? I'm at the end of my rope.

Dear Starved: In trying to be so loving to your husband—so gracious and kind and such a good wife—you are actually shielding him from the consequences of his actions. You have tolerated his behavior and failed to confront him with loving toughness. Just as rebellious preschoolers can profit from a well-timed spanking, so guilty adults should experience the consequences of uncaring behavior. There's nothing quite like a dose of reality to awaken dreamers from their fantasies.

The secrecy you've maintained prevents you from getting the emotional support you need to keep yourself together. It is almost masochistic of you to refrain from telling anyone about the agony you are so bravely suffering in silence. This martyrlike approach can take people to the brink of suicide—that's why I'm urging you to see a counselor immediately, whether or not your husband will.

You indicated you felt you must tolerate the relationship for the sake of the boys. I admire your tenacity, but your perspective is shortsighted. In the process of giving your boys a home, you are also giving them a severely depressed, emotionally starved mother.

Becoming angry and throwing a temper tantrum is no more effective in dealing with emotional rejection than it would be in dealing with a rebellious teenager. Screaming, angry outbursts and berating are rarely successful in changing behavior. What is required is a course of action that demands a specific response and results in a consequence.

A separation might be in order, but don't use it to end your marriage. Do it to rescue your marriage—to awaken your husband to the responsibilities that he carries as your husband and as the father of his children. You might find a temporary separation the only method of forcing your husband to recognize that you need professional help to salvage your marriage. This crisis of loneliness may be the last step in jarring him to his senses; you could be doing the most loving thing by temporarily making him more miserable. If this would be your motive in separating from him, then I could find no scriptural condemnation against your decision.

Before you attempt a separation, however, I recommend you attend a tough-love or assertiveness training class while tempering it with biblical principles. (See appendix for information on co-dependency.) Then tie a knot and hang on.

Rebuilding a relationship takes hard work and effective communication. Without that kind of communication, one person tends to control the other, as in the following letter.

Dear Nancy: *I'm married to an angry woman. When Denise is angry, she'll say anything, no matter how much it may hurt me. Her words are often hostile, bitter, and nasty, and she makes some serious threats. She has a long history of using anger to get what she wants. I am lost in a vicious cycle of anger and can't take much more.*

Dear Lost: People who use anger in this manner feel a sense of power when the adrenaline is pumping. When they shout, pound, and spit out angry words, they actually think they are getting some respect, that others will listen, that they are in charge and doing something that will benefit themselves. Actually, of course, the opposite is true.

Denise's outbursts may be offensive and unreasonable, but she has the right to be angry. And though her anger may not be pleasant, it doesn't signal the end of your marriage. The best marriages allow room for some turbulence. Here are some suggestions to help you maintain your sanity when she blows it.

Denise may attempt to blame you for her anger. Refuse to accept this kind of faulty thinking. You are not responsible for nor are you the cause of her anger, despite what she says. She is choosing to display anger, and in all probability, it is an attempt to get you to conform to her wishes. Refuse to let her manipulate you through anger.

And stay reasonable. Even though Denise curses, yells, and acts disrespectful, you can stay reasonable. Quietly confront her with the reality of the situation. With controlled assertiveness, state your thoughts, feelings, and convictions in I-message form: "I'm really hurt when I'm threatened with divorce because it breaks the ground rule we laid down and makes me feel insecure in your affection." Continue stating your comments in a logical but caring manner.

Should she become increasingly abusive physically or emotionally, you may have to exit the scene. Calmly state that you will be happy to discuss the matter further when she gets her anger under control. Then retreat to another room or go out for a walk until she calms down.

Through all of this, refrain from apologizing to her. Some people become so terrified of precipitating another tantrum that they rush to avert it through apologies. But a verbally abusive partner doesn't deserve an apology. You may be partially responsible for the problem, but to reward her offensive behavior with apologies teaches her that such behavior succeeds. An apology may be appropriate later, when she is under control. Save it for then.

Should Denise show progress in controlling her anger, reinforce her positive behavior by expressing your willingness to listen and negotiate. Don't let her verbal abuse devastate your self-worth. Her put-downs don't make you inferior.

If after all this you see no improvement, consult a counselor who specializes in anger management. Insist that Denise attend an anger-management class. If she refuses, you may have to resort to "the ultimate ultimatum." (I've described "the ultimate ultimatum" in my book *Smart Listening for Couples,* see the appendix. There's an example of it on pages 119, 120 of this book.)

Professional support is often necessary as a less-than-perfect marriage begins to disintegrate after the first flush of passion begins to wane. The next question is typical for many who married before they got to know each other properly.

Dear Nancy: *My husband, Jim, and I married ten years ago for all the wrong reasons. We both had difficult childhoods and didn't have many friends and were very lonely. Neither of us had much money, and we both thought we'd be more financially stable if we married. Both of us felt a profound passion for each other and became more intimately involved than we knew we should before marriage. Now, we both feel empty and are not as happy as we thought we'd be. We're committed to staying in our marriage, but I can't stand the thought of living such a drab life. Where did we go wrong, and what should we do now?*

Dear Unhappy: Thank God for the commitment you've made to stay in your marriage despite the problems you face. In my opinion, your problems stem from rushing through the pair-bonding process or even entirely skipping some steps (see chapter 2 in *Smart Listening for Couples*). Can you repair a damaged or weak marital bond? Yes! You do so by filling in now some of the steps you skipped during the bonding process.

First, spend time communicating with Jim daily. It's likely that you and he never established good communication habits. Once couples turn their sexual motors on, they neglect verbal communication. Then many get caught in a web of ineffective communication habits from which they think there is no escape—especially if the habits have become deeply ingrained through time.

Here are some of the symptoms of communication problems: The couple functions poorly as a team. Their conversation doesn't flow easily. Their talk sounds more like speeches. They often use silence to communicate their dislike about something. Power struggles often dominate their relationship—along with anger, judging, and blaming during times of stress.

Well-bonded couples learn how to keep the channels of communication open. They listen with respect and accept all their partner's feelings even when they don't agree. Each is free to interrupt the other on occasion without hurt feelings. Sentences may not always be completed, yet the other understands the message sent. Each enjoys hearing the other's daily experiences and expresses empathy and support when needed. There's an atmosphere of respect for themselves and each other. And these couples spend more time looking directly into one another's eyes than do those who don't communicate well.

Jim and you can recapture the magic you felt when you first met, but it will take time, eye contact, touch, and persistence. Begin by sitting across from Jim at a table. Look directly into his eyes and say something like this: "Something is gone from our relationship, and I'd like to see what I can do to bring it back."

And spend more time in loving touch. The most troubled couple can experience a dramatic change in their marriage simply by touching each other more in affectionate ways. For example, give Jim a loving pat, hold his hand while riding in the car, spoon your body next to his at night, sit close to him while watching TV, greet him with a hug when he comes home from work, kiss him every morning and night, and hold his hand during prayer. It brings emotional healing and satisfaction to be touched and held outside the bedroom.

Jim and you can have a successful marriage, but you'll have to learn some basic communication skills. If the two of you can learn to communicate, spend time looking into one another's eyes, and re-establish touch, your relationship can not only survive but also drastically improve.

Self-help books are good, but what if only one partner is interested in change?

Dear Nancy: *My husband and I both came from broken homes and married when he was eighteen and I was seventeen. We have two beautiful children, but I don't feel that either one of us are educated as to the true meaning of marriage. However, I've read many Christian books on marriage and have learned many things. My husband won't look at any of these books. He was abandoned as a child, and as he grows older, he seems to withdraw further and further into himself. This distresses me greatly. How can I get him to read and learn more about marriage?*

Dear Distressed: Face it—you can't get your husband to read books that he doesn't want to read. You are making yourself sick over something you can't change. Give it up.

For your own sanity, you must accept your husband the way he is with no thought of change. You are married to a man who, for whatever reason, has no interest in learning more about marriage or lifting a finger to improve it. Learning to accept this fact will take a lot of pressure off him to conform to your wishes. At present, he may be resisting you to protect himself. Eliminating the pressure to conform to your wishes just might free him to move in a positive direction. No promises, mind you, but it's worth a try.

Here's another prime recommendation: get him to a Binding the Wounds seminar with Drs. Ron and Nancy Rockey. Their seminar explores the effect of traumatic early childhood experiences and the effects people experience as adults from when their childhood needs weren't met. This exciting seminar helps individuals move toward emotional wholeness and offers a path to recovery and joy (see appendix). Your chances of getting him to a seminar probably aren't great if he won't read a book, but again, it's worth a try.

You can't force him to do something he doesn't want to do. This isn't even biblical: "Love does not insist on its own way" (1 Corinthians 13:5, RSV). So your only option is to give up the idea of changing your husband and work instead on changing yourself.

How does a henpecked husband who tries hard to please deal with a controlling wife?

Dear Nancy: *I'm married to a very domineering woman whom I am always very anxious to please. In short, I am henpecked. I'm tired of trying so* *hard to please a person who has all the control. Can a henpecked husband build a good marriage with soft leadership, or does his leadership style have to be tougher?*

Dear Henpecked: Picture two gates leading into heaven. A sign over one reads, "All men who have ever been bossed by their wife line up here." Several hundred men are standing in front of that gate. A sign over the other gate reads, "All men who have never been bossed by their wife line up here." One bewildered-looking man stands by this gate. Saint Peter approaches the lone man and asks why he's standing there. He says, "My wife told me to."

Following this pattern in marriage causes ridicule, which is precisely why so many jokes about henpecked husbands exist. It damages the male ego, there's no biblical support for it; and society disrespects it.

You said your wife was domineering, but you didn't indicate whether you were weak, wimpy, and passive. Does your wife have to do everything alone because you take no interest in her, the children, or the home? Do you sit back as a silent partner to avoid conflict, which forces your wife to take over and have all the say as well as make all the major decisions in the family? Do you escape into yourself, the television, newspaper, work, or some hobby? Have you left the running of the home and family entirely to your wife—perhaps like your father did? Do you, for the sake of peace, withdraw rather than argue with your strong-willed wife? If any portion of this description fits, you must wake up and face the fact that you share her guilt.

You asked if a henpecked husband could build a good marriage with soft leadership. Yes. And this is precisely what a woman wants when it comes to leadership—both tough and tender qualities. Such traits may sound as if they conflict with each other, but men can maintain a balance between being strongly decisive when making hard decisions that keep a family operating and communicating lovingly with their families.

Most women, regardless of how traditional or liberated, desire a politely aggressive male who radiates masculinity—one who is sensitive to her needs and can evoke a positive feeling in her. But few men know how to provide this type of soft leadership. You can do it only when you determine—deliberately, intensely, and faithfully—to become God's man. If you are going to lead your family effectively and survive the crises of life, you must ask God to come into your life, forgive your sins and failure, and make you into the kind of leader needed to guide your family. It's never easy to become God's man, because Satan lurks at every turn to thwart your plans, divert your attention, and sidetrack your efforts.

You and your wife can learn to function in a mutually supportive manner. When you do, you will have fewer arguments and less contention. A natural peace and harmony will settle over your marriage. A closeness and intimacy will result that you couldn't achieve any other way. You will grow in self-confidence. And your wife's attitudes toward herself and your marriage will improve as she responds to your leadership. Your children will learn a natural respect for family organization, which will grow into respect for school, church, and society as a whole. Get with it. Ditch your wimpy ways and try soft leadership. (For more on this subject, read chapters 15 through 18 in *Highly Effective Marriage*.)

Making each other happy should be a major goal of all married couples. What happens, then, when a spouse emotionally withdraws because of negative character traits? Read on.

Dear Nancy: *My husband complains that I am a very negative and critical person, and he is emotionally withdrawing from me. We've been married for twenty-eight years and have no children. I feel he's a selfish person, and I deeply desire a husband who has the character traits of my father. I want to make him happy and communicate in a more positive way. Is that possible?*

Dear Critical Wife: Criticism heads the list of behaviors most likely to end a marriage. Constant criticism ends in a vicious circle. The wife criticizes or blames her husband. He becomes defensive and either withdraws from the discussion or goes on the attack. The latter results in a highly destructive verbal battle and, sometimes, physical abuse. All this brings on more criticism. Then the negative emotions so overwhelm the couple that further discussion is fruitless, and someone must call timeout until they've calmed down. Third-party intervention is often necessary to help the couple control this negative cycle.

Constant criticism makes it impossible for your husband to feel tender love toward you. Criticism kills love. He may not even want to be in the same room with you or touch you. The thought of a sexual encounter at this point is out of the question. A man once told me that his wife had berated him for so many years—criticized everything he said or did, emasculating him in hundreds of insidious ways—that he had no sexual desire for her whatsoever. He had plenty of sexual desire for other women, whom he vigorously sought, but feelings for his wife were dead and without hope of resurrection.

Criticizing your husband endangers your love relationship. Every negative comment takes something away from it. Lovers should not become each other's critics. On a church marquee, I read, "If your attitude stinks, even breath mints won't help." Paul warned us, "If you keep on biting and devouring each other, watch out or you will be destroyed by each other" (Galatians 5:15, NIV).

Changing someone with a serious problem is nearly impossible. Therefore, those who recognize problems in their marriage must change themselves.

Dear Nancy: *My husband and I have been married for thirty-four years, and all during this time he has criticized me severely. Nothing I ever do seems to be right. I try so hard to please him, and it seems that all my efforts are in vain. Even if I were perfect, he'd still find something to criticize. I'm about to give up and move out.*

Dear Criticized: How are you responding when he attacks you? Do you clam up? Counterattack? If I may borrow a line from Dr. Phil, "How's that workin' for you?" It isn't, or you wouldn't have written!

Face it. There is next to nothing you can do about him or his behavior. But you can do something about your response pattern. *Change it!*

Here's a plan of action. The next time he criticizes you, rather than reacting the way you normally do, say nothing, but reach for a notebook that you have ready for the occasion. Write down what he said to you, noting the date and time. When he asks what you are doing, explain—without a trace of rancor in your voice—that sometimes he says very memorable things. Tell him that your relationship is so important to you that you want to have a record of everything memorable that he's said.

At first, he may accuse your shrink of putting you up to this. Or he may get angry. Whatever his reaction, refuse to be drawn into a discussion of what you are doing or why. Most important of all, don't become angry yourself, explain yourself, or debate him. This may take some effort on your part. Without fail, every time he criticizes you, grab your notebook and begin writing. But say not a word. If you're consistent, you'll likely note a decrease of incidents even within the first week. After that, he may slip and apologize.

You're raising his consciousness level to a specific situation. You can change the situation by changing your reaction to it, but be consistent—he has a thirty-four-year-old habit to buck.

Changing our behavior can be difficult, especially when the habits have become deeply ingrained. What's a man to do when his wife doesn't keep a clean house?

Dear Nancy: *My wife is a terrible housekeeper, and I can't stand living in filth and disorganization anymore. Beds are rarely made, the bathrooms smell, I can hardly find a place to sit down in the family room, the kitchen counters are covered with dirty dishes and clutter, and dishes remain in the sink for days, although we have a new dishwasher. And if I want clean clothes, I have to wash them myself.*

If my wife worked outside the home, I'd make more excuses for her, but she doesn't and never has. Our kids, six and eight, are growing up with terrible habits because she has terrible habits. I've tried talking to her about this, but it goes in one ear and out the other. If you can't help me help her get a handle on housekeeping, I'm out of here.

Dear Swamp Dweller: I am a firm believer that women, as "keepers of the home," should learn how to manage a family and home—to cook, clean, and maintain a clutter-free living space. (Or they should learn how to delegate these tasks.) You have a right to expect that your wife handle household tasks and your children in an organized, efficient manner. To put it simply, you need a home environment that offers a respite from work pressures.

This is not to say that you can't contribute to maintaining the home, both by pitching in and sharing the load and by not adding unnecessarily to clutter, chores, and disorganization. But largely it is a trade-off for husband and wife. If your wife expects you to provide financially for the family, she needs to supply a home environment that provides the rest and peace you need in order to contribute the necessary income.

There are several solutions to your problem. You can accept your wife as she is—a terrible housekeeper—and continue to live in filth and disorganization, clutter, and mess. You might instigate a family cleanup hour, during which everyone in the family takes part. Everyone works together in teams, and no one tackles a mess alone, even though only one person may have made it. No one stops or plays until either the work is done or sixty minutes is up, whichever comes first. You can go on strike (see page 179 of my book *Get Organized*). Or you can hire a cleaning service to come weekly or bi-monthly. This will cost you, but the clean, organized living space might be worth the cost. And who knows, it just might provide your wife with the encouragement she needs to get her act together.

If your wife is really as bad as you say, she may be depressed. Make sure you are doing your part to meet her legitimate needs. And then try one of these ideas. In any case, do something—don't just sit there, buried in clutter!

Can a marriage be highly effective when one partner doesn't drink and the other does?

Dear Nancy: *I recently learned that my husband, a member in good standing of our church and on the church board, has been drinking alcohol for some time. We've been married for over twenty years and have three teenagers. Since we were first married, we've had problems regarding communication, sex, spirituality, and child rearing. Should I divorce him?*

Dear Wife of Closet Alcoholic: Scripture gives one—yes, *one*—reason for divorce. Nowhere do I read in Scripture that alcoholism, difficulties with communication or sex, or differing views on spirituality or child rearing are justifiable reasons to seek divorce. Unless your husband has committed adultery, you do not have grounds for remarriage (see Matthew 19:9).

Don't be so willing to throw your marriage away. Fight for it. Join Al-Anon and get the support of the group in understanding and not enabling an alcoholic (see appendix). Get yourself and perhaps your teens into therapy. Read *Highly Effective Marriage* along with other self-help books. Attend a marriage seminar. And last but not least, pray that God will change you.

Remember, it is infinitely easier to rehabilitate your present marriage than to go through the trauma of divorce and attempt to build a new future on the rubble of a troubled past.

Some couples have opposing views regarding leisure-time activities. How can you close the distance between sports and the symphony?

Dear Nancy: *My husband is having an affair—not with a woman, but with sports. We have season tickets to football and basketball games. In between* *games and seasons, he is glued to sports on TV. During baseball season, he plays in a local league. He doesn't consider my interests important. If we had children, he'd win the "Negligent Father of the Year" award. I've tried to talk to him about this to no avail. I am nothing more to him than a servant, a housekeeper, and a sex partner. He says if I don't like it, I can get a divorce. This is a crisis, and I don't know how to handle it.*

Dear Second-Place: I don't condone your husband's behavior, but let me help you understand it. Author Willard F. Harley, in his best-selling book *His Needs, Her Needs* (see appendix), lists recreation as men's second most pressing need—second only to his need for sexual fulfillment. From the time boys are young, they enjoy playing in groups and participating in activities. From childhood on, girls enjoy talking, which to them proves intimacy. Boys prefer activities, with less talk.

An adult man looks to his wife to help him satisfy this longing for group recreational activities—he wants to enjoy these activities with her. Through her interest in his activities, he gains a sense of closeness and intimacy. When she joins him, he experiences similar emotions to those she feels after a heart-to-heart talk.

I seriously doubt your husband developed this consuming passion for sports after you married. He was probably just as involved while you were dating. And you likely joined him then without a word of complaint. You likely showed a great interest in sports—feigned or not!—to demonstrate what a perfect partner you would be. He thought he'd found a woman who loved what he loves as much as he does. He felt closer to you than he'd ever felt to any woman before. Now, after marriage, you resent his interest in sports and have a different agenda. How fair is this? He may be neglecting you, but my guess is that you aren't being fair to him either.

Men and women usually have very different tastes when it comes to having fun and pursuing leisure activities. But women who let opportunities pass to share their husband's passion may find that in spite of all their efforts and longings, they never build an intimate relationship with their husband. Such women are often quick to point the finger of blame at their husband while never considering it important to take time to play with him.

Unless you learn to adapt and go with your husband, he'll go alone or with his buddies. This also means that you'll never share what he enjoys most. If you refuse to allow him to pursue sports, he'll resent the time he is home.

So, invite friends over to watch the games on TV with you. Get season tickets to games next to a couple you enjoy. Don your baseball cap and cheer your husband on when he's at bat. Strike a deal with him. "I'll go with you to the games. Please go with me to the symphony." Then thank God you have a husband who has a passion for a healthy activity.

Unless you recognize and help your husband satisfy this need, you'll miss the opportunity of becoming his best friend and having a lot of fun with him.

One of the many components of a highly effective marriage is faith in God. What happens when one partner is spiritual and the other is not?

Dear Nancy: *I am married to a man who is not of my faith. He doesn't want to hear anything about my religion. I have to go to all church functions alone. I am totally responsible for the spiritual training of our children. I feel so lonely sometimes because I have no one with whom to share spiritual insights. Sometimes I think it would be easier to give up my faith. It would certainly benefit my marriage.*

Lately my husband has been acting as if he does not care for me at all, and I suspect he may be in love with another woman. We've gone four years with no sex, and nothing I do pleases him. My birthday and Mother's Day come and go with no notice from him. I am so hurt and unfulfilled in my marriage, I am thinking of trying to find a boyfriend. In fact, I am finding it difficult to resist other men. I just want someone to love me and share life with me. I am praying so hard that God will help me.

Dear Wife of an Unbeliever: Some women become convinced that it is their obligation to convert their unbelieving husbands. Through nagging, moralizing, lecturing, or begging, they attempt to coerce or trick their husbands into attending church. This demanding, self-righteous attitude is probably as offensive a sin as is their husband's alienation from religion.

So, what's the answer? The answer lies in acceptance. God has not laid on you the responsibility of converting your husband to your beliefs or of changing him in any way. Attempts on your part to convert him to your religion will only antagonize him further. Leave this work to the Holy Spirit. A common spiritual foundation makes marriage easier, but it is not the sole determiner of a healthy marriage. Your husband doesn't need your suggestions or improvement plan, but he does need your acceptance and encouragement.

To maintain a friendship with someone, we must practice acceptance. Regarding your husband, this means that you accept him at face value, as an unbeliever. It means that you like him just the way he is. That you respect his right to accept or reject religion. That you allow him to possess his own feelings about religion regardless of how they may differ from yours.

Forget about abandoning your faith. This would only be a temporary fix that would end in failure. Satan would gain victory for a time, but why give him this advantage? Bury this idea. If you understand what motivates your husband, you will not take the guilt upon yourself for his actions. He would act this way even if married to someone else. Nor will you find the solution to your problem in the arms of another man. That would only compound the problem and leave you with tremendous guilt. I received a letter from another woman who experienced a miracle on the part of her husband. This was one of the most hopeless and pathetic cases I've ever seen. Even I felt there was no hope, because this man closed himself off from her for up to six weeks at a time. He seemed to be totally unfeeling. But as she turned her problems over to God and followed His plan, she experienced a miracle. She changed her behavior and accepted her husband, and the outcome was positive.

The woman in the next letter is about to go to her spiritual death because her husband is not willing to become the spiritual leader of their home.

Dear Nancy: *My husband of eight years is just not a spiritual person, even though we attend the same church. I am very unhappy, and my children are beginning to notice. We don't have the companionship I want. We are doing little more than putting on a big show at church and with our friends. Paul says, "Be content with what you have," but I want my husband to be more spiritual. I need a strong spiritual force in my life to stay consistent. I know that people can change when God works in their life. What can I do to help my husband become the spiritual leader of our home?*

Dear Unhappy: You have expressed a concern that many women struggle with. Many men besides your husband have abdicated the spiritual leadership in their home. Some men think of spiritual leadership as being as much a woman's job as having babies and cooking the evening meal. Men sometimes plead their cases by saying they attend church every week (usually at their wife's insistence) or they serve on church boards or they say grace at the table. But this type of spirituality isn't what a wife wants, and it certainly won't hold the family together when a major crisis arises or the children hit their teen years.

There's one important fact that you must learn to deal with: You are not responsible for your husband's spirituality or for his salvation. You are responsible only for your own. Don't take on responsibility for saving your husband. Learning this concept of acceptance will free you from a heavy load and change your attitude. It will also free your husband to grow because he'll no longer have to fight your lack of acceptance and your demands—verbal or nonverbal—that he change. There is no magical way of transforming your husband into the spiritual leader of your home. But an unaccepting attitude will certainly complicate things.

If your husband refuses to take charge of family devotions, do it yourself. Should an opportunity present itself to invite him to join, you might say, "Honey, let's tuck the children in and hear their prayers," or "Would you read the children their Bible story tonight? They love to sit in your lap and listen to you read." If he declines, carry on alone. You may ask one of the children to bless the food at the table if he isn't interested. Should he go so far as to tell the children there is no God, you can later teach them that there is, explaining that Daddy says this because he doesn't know God yet.

You need not parade your prayer and devotional time before him as evidence of your spirituality. Rather, make your life a silent witness. Daily Bible study and prayer will provide the wisdom you need to know how to make the best of the difficult circumstances facing you. You will also find benefit in having a faithful prayer partner and counselor who can guide you through trying times.

The benefits of spiritual oneness cannot be overestimated. When couples don't participate in religious activities together, many problems can develop.

Dear Nancy: *When we got married five years ago, there were things about my husband that bothered me. For example, even though we are of the same religion, he doesn't attend church with me on a regular basis. His father was the same way, and my husband says I shouldn't nag him, because he can never be any different. I am sad most of the time, and my husband says he's tired of my* *negative spirit. I'm reaching the place where I don't want to do anything for him. Can you help me?*

Dear Sad Wife: Your husband may never change. That may not be easy to face, but the sooner you do, the sooner you can get on with life. As it is now, you are feeling sorry for yourself and wallowing in self-pity. I only say this to help you understand yourself. As long as you are consumed with these feelings, you'll find filling your husband's needs next to impossible.

You'll need to spend extra time with God each day, seeking divine strength to handle the multiplicity of pressures you face. Marriage is difficult enough when both partners work together to achieve mutual goals. When a husband opposes his wife's spiritual beliefs, she has an even greater need to maintain harmony in the home.

After you stabilize your mental attitudes, here's a project I'd like to see you try. Lay your own needs aside for a week, and do everything in the world to meet your husband's needs. Fix his favorite foods. Be a stimulating sex partner for him. Tell him how handsome and wonderful he is three times a day for seven days. On a daily basis, demonstrate the benefits of a Christlike life. Make your home a heaven for your husband. With his present attitudes, home may be the only heaven he'll ever enjoy.

Your current nagging and negativity are driving him away from you as well as from the church. You mustn't let anything he does or doesn't do, or whether or not he goes to church with you, control your attitudes toward life. You control your own attitudes. Invite Christ into your heart, your mind, and your marriage. Especially ask that He change your negative spirit and replace it with love and acceptance for the husband God gave you.

I pray that God will grant you wisdom as you seek new ways of treating your husband so that you may be more concerned with meeting his needs than having your own met—which is the essence of true love.

True love includes forgiveness. The next letter illustrates how much some need to forgive.

Dear Nancy: *My wife and I have been married for eighteen years, but she left me six weeks ago. This forced me into looking at my own behavior. I have been guilty of everything from lying and stealing to unfaithfulness. I didn't want my wife to leave, and I miss our two children terribly, but her leaving has been* *a blessing in disguise. It was the jolt I needed to get desperate enough to work for a change in my life. My wife isn't home yet, but I am working to become so attractive to her that she'll eventually be eager to return. I've read all of your books, and the concepts you've written about are so important for couples to know. I'm not giving up but hanging in there!*

Dear Unfaithful: I am pleased to learn that the crisis of your failing marriage and the message of my books have had an impact on your life. Hang tough. Your wife may not be home yet, but allowing her to observe the changes in your life is one of the best things you can do. Let her see and know that you are not the same man she left. Don't bug her with this information; let her hear about it from others and observe it in your quiet demeanor. Let her wonder if she hasn't made an enormous mistake. Be such a kind and godly man that she'll realize she'll be the loser if she gives you up.

* * * * *

I hope this chapter has brought you a few chuckles, a few inspirational thoughts, and a new determination to make your marriage the best it can be. Continual challenges lie ahead, regardless of whether you are just starting out as husband and wife, are enmeshed in the turmoil of the child-rearing years, or have launched your children on their own.

Every couple goes through difficult stages. Highly effective marriages arise out of the crises in which husband and wife work to resolve unsettling issues before they become major disasters. It takes teamwork to do this—two people who love, trust, and respect each other, that are totally committed to allowing God to rule in their lives.

You will find that working through each crisis leads to a stronger, more fulfilling, and more successful marriage—one that will last through all the years to come. So, meet each new stage enthusiastically and confidently.

And be willing to risk opening yourself honestly to that special person you married. The reason we marry in the first place is to share our lives with someone we care about.

During our early married years, Harry and I experienced numerous problems. We were young, naive, and unlearned in the disciplines of married life. We felt as though we had been thrown together to work out problems on our own, and we weren't doing very well!

During this time when we were just stumbling along, Harry was training for and subsequently entered the ministry. We went to church, read our
Bibles, and did all the good things Christians are supposed to do, but things
continued to worsen.

Had it not been for our faith, we might have thrown it all away, figuring
that what we had together wasn't worth saving, that it might be better for us
to go our separate ways and not "torment" each other any longer. But the
closer we faced the reality of separation, the more we wondered how we
could disgrace our church and sin against our God. The faith in which we
had been reared would not let us go. Ultimately, it became a stabilizing
factor.

Then I began studying the principles that make marriage work successfully. As God led, I followed. It was difficult, but change did come about.
Today we are stronger than ever in the Lord's love and our love for each
other. Harry became my pride and joy then and remains so today.

What lies ahead, then, is up to you. You can stay where you are or you
can look up. You can say, "Lord, I can't do this; I can't take any more," or
"Lord, I will follow where You lead." Success will not come merely through
your own efforts, but much can happen when you link your efforts with
divine power.

Strangers in the Night

Good sex doesn't seem to be happening much anymore—at least not according to the reports. *Newsweek* noted the yuppie syndrome of decreased sexual activity. And *U.S. News & World Report* declared that millions of people are unhappy with the sexual side of their relationship.

One study of Christian men found that one out of three reported their sex life as fair or not good, and one in twelve had a major complaint about their sexual needs not being met. Since the current divorce rate is about one of every two marriages, having one third of married men dissatisfied with their sex lives spells problems for marital stability.

However, according to the Sex in America survey, monogamous partners enjoy the best sex. The epidemic of dissatisfaction may be the result of our complex and busy lifestyles as well as the belief that good sex just happens.

What happens on television or in the movies may be perpetuating this epidemic. There, when a couple find themselves irresistibly attracted, within moments they're having passionate sex. Every couple wants to have that kind of gut-grabbing sex.

If you think good sex just "happens," you may also think that when it doesn't happen, you're no longer in love. But maintaining a fulfilling sexual experience that lasts for decades of loving together requires deliberate thought and action.

Many women, when first married, have high expectations and little real knowledge about sex. Read on.

Dear Nancy: *I've been married a year and nine months, and I love my husband very much. But I must have some answers to questions about sex. I expected I would always be in the mood for sex and enjoy all aspects of it. I imagined it would be very natural and would hurt only the first time, after which it would be OK. But it still hurts if we don't use some lubricant. I imagined foreplay to be as great as orgasm. And often I have to work so hard to get in the mood that I wonder if it is worth the effort.*

I knew my husband would be gentle, and he always is. He never forces me, is romantic with low lights and candles. He plays soft music, draws my bath, rubs my back and body, teases me, reads my signals, and knows what I like. He looks me in the eyes and is extremely concerned about my enjoyment. Afterwards I feel so close to my husband—at peace, secure, loved, cherished, fulfilled, and at one with him. But I had the misconception that his penis would naturally give me an orgasm. I'm disappointed that he has to use his hands to stimulate me. I especially don't like it when he touches my breasts or any other part of me before I'm ready. And I don't like the mess of sex or the smell of my juices or his semen. Both gross me out. I also thought every time was going to be a mutual orgasm.

While my husband is always gentle, somehow that doesn't seem to be enough. I'm not in the mood nearly as often as he is, and I don't like to make love when I'm not in the mood. I keep telling myself that I'll get there if we keep going. Usually I eventually do, but I don't like wondering if I'm going to make it this time; it doesn't seem natural to me. It makes me feel like a hypocrite for going with the flow until I feel like it.

Dear Grossed-Out Wife: Your letter indicates that you married with little specific information about the physiology of sex. You, like many, thought you could attain instant sexual harmony. The harsh reality is that it takes time to adjust sexually after marriage.

Why is it that the most fascinating subject known to humankind is the most difficult for a couple to talk about? When your husband touches your breasts before you are ready, you must convey to him either verbally or nonverbally that you aren't ready. Don't expect him to read your mind.

According to studies, only 30 to 40 percent of women can attain a vaginal orgasm without clitoral stimulation. This means that for 60 to 70 percent of females, penile thrusting does not lead to regular orgasm. God designed the female clitoris to be used in sexual expression, and manual stimulation constitutes acceptable love play between husband and wife. For a majority of women, which obviously includes you, it offers the only path to sexual fulfillment.

Since God designed males to become aroused primarily by what they see, they can become aroused much more rapidly than females can. God designed females to become aroused through emotional factors, which takes longer. On the average, it takes a female fifteen to twenty minutes to reach her maximum level of sexual responsiveness. But there is nothing wrong with a woman who takes thirty to forty-five minutes, and an inexperienced bride can take longer. What's the hurry anyway?

A mutual orgasm, in which both partners achieve climax at the same time, is not necessary. It's more important that you both enjoy an orgasm, that you both experience pleasure, and that the experience renews your love for each other. Most couples find it satisfying when the husband brings his wife to orgasm first, and then climaxes soon after. This way each can contribute to and share in the other's pleasure.

Regarding the mess and smell: The male ejaculate includes about a half teaspoon of semen. This is primarily protein, similar to the white of an egg, and is neither dirty nor unsanitary, although it has a distinctive odor. Since the odor is distasteful to you, use an aromatic candle to mask or cover the smell, and keep a small towel handy to wipe up the "mess."

Wake up, little girl. You have an extremely romantic husband who is gentle, makes you feel loved, and is concerned about your enjoyment. The expectations you hold are unrealistic. Give yourself more time to learn and to adjust to marital sex. And thank God every day for a husband who puts so much caring into your sex life.

Many men want to create powerful passion. Doing so can be difficult.

Dear Nancy: *I've been married seven years, and I dearly love my wife. But I'm not sexually satisfied. Yes, she gives me sex, but rather reluctantly. I'm sure she achieves orgasm most of the time—either that or she's very good at faking it. But I'm a caring husband who wants her to achieve orgasm every time. I think something is missing in our sexual relationship—something that I long for. But I can't identify it. Is there something wrong with me? Or is there something wrong with her? Or is this just normal for couples who have been married as long as we have?*

Dear Longing for Something More: What you describe may be "normal" for many couples, but married sex doesn't have to be that way. I think you may need a little education about what a woman wants and needs from her husband in order for her to respond eagerly to his advances.

A woman responds to her husband in direct proportion to his ability to fulfill her emotional needs. If you fail to create an atmosphere in which your wife can respond, you can deprive yourself of the sexual pleasure that is so important to your happiness. You wonder how she can say she still loves you and yet deny you what you want and need most. But when things are out of balance in the sexual department, you might well look to yourself. There are not as many lukewarm or frigid wives as there are husbands who fail to meet the needs of their wives.

Most men don't understand that lovemaking is a deeply emotional experience for a woman. She is stimulated by the amount of romantic love her husband has shown for her throughout the day and considers each lovemaking encounter a moment of profound love and a deep part of her life. If her husband seems to take their sex life for granted, she can feel deeply hurt and offended. He may consider repeated assurances of his love unnecessary and theatrical, but she doesn't. She doesn't need reassurance because she seeks flattery, but because women instinctively withdraw from sexual encounters devoid of love and adoration.

A woman has a special need to feel respected as a person. Unless she feels her husband's constant approval of her as an individual, she won't be able to enjoy making love. Since her self-esteem is closely related to her sexual enjoyment, she will seek reassurance in areas where she feels the weakest. Are you fulfilling this need?

If your wife feels ugly, she won't be able to respond without embarrassment. A shy person with deep-seated feelings of inferiority will act shy and inferior in the sexual life, just as a self-confident, emotionally healthy individual is much more likely to have a well-adjusted sex life. Do you ever tease your wife—even in fun—about small breasts, skinny legs, or fat? If so, this could contribute to self-consciousness during sex, and you may never see her out from under the covers again.

A woman doesn't have to achieve an orgasm every time in order to enjoy sex. Many women can participate in sex and feel fully satisfied even though they enjoyed no ecstatic climax. You should never demand that your wife achieve an orgasm. Such a demand would push her in one or the other of two wrong directions. She might lose interest in sex altogether, or she might begin to fake orgasm. Most men despise the latter. As Dr. Dobson puts it, "Once a woman begins to bluff in bed, there is no place to stop. Forever after she must make her husband think she's on a prolonged pleasure trip when in fact her car is still in the garage."

Women need to hear certain words and to experience certain feelings before they can respond in the bedroom. Any husband who thinks he can merely walk into the bedroom and expect his wife to "turn on" with no preparation doesn't understand female sexuality. And contrary to popular belief, women want more imagination and variety in sex, too. Any husband whose advances are always on the same night, at the same time, in the same place and position, has no imagination. The man who wants the wife of his youth to respond for a lifetime needs to create variety.

For the most part, men are the pursuers and women the responders. But women must have something to respond to. Even an inhibited woman can become responsive if her husband woos her gently, slowly, patiently, and creatively. You are searching for ways of improving your sex life. You are on the right track. Carefully read and evaluate the suggestions I've made. Makes changes where changes need to be made. What could be more exciting or challenging for a man than improving his sex life? You can become a better lover or even a great one if you work at it. Have fun!

After reading the next problem, you can understand the man's frustration.

Dear Nancy: *Three nights ago, my husband set me up for sex. In the middle of it all, he got so frustrated that he said some hurtful things. He called me frigid and said he was fed up with my cold and tired thinking about sex. He threatened some drastic things if I didn't get my act together and get some new attitudes.*

I've spent three days crying about it. Now that I'm all cried out, I'm beginning to think straight. Maybe he's right. My parents had very negative attitudes toward sex. The only thing I ever learned about sex before I married was that it was "bad," something you didn't talk about, and something you only did to have children. I'm afraid to release myself to enjoy a sexual experience. Maybe it's time to do something about these attitudes. Where do I begin?

Dear Frigid Wife: I'm happy to hear that you're willing to do something about your tired attitudes. Let's get to work. The only part of the sexual experience that a man enjoys more than ejaculation is the satisfaction he derives from an amorous wife who finds him sexually stimulating. Obviously, you haven't seen creativity and responsiveness as part of a woman's role in sex. You might be surprised to learn that in a study I conducted, 65 percent of the husbands wanted more interest, response, and creativity from their wives. Only 35 percent were satisfied with the status quo.

Whereas experiencing the emotions of love stimulates you, your husband is stimulated to a greater degree and more quickly by sight. Men love to look at the female body. They turn on at the glimpse of a nude or partially nude female—and they're not "dirty old men" because they do this. Men react this way because God designed them to do so. What's in your wardrobe for nighttime wear? Flannel pajamas? Rag-bag nighties? Stained bathrobes? Here's a little assignment: You needn't cavort in see-through negligees and high-heeled boots, but I suggest that you purchase a new wardrobe of attractive nighties in all lengths and colors. (No husband has ever complained about this expenditure!)

And make sure you're getting enough rest. Fatigue is a big hindrance to a woman's interest in sex. That's like the last item on your mind after you've struggled through an eighteen-hour day—and whatever gets done last probably gets done poorly. Sort out your priorities so that sex doesn't languish in last place. Fight the urge to begin one final project at 9:00 P.M. When you start giving the sexual side of your marriage the priority it deserves, you'll save time and energy for it.

In addition to what I've said here, I recommend that you read "How to Satisfy a Man Sexually" in *Highly Effective Marriage;* Tim and Beverly LaHaye's book *The Act of Marriage;* and Clifford and Joyce Penner's *The Gift of Sex* (see appendix). Men should lead out in initiating creativity during lovemaking, but women must be responsive to such efforts, or it will be in vain. You too can be creative.

Wise King Solomon said, "A constant dripping on a rainy day and a cranky woman are much alike! You can no more stop her complaints than you can stop the wind or hold onto anything with oil-slick hands" (Proverbs 27:15, 16, *The Living Bible*). Nagging has such debilitating effects that it can kill love as well as sexual desire.

Dear Nancy: *My husband and I have been married for only seven months, and we haven't made love in four weeks. We're both twenty-two years old. When*

I try to talk to him about it, he says, "All you ever do is nag." It seems that lately there are virtually no good times, only fighting. I so much desire a loving, close relationship with my husband. What should I do?

Dear Nagging Wife: Nagging is something you can work on by yourself. When a man complains that his wife is a nag, frequently she'll counter, "I am not! I never say a word. He's making that up!" What she doesn't realize is that nagging has as much to do with what you don't say as with what you say. My favorite definition of nagging is "repeating known facts unnecessarily." But here again we are skirting the issue. Usually, nagging is more a matter of the attitude projected than the words said.

I think your husband is saying, "I don't feel like you like me. You're always trying to change me. You won't leave me alone. When I get home, I never feel like you want me just the way I am. I can't relax around you. You're always passing judgment on me."

Take a careful look at what I've said, and see if you do any of those things. Acceptance could be the factor that is affecting everything else in your marriage. You're both young. With the difficulties you face, saving your marriage will require maturity on the part of both of you. You've been married only seven months, and already things are not good. What will you be facing after seven, seventeen, or twenty-seven years if things continue as they are right now? There won't be anything left. Men don't want to communicate with someone who nags all the time. Making your husband feel loved will make him want to spend time with you.

Something is definitely wrong in a marriage if a man doesn't desire sex for four weeks—especially a newly married man who's twenty-two! The problem doesn't lie in the sex relationship itself but in something about the way the two of you are relating to each other. He might see you in a mother role. Acting like his mother isn't going to help him grow up. He needs a loving wife who admires and encourages him.

The fact that you are fighting a lot indicates that both of you have a lot of anger and hostility building up .The two of you need help, and you need it *now!* Locate a knowledgeable Christian counselor as soon as possible (see appendix for chapter 1). Then prepare to hang in there with this counselor until you stabilize this relationship. If your husband is unwilling to go, you go alone. When he sees you making changes in your behavior, he may become willing to make some changes too.

Marriage isn't designed for kids. It requires self-control and unconditional love. You can learn to meet these requirements, and you can be happy together. Make yourselves teachable so that the Holy Spirit can work with you.

Let's explore what could be causing the next woman's loss of sexual desire.

Dear Nancy: *I'm a thirty-three-year-old mother of three, and I have a big sex problem. Maybe I should say I have a big problem in that I lack the desire for sex. I love my husband very much, and there are no major problems between us outside of this sex thing. But sex is the last thing on my mind after working an eight-hour job and feeding the family and caring for three kids. I have NO— and I do mean NO—sex drive. I could easily live without it forever. When I refuse my husband, he storms out of the bedroom, and I end up going through with it just so we don't go to bed angry at each other. Then I feel guilty for not responding as I used to and angry for giving in when I'm not in the mood.*

Dear Not in the Mood: First, talk to your physician. Only your physician can tell you if your estrogen levels have declined, which might explain your loss of interest in sex. This is worth checking out.

I am more inclined, however, to blame your lack of desire on stress. You must have sexual energy available to have sexual desire. Sexual desire is different from sexual arousal. Arousal occurs when the body has been stimulated, but sexual desire shows up in our sex drive or libido. When you use all your energy on other projects—working full time, caring for children, or managing a home—little remains to fuel the sex drive.

Sexual desire grows out of energy derived from proper nutrition, exercise, and sleep. Those who live complicated, busy lives may never have enough time or energy to feel sexual desire. To correct these problems, you must eat properly and get enough exercise and sleep. You will also need to clear away some of the distractions currently cluttering your life. Begin by turning off the TV. Eliminate outside commitments that currently keep you from having enough time to nurture your marriage. You may need to curtail even church commitments.

Your problem is serious enough for me to recommend that to restore the love you and your husband once had for each other, you should go on a vacation where you can spend the entire time restoring the intimacy you've lost. This vacation must be one for just the two of you. Don't take your children. Should you be thinking that you don't have time or money for this, let me remind you that if either of you were carrying on an affair, you would find the time. It is a matter of priorities. You can learn to re-create the type of romantic occasions you enjoyed while dating and restore the desire you once had for each other.

I hear despair and exhaustion in your letter. Put behind you all the empty feelings that have replaced sexual desire. You don't want to lose a good marriage or the husband you love. Once you have re-established desire, you can anticipate and plan for sexual times, allotting time regularly to connect physically. And remember, even if you do not climax every time, you can still—out of love for your husband—allow him to make love to you. And you might even enjoy it!

Satisfying marital relationships involve much communication and mutual affection. When one partner withdraws, it's maddening.

Dear Nancy: *My husband and I have sexual problems, which I feel are due in part to our lack of communication. He has always reacted to problems by shoving them under the rug. He rarely ever touches me except when he wants sex, and then he wonders at my lack of enthusiasm. I've told him how hard it is to bridge the gap. When I put my arms around him to try to get close, he stays only for a second and then moves away. He has a high need for sex, but I am ready to give up and am considering divorce.*

Dear Longing to Be Touched: Your communication problem will be more difficult to solve than your sexual one. First, your husband must realize that there is a problem. We don't do anything about things we don't see as problems. Pray that the Holy Spirit will impress both of you regarding what you should learn and do. Then read my book *Smart Listening for Couples.* Chapter 5, "Anger Workout: Coping With Conflict," is key. Pay special attention to the "Share-Care Plan for Conflict Resolution." Read also the sections on "Shifting Gears," "Setting the Stage Before the Conflict," "During the Conflict: Resolving the Big Stuff," and "After the Conflict: Harmony Restored." If he refuses to read, you can read key sections aloud to him. The Holy Spirit may use this material to help him accept that you have a communication problem that is affecting your sex life.

Men frequently do not understand the necessity of nonsexual touching outside the bedroom. In my seminars, I teach men that two things arouse a woman most—touch and words. I tell them to romance their wives with loving touches, pats, and hugs throughout the day—to hold their hand while walking or riding in the car. I emphasize that if he touches her only when he wants sex, she'll begin to think that every hug or touch means a trip to the bedroom and resent it. That's where you are right now.

Don't call it quits. Divorce is a devastatingly long process that produces broken lives and depression. From the outside looking in, it may look easy. Many fantasize unrealistically that another relationship would be better and solve their problems. But the real answer lies in fixing yourself first so that you are not the problem. Don't give up!

Does this next question have a familiar ring?

Dear Nancy: *My husband is a good man and a wonderful father to our children. In most ways, he's great, but there is one thing that turns me off so badly that it's hurting our sex life. Before we make love, he hugs and kisses me and tells me how much he loves me, but when we finish, he turns over and falls asleep within minutes. I feel like a prostitute whom he can't wait to get away from. I can't figure out who has the problem—him or me.*

Dear Can't Figure It Out: Following sexual climax, men's bodies typically return abruptly to normal levels of calm. Therefore, they're relaxed and ready for sleep. But women's bodies usually take ten to fifteen minutes to subside. For women, orgasm signals not the end of lovemaking but merely entry into another phase known as "the afterglow." In a survey I conducted, women shared their feelings by saying things such as "I wish my husband wouldn't go to sleep so soon after intercourse." "I wish he would hug and kiss me more after intercourse." "I wish he would be as affectionate after his orgasm as before." "I like to feel him near me after intercourse."

In order to teach him about your needs, ask him to play the "Let's Talk It Over—Sexual Attitudes Game." Couples play this game using open-ended sentences that help them get started talking about sexual topics. Here are some suggestions: "A funny thing I learned about sex when I was a child was _____." "The type of foreplay I enjoy most is _____." "When I talk to you about sex, I feel _____." "The best sexual experience I ever had with you was when _____." "One thing I would like more of when we are making love is _____." Right there is your opportunity. Tell him you want more holding after lovemaking. I highly recommend you read chapter 7, "Sexually Speaking," in my book *Smart Listening for Couples*.

One caution: Feelings of worth are never more at stake than in the bedroom. Many opportunities to make a partner feel loved, adequate, and attractive lie behind closed doors. Words such as "You were terrific last night" or "On a scale of one to ten, you rate eleven as a lover" cause one to take pride in his or her sexuality. Sexual compliments will work to your advantage now, because they encourage your husband to live up to your views of his performance. So, sandwich your request between a couple of great compliments. This will promote a stronger sexual bond between you.

The next woman needs patience and understanding—along with a thorough familiarity with her partner's body—to solve the problem she and her husband face.

Dear Nancy: *I am nineteen, and my husband is twenty-one. We've been married for seven months. We already have sex problems, and I don't know what to do about it. My husband ejaculates so fast that I get nothing out of it and am quickly losing interest in having sex at all. We haven't had sex for an entire month now, and I am becoming very angry with him. What will happen to us if we keep on like this?*

Dear Quickly Losing Interest in Sex: Ejaculatory control should be natural, easy, and voluntary. Unless it is, a couple's sex life can be damaged or even destroyed. Although premature ejaculation (PE) is essentially a male problem, it requires teamwork to rectify. While it can be cured, you shouldn't expect an immediate solution. Your husband will have to learn new habit patterns, which takes time. He'll need to admit his problem, and you'll need to exhibit patient understanding. Lashing out at him will only heighten his feelings of inadequacy and complicate the situation.

There are two main methods of treatment for PE. The first is Masters and Johnson's "squeeze technique," and the second is the "stop/start" procedure, which I believe to be more effective and which is the one I will explain to you. It works as follows:

1. The husband brings the wife to orgasm first. Your husband should help you reach a climax first so that he can concentrate completely on his own sensations as the two of you begin to work on his problem. He can help you achieve orgasm by manual stimulation of the clitoris or another agreed-upon approach.

2. The couple spends time in loving foreplay. Recognizing that increased fondling heightens a man's excitement, a wife will often eliminate touching her husband's penis. In the couple's effort to short-circuit excessive sexual tension, they proceed directly to intercourse. However, when penetration of that warm, familiar environment occurs without prior stimulation, a husband may actually thrust and ejaculate more quickly because of the total shock to his system. Therefore, you should lovingly fondle your husband's genitals—especially caressing the underside or head of the penis, but not to the point that he ejaculates.

3. The husband begins to penetrate. During this stage, your husband inserts his penis *slowly* into the vagina. (He should do this from the man-above position, in which he can maintain better control. And since the friction of total withdrawal may trigger ejaculation, he should keep the head of the penis in the vagina if possible.) Stopping the motion will not cause the erection to subside but will only curb the desire to ejaculate. When your husband feels in control, he can slowly begin penetrating again. If the desire to ejaculate increases once more, he should stop movement immediately. The objective during this phase is to penetrate until he senses imminent ejaculation. A man with a severe problem may not be able to insert more than the head of his penis before stopping to gain control.

4. The husband finds his "point of no return." Sooner or later, every man reaches the "point of no return" when there is no turning back—he continues to thrust till he ejaculates. So, your husband should approach the point of no return but maintain control by suspending motion. After deferring ejaculation, he then should rest from fifteen seconds to two minutes or more, depending on the severity of his problem. He should carefully time himself by means of a clock with a sweep-second hand. Although this sounds unromantic and clinical, it is important that he do so until he can consistently recognize the sensation preceding ejaculation. During this time of suspension, he does not thrust, and you avoid moving, coughing, sneezing, and winking, because the slightest movement could push him beyond the point of no return.

5. He extends the act of intercourse. Once your husband learns the feeling that occurs just prior to the point of no return, he can begin light thrusting motions. The objective is to tolerate gradually increasing amounts of movement. At first, he will have difficulty controlling his movements because his instincts and excitement motivate him toward deep thrusting. However, such deep thrusting doesn't usually produce the greatest amount of satisfaction for you and can actually produce discomfort. Concentrating the motion closer to the vaginal opening is more advantageous for both husband

and wife than deep penetration. It is better for you because only the first two or three inches of the vagina contain primary sensitive tissue. And it's better for him because it will reduce his excitement and thus assist him in learning ejaculatory control.

6. *He achieves lasting ejaculatory control.* Once your husband learns the sensations that precede ejaculation and can tolerate light thrusting with periods of rest, he'll be well on his way to ejaculatory control. After he can control ejaculation for fifteen seconds, he should increase the time to four fifteen-second periods. If he can learn to last one minute, he can eventually last two. And if he can last two minutes, he can last a third. Soon he'll be able to engage in light thrusting, approach the point of no return, stop thrusting, and lose the desire for immediate ejaculation. After extensive practice, he'll be able to maintain intercourse as long as he and you desire. A man attains complete ejaculatory control when he can select the time when his orgasm occurs.

You may find that the stop-start training sessions will produce increased pleasure for you also. You may begin to experience sexual arousal unknown to you before. If you have not previously had climaxes, you may now have them. If you've already reached this plateau, you may go on to enjoy multiple orgasms. This will also free you to experiment with various positions— an option never open to you previously, due to how quickly he climaxed. Through teamwork, you can develop valuable verbal and nonverbal communication skills as well as a new awareness of your interdependence in bringing one another sexual fulfillment.

Now, get to work on your new project, and have fun while you're doing it! (For more information on premature ejaculation, see appendix.)

God designed lovemaking to be enjoyable. What then about the person who feels repulsively removed from sexual pleasure?

Dear Nancy: *On page 131 of* The Compleat Marriage, *you quote a survey that shocked the world by announcing, "Religious women make better lovers." This isn't true in my case. I've gone to church all my life and consider myself a committed Christian. Yet after twelve years of marriage and three children, I've never had an orgasm. This is not a major concern for me, but my husband is letting this hinder his sexual enjoyment. He thinks perhaps we should try oral sex, but giving or receiving sex orally is repulsive to me. My doctor has checked me and says there's no reason I shouldn't have an orgasm.*

Dear Preorgasmic Wife: Not many years ago, women like you were left to rot in their own sexual frustration. But that day is over. Research has proved that all women are capable of achieving orgasm—including you. The word "frigid" is no longer used for women who aren't achieving orgasm. "Preorgasmic" is more descriptive, since orgasm for the female is a learned experience. This means that you simply have not yet learned how to achieve an orgasm. Certainly, no wife—you included—should settle for less. You owe it to yourself and your husband.

Your orgasmic response is closely connected to your feelings about yourself. Resentment, bitterness, misinformation, and tired attitudes erect barriers. This can make it difficult, if not impossible, to respond to your husband. Our most important sex organ is the brain; for you to be sexually satisfied, your brain must say, "OK, go ahead."

You can help yourself adopt attitudes that are more positive by reading such books as *The Gift of Sex,* by Clifford and Joyce Penner, and *The Act of Marriage,* by Tim and Beverly LaHaye. Such books may offer insights into your problem. If such self-help efforts fail, you should contact your physician or ask for a referral if necessary.

You may be able to increase your sexual pleasure and possibly achieve an orgasm by strengthening the pubococcygeus (PC) muscle. In 1940, Dr. Arnold H. Kegel, a specialist in female disorders, inadvertently discovered that an exercise to strengthen a weakened bladder muscle also increased sexual satisfaction for women. Not only did the Kegel exercise cure the urinary problem one of his patients was experiencing, but this patient also experienced orgasm for the first time in fifteen years of marriage. Widespread reports confirm Dr. Kegel's discovery, and many physicians have adopted the Kegel exercises to improve the sexual response of their patients.

The PC muscle runs between the legs from front to back like a sling. It supports the bladder neck, the lower part of the rectum, the birth canal, and the lower vagina. In two out of every three American women, this wide muscle is weak and sags, interfering with sexual functioning.

The Kegel exercises to strengthen the PC muscle consist of a series of contractions first done as the woman is voiding urine. If she can interrupt her urination, she has contracted the PC muscle. Once she has learned control of the muscle, she can practice the exercise any time. See if you can find and contract the muscle that squeezes off the flow of urine. If not, try sitting on the toilet and letting go of a tablespoon at a time. (No need to measure!)

I encourage women to pretend they have an elevator in there that must get to the fifth floor. While I count to five, women squeeze and lift, while tightening and lifting that muscle. At the count of five, they relax the muscle for another count of five. Then they begin the next contraction. They repeat this process until they've completed the desired number of contractions. Begin with five to ten contractions six times daily for a week. Over a six-week period, increase the number of daily sessions to fifty. You should note changes in your sexual performance within three weeks. After six to eight weeks, you can maintain the muscle tone with just a little exercise.

Strengthening the PC muscle will tighten a vagina stretched by having children. A stretched vagina can result in significantly reduced sensation for both partners. Squeezing these muscles during intercourse (and adding your pelvic movements to your husband's) will intensify pleasure. Get busy with these exercises, and see if you can't experience what God created you to enjoy with your husband.

And, yes, I did state, "Christian girls are more fun in bed." Religious women have a higher rate of orgasms and are the most sexually satisfied and sexually active, according to the surveys. Religious women view sex as a gift from God. Seeing sex as God-given and God-inspired frees them to enjoy it. It's not often that religious women see sex as sinful or dirty.

You said that you didn't consider your not having an orgasm a major concern. But it certainly is an important part of your husband's life. God made this strong desire a part of the makeup of men. And God intended His family here on earth to enjoy sex. When a woman denies her husband something so pleasurable, she will have a very dissatisfied and unhappy husband. I can understand why your husband is never satisfied in sex.

No one can tell anyone else what sexual practices he or she can or cannot do. That is up to each couple to decide. Christian couples will be guided by their consciences. In your case, since oral sex is objectionable to you, your husband should not force it upon you. On the other hand, you should consider whether you have approached this with an open mind, with a sincere desire to please your husband. It might be that if you approached it in this manner and tried it, you might change your mind. If you try oral sex and you still object, your husband shouldn't force the issue.

If a doctor has pronounced you physically capable of reaching orgasm, I would hope that you could come to view your sex life with your husband differently. God created sex and blessed the marriage relationship. If you absolutely cannot solve your problem on your own, I recommend that you see a professional counselor. I also suggest that you read the section in *Highly Effective Marriage* that begins on page 191. There are also exercises you can do that might help you become orgasmic. If you have any trouble with them, see a gynecologist. It is my belief that you can be helped to change the course of your life and marriage.

Can dredging up painful past experiences have anything to do with present problems?

Dear Nancy: *I am a woman in my thirties who does not desire sex at all. I'm wondering if it is connected to hormones—or could it be because I was molested when I was five years old?*

Dear Wife With No Sexual Desire: You could be among the 2 percent of women who are totally unresponsive in sex. To make certain your lack of desire isn't due to a hormone imbalance, you may wish to see your physician and have this checked out. However, your lack of sex drive is more likely connected to the molestation you mentioned. Have you had counseling for this and worked through the trauma? This problem is not an easy one to confront, especially when you've kept it buried for years. Regardless of how long the problem has existed, though, it is worth the effort to work through it rather than to try unsuccessfully to bury it. Until you've had extensive counseling, you'll continue to struggle.

What you said in your letter makes me think you're ready to begin. Read *The Wounded Heart* (see appendix). And I highly recommend that you see a Christian counselor—preferably, a female—who specializes in sexual abuse cases. Like physicians, many counselors now specialize. You might also find it helpful to request prayer from a person who can hold a confidence and who understands intercession and can petition God for your healing. God bless you in your recovery.

Is it possible for a wife to recover lost sexual feelings? Read on.

Dear Nancy: *My wife and I enjoyed satisfying sexual relations during the first two years of marriage. But lately she is refusing to let me even kiss or touch her. I have tried to talk to her about this, and she doesn't want to discuss the issue. I'm at a loss as to what to do.*

Dear At a Loss: You and your wife desperately need in-depth counseling to get at the seat of the problem. God's plan for marriage includes having healthy, satisfying sexual relations. Something's wrong when either partner withholds this. Your marriage is headed for trouble if you don't remedy this problem soon.

Since I've taught and counseled with thousands of women over the years, let me make an educated guess at what the problem might be. When a woman resists being touched or kissed by her husband, I immediately suspect either that she is angry with her husband or that she has been sexually abused or molested, perhaps as a child. Your wife may have successfully masked her problem or buried it deep within herself till now. But something has triggered the memories that she has desperately been trying to avoid. Often women bury such memories for ten or even twenty years before they have the courage to confront them. Has she ever told you about experiencing sexual abuse? A father? Stepfather? Brother or stepbrothers? An uncle? A rape experience?

You aren't equipped to deal with these issues. Counseling is a must. If she refuses to go, engage the help of your physician. Explain the circumstances. The physician can encourage your wife to get help from a counselor.

When searching for a counselor in sexual abuse cases, look for three criteria: (1) The counselor must be a Bible-believing, committed Christian. (2) The counselor must specialize in sexual abuse cases. And (3) in most cases, the counselor must be a female. Women who have been sexually abused rarely relate well to males in general, let alone a male who is delving into this aspect of her life. Waste no time in seeking help.

The next letter asks about sex on the Sabbath.

Dear Nancy: *My husband and I had thirty years of stress in our marriage. Then, a year and a half ago, the Lord gave us a wonderful miracle, and we'd been on a honeymoon ever since—until a month ago, when the issue of sex during Sabbath hours came up. He thinks we should abstain, but I don't. And now the total freedom I had enjoyed in expressing myself to him has been cut off. I'm not happy about this, and it takes two to three days after Sabbath to bring our relationship back to where it was. If you can assure me that God wants us to abstain from sex on Sabbath, I'll willingly adjust.*

Dear Willing to Adjust: The subject of whether a couple should engage in sex on the Sabbath has the potential of getting people into sin.

First, if someone thinks something is a sin, he or she had better be careful about engaging in it. Yet I believe you can find an acceptable answer.

Some people use the part of Isaiah 58:13, 14 that states that we are not to do our own pleasure on the Sabbath to forbid sex on that day. Let me ask some questions regarding this thought: Do people find pleasure in going to church on Sabbath? Do they find pleasure in singing hymns, reading the Bible, or eating on the Sabbath? If Isaiah were talking about all that is pleasurable, then Christians had better put these activities—which many people find pleasurable—on their list of "Thou shalt nots."

In my opinion, Isaiah was talking about my seeking my own selfish pleasure. If sex is nothing more than "my pleasure," it is selfish and therefore wrong not only on the Sabbath but on every other day of the week as well. But if my sexual relations are motivated by love and a desire to bring pleasure to my mate, they might be appropriate on the Sabbath. After all, we should be more loving to others on that day than on any other day of the week.

Let's also look at Creation. Adam named all the animals and suddenly recognized that although they had mates, he was alone. God put Adam to sleep and created Eve from his rib. Adam woke up, took one look at Eve, and said, "Wow, God! You outdid Yourself!" Then God instructed Adam and Eve to be fruitful and multiply. All this took place on Friday afternoon, just before the beginning of the Sabbath. We could assume, then, that God made a terrible mistake if He didn't want them to have sex during Sabbath hours. I have trouble believing that God arranged all this and then instructed Adam, "This is Eve, your mate. You are to be fruitful and multiply. But don't touch her until after sundown tomorrow night."

I'm not suggesting that a couple must have sex every Sabbath or even that the views I've expressed here are right for every couple. Each person must ask for wisdom from God. In the end, you must answer to God, not to me or any other human being. If after sharing this information with your husband, he continues to think it wrong to have sex during Sabbath hours, it would be wrong for him to do so. However, if sex is an expression of mutual love in which one is more concerned with the pleasure of the other than with his or her own pleasure, I can't see the sin in that expression of mutual love.

This couple faces more than one problem.

Dear Nancy: *I am thirty-five, and my husband is thirty-eight. We've been married twelve years and have four small children. My husband is very rigid, cold, and domineering. He puts me down constantly and calls me names like "Satan's Daughter." He is never affectionate or tender with me and refuses to allow me to hug or kiss him when he comes home from work. Yet in the same rigid, cold, and domineering way, he has demanded sex every day since we were married. It must always be in the morning, rain or shine, summer or winter. I have never been orgasmic, and this is a big disappointment to him because his first wife was very sexy. Recently, his doctor put him on medication to control his blood pressure, and now he has trouble with his erections. He demands that I masturbate him every morning to ejaculation, but he makes no attempt to stimulate me. I'm one worn-out wife.*

Dear Worn-out Wife: If your husband is as unsympathetic, cold, and unaffectionate but as demanding as you describe, no wonder you're worn out. I hope you got time off for good behavior on days when your babies were born! Obviously, this man needs help. If you've tried to talk with him about it, and he refuses to listen, it's time for "the ultimate ultimatum" (see page 223 of *Smart Listening for Couples*). Write out in letter form precisely the changes you must have in your marriage if it is to continue. Prepare yourself for this occasion by having a suitcase packed and ready beside you so that he understands you are serious. He needs counseling to stop the verbal abuse and to get a grip on his domineering ways. Sexually, he needs to learn that a woman responds to a man in direct proportion to his ability to fulfill her emotional needs. He doesn't realize that by not creating an atmosphere in which you can respond, he's depriving himself of the sexual pleasure that is so important to his happiness.

Your husband is suffering from erectile dysfunction (ED). For many men, this creates such mental stress that discussion can be difficult and embarrassing, even with people he trusts. There have been many advances in the treatment of this problem, yet many refuse treatment because it so strongly affects their self-esteem and virility. The first step to recovery is admitting he has a problem and asking for help. (For information on ED, see appendix.)

You are not frigid but preorgasmic, meaning that you have not yet learned to attain an orgasm. For a woman, orgasm is a learned response. In some women, strengthening the PC muscle solves the problem (see my reply to "Dear Preorgasmic Wife" (p. 52), above). It's also my guess that this problem will diminish when and if your husband gets help. When things are out of balance in the bedroom, the husband often must look at himself. Where you find a lukewarm wife, you will most likely find a husband who fails to meet her needs.

The next question concerns someone who obviously wants more than she feels she's getting out of her intimate love life.

Dear Nancy: *You write in your books that a man should have his sexual needs met every two to three days. What about a woman? After thirty-three years of marriage, I have been sexually and emotionally abandoned. Surely I'm not the only woman to suffer like this. Is there any hope?*

Dear Abandoned Wife: I suspect something is going on in your husband's life that he hasn't mentioned to you. Has he ever experienced erectile dysfunction (ED)? Since you've been married thirty-three years, I'm guessing you're most likely in your fifties. That's an age when a couple is most likely to be matched sexually and emotionally. Their careers are under control, and they have more time, less pressure, and fewer worries than they did a decade earlier. But men sometimes greet their fifties with trepidation because they sometimes experience a slight drop in frequency of erections, and it takes more than visual stimulation to produce one. Men often have an increased need for touching at this time. This is where you come in. What men don't realize is that the erections they do get will last longer and may be fuller than in earlier years.

While you are in your fifties, you should enjoy deeply gratifying and unhurried sex because you have more time to spend on foreplay. Perhaps your husband has suffered from a bout or two of impotence and thinks he is finished sexually. But erectile dysfunction, or impotence, is not permanent. However, the biggest hurdle is a person's attitude toward the problem. The more firmly a man believes he is sexually finished, the more real the possibility becomes.

In about 85 percent of the cases, disease and/or the medications used to treat the disease cause the impotence. Two major culprits are diabetes and heart conditions that restrict blood flow. Even though most impotence results from physical causes, once erection troubles begin, emotional factors often compound the problem.

Many advances have occurred in both the diagnosis and treatment of erectile dysfunction. About 95 percent of all cases can be treated successfully. So, don't just sit there. Pick up the phone and make an appointment with the best urologist in your area who specializes in impotency (see appendix). Make sure you go with your husband so that you can become informed and involved in his treatment. Your attitudes toward his recovery will play a key role.

The next woman says she's not getting enough sex—she's certain of that fact! So, what's the answer to the questioner's deprivation?

Dear Nancy: *My husband and I have been married for thirty years and always had a good sex life. He has been a patient, loving sex partner. During the past couple of years however, our sex life has dropped to near zero. We haven't had sex in five months now. Our relationship continues much the same as before—good most of the time, with occasional arguments that we usually settle the same day. He hugs and kisses me almost daily, but I miss the closeness of sexual intimacy. I'm pretty certain he thinks he's impotent. He is on blood pressure medication as well as antidepressants. I think the medication may be causing his impotency, if that is the problem. What suggestions do you have for this sex-starved wife?*

Dear Sex-Starved Wife: Get some help now! Don't just sit on this problem without making a full-fledged effort to investigate it. Between ten and twenty million men in America suffer from impotence at some point in their lives. Its occurrence increases with age as a result of specific illnesses, and drugs can often be the cause.

Erectile dysfunction (or impotence) is not permanent. Nor is it just a man's problem. Because it disrupts marriage and the way people feel about themselves, it becomes a couple problem. Treatment is more successful when both partners become involved. Your husband should have a complete physical examination, making certain the physician is aware of his sexual problems. You should accompany him to the appointment so that you are fully involved and informed about all causes and treatment.

Don't let another day pass without doing something about this problem. You've got too much to lose. (For assistance in finding help, see the appendix.)

The next man obviously did something very "right" during the prime years of his marriage, and the satisfied lady isn't willing to give up the pleasure to which she's grown accustomed.

Dear Nancy: *My husband and I are in our elderly years. We've had a wonderful life together, but lately he goes flatter than a deflated balloon during sex. What should I do?*

Dear Elderly Wife: The correct term for the problem your husband is experiencing is impotency, or erectile dysfunction (ED). The likelihood of ED increases with age, but it isn't an inevitable consequence of age. Most often, ED occurs because of illness or medical treatment for certain illnesses. The most common causes include vascular disease, diabetes, neurological impairment, pelvic injury, prescription drugs, hormonal imbalances, and Peyronies disease.

Your husband should have a complete physical exam after telling his physician about his impotence. Accompany him on his visit so that you can become informed and involved in his recovery (for information on ED, see appendix).

The fact that your husband is experiencing impotence doesn't necessarily mean that you and he are sexually finished. The later years can be the sexiest time of life. Most women have frequent if not multiple orgasms at this time of life, and men are not so hurried. One study noted that those seventy and over said sex was as gratifying as ever, and some said it was the best. Even those in their nineties who had partners and were in good health said sex was still good. So, get your husband the medical help he needs, and then hang on for the ride. You have some great times just ahead of you!

The aging process can affect how our bodies work. Understanding each other can help us to avoid major problems.

Dear Nancy: *I am a professional man eighty years old. My wife and I have been married sixty years and have had a happy marriage, until five years ago when I became impotent. My wife (age seventy-nine) enjoyed sex most of our lives, but now she doesn't want to be touched or to touch me. She tells me it hurts her to touch me. I desperately desire more closeness, such as hand touching, caressing, etc. Am I being unreasonable to expect this much?*

Dear Professional Husband: My guess is your wife is angry over your impotency. Very angry. At first, she likely hoped the problem would be solved and life could go on as usual. But after five years of little or no sex or sexual advances, she feels she's unloved. After all these years with you, she feels abandoned and without hope for future closeness with you. At first, she may only have been confused. But her confusion turned to hurt, and her hurt to anger and bitterness. She's closing the door on these emotions by rejecting any attempt on your part toward closeness.

You should have sought help immediately, when you first experienced impotency, rather than waiting five years. Here's our plan. Send her a large bouquet of flowers with a note that says, "I'm sorry." When she asks what you're sorry for, explain that you are sorry for depriving her of marital love for five years. Tell her you are going for medical treatment. Have the appointment already confirmed. Then ask her to accompany you to the doctor.

Since you've been married sixty years and have enjoyed a good marriage, you have a strong bond to work with. But you have no time to lose in repairing the damage that has occurred in the last five years. Your future happiness as well as that of your wife rests with how well you carry out the plan outlined. Seek help until you find it. God wants the best for your marriage, even into the golden years.

This woman faces a difficult decision.

Dear Nancy: *I am forty, and my husband is forty-seven. We've been married four years but have never had sex. He accuses me of not being sexy enough for him, and I feel very guilty. But I wonder if he doesn't have a problem. During these four years, we've attempted intercourse only four times. He hasn't been able to maintain an erection, and so it goes no further.*

My husband is under a psychiatrist's care and takes many medications. His doctor prescribes medication for him, but he also self-medicates. (He's a doctor too.) His psychiatrist says he's severely depressed and can't stop taking the prescribed medications. My husband was married once before, but that marriage ended in divorce after only two years. I wonder now if he and his former wife had the same problem. Before we married, he told me he took medication for depression, but he made no mention of impotency.

I love this man, but he is rarely affectionate with me. My love is beginning to die, and I fear for my own emotional health. I'm having difficulty sleeping, I have little appetite, and I cry a lot. I'm nervous all the time, forget things, and feel depressed. I wanted to have children and a happy home with this man. All my dreams for the future are lost. We're currently separated, and he refuses counseling or help of any kind. I am lost in misery.

Dear Lost in Misery: You are at a crossroads. You're married to a totally impotent man who refuses to seek help for his problem. And help exists. About 95 percent of all cases can be successfully treated once the cause has been determined. According to Dr. Bob Phillips, where there is depression, there is also anger. Until your husband deals with his anger, other treatments aren't likely to work. (See the appendix for information on Bob Phillips's book *What to Do Until the Psychiatrist Comes.*)

In all likelihood, your husband will need to continue taking medications to control his severe depression, but there are new medications on the market that won't interfere with sexual functioning. Under a competent physician's care, he should try various medications for depression until he finds one that doesn't cause him to suffer erectile dysfunction. In addition, he should investigate the other treatments that are available—among them vacuum therapy, self-injection, penile implants, and intraurethral pellets. And now, pills promise to restore sexual function without the discomfort and embarrassment of traditional therapies.

I also recommend that you read *Depression: The Way Out* by Dr. Neil Nedley (see appendix). Dr. Nedley specializes in treating depression through nutrition and lifestyle. Gradually, his patients are weaned off medications. He claims a 90 percent success rate.

If your husband refuses to change medications, go to treatment, or search for a solution of any kind, you'll have to make a tough decision. You could remain separated from him and live as you are forever. If you opt for this choice, I fear for your emotional health. You could reunite with him and live like husband and wife even though a marriage in the true sense of the word wouldn't exist for you. Again, I fear for your emotional health. Or you could divorce. Since the marriage has never been consummated, you may even be able to get an annulment. You may wish to check on the laws in your area.

So, you are at a crossroads. Each road leads to a destination, a life decidedly different from the other possibilities. You face a difficult decision that only you can make. I know you didn't want or imagine such massive problems on your wedding day four years ago when you pledged your love to this man forever. Life can be cruel. But we serve a wise and loving God who will help you pick up the pieces of your life. He can and will turn ashes into gold!

This next problem involves the expectations of a husband who is seeking increased sexual excitement.

Dear Nancy: *My husband and I enjoyed sex until he reached his fortieth birthday. Then he said that he felt "old and not able to perform as quickly." He has suggested that we try some of the acrobatic sex acts he has seen in some magazines and videos. I am hesitant about this. He also says he wants to spice things up by watching some sexy videos with me. I know he's getting some of his ideas off the Internet. I really want to please him, but I don't want my husband to be dependent on pornography for sexual arousal. How far should a wife go in trying to please her husband's sexual desires?*

Dear Wife of Slowed-Down Husband: It sounds like your husband is searching for the ultimate sexual experience. Might he have reached some midlife crisis and come to feel that his masculinity, virility, and sex life have gone over the hill? Many men just like your husband use pornography as a sexual stimulant even within marriage. Having a regular sex partner doesn't remove their need for pornography because they've established a habit. People may turn to pornography to satisfy curiosity or to revitalize a sagging sex life, but they tend to become habituated to its stimulation.

Unfortunately, the Internet has opened a new era of pornography and sex addiction. No longer must seekers cruise the seedy side of town. Now they can cruise the Net and indulge in pornography or "cybersex" or even have an affair online. The accessibility to inappropriate sexual activities creates problems for many wives. Weak, struggling men, including Christians, become deeply entrenched without ever leaving their home or office. This leaves wives calling addiction counselors in anguish, not knowing what to do about their husbands' involvement with Internet porn. Some men try to defend their actions by saying they don't see that they're doing anything wrong as long as they don't have physical sex with another person. But infidelity begins at the point when a person makes a strong emotional connection. This means it doesn't take a physical act to betray one's marriage vows.

Pornography destroys intimacy because it introduces a third person, or more, into the relationship. A man's dependency on it not only hurts the man himself and the couple's sex life but also devastates the wife's self-esteem. It undermines her sense of safety within the marriage and damages her trust in her husband.

People can break sex addictions such as this, but only when they admit their problem and get into a program designed to break it (see appendix). Spend much time on your knees, and then hold the line wherever your good judgment tells you not to follow him. *No counselor can settle where that line is for you—only you can do this.* God gave you a brain and a conscience. You have sought counsel. Now, through prayer, you are going to have to make up your own mind about what is right and what is wrong. God will guide you.

The use of pornography often escalates into even worse sexual practices.

Dear Nancy: *My husband is into pornography big time, and I don't know how to handle it. At first, it was only magazines, which he tried to hide from me. He started out with relatively mild stuff but over time graduated to the hard-core stuff. I suspect he is going to X-rated films. He wants to watch porn movies before we have sex and sometimes while we are making love. Now it seems we can't make love without him having some stimulation from an outside source. I can't stand watching that stuff. My self-worth is about one inch high, and I don't know how much more I can take. This is really getting me down.*

Dear Tired of Porn: Some men turn to pornography to restore lost interest or to revitalize a tired sex life. They may also use it because of early conditioning, as a way of satisfying curiosity, or in an attempt to improve their sexual performance. Whatever the reason, they tend to become habituated to its stimulation, which continually diminishes their gratification. Consequently, as in all addictions, they want increasingly stronger stimulation. Eventually, several sex experiences every day still leave them unsatisfied.

Sex addicts typically begin to live a double life. They must hide from their spouses and others their masturbation, porn-shop visits, prostitutes, etc., because they're consumed with shame and afraid of being discovered. And they lack intimacy. They become very self-absorbed and can't develop relationships outside of sexual ones. To addicts, sex becomes a mechanical process that involves another person—but that person isn't really a partner, only an accessory to fantasy, a means of indulging their obsession.

Like all other addictions, sexual addiction becomes progressively worse. In his book *When Sex Becomes an Addiction,* Stephen Arterburn identifies four levels of sexual addiction:

Level 1: Fantasy, pornography, and masturbation. Arterburn calls pornography the "gateway drug" to most sexual addiction. Society views pornography as harmless, yet it is the fuel that burns in the fires of lust gone out of control. Through the use of porn, the addict can masturbate while fantasizing about sex with another woman, a child, multiple partners, or while inflicting pain or violence. To state it bluntly, pornography is about masturbation, because that's what people do when they use porn. Porn is an aid to masturbation. Compulsive masturbation is a quick escape from intimacy and becomes a one-sided process of self-gratification.

Level 2: Live pornography, fetishes, and affairs. In level 1, the addict's only contact with another person is through film, video, or paper. In level 2, the addict makes contact with another person. Activities at this level include frequenting bars that feature nude dancing, having an affair, and indulging in phone sex and in fetishes—such as clothing—that become erotic stimulants. Addicts functioning at this level may also practice perverse forms of sex, such as bondage, masochism or sadism, multiple partners, and sex with prostitutes. All these sexual encounters are devoid of intimacy.

Level 3: Minor criminal offenses, prostitution, voyeurism, and exhibitionism. When sex addicts reach this level, they cross the line to minor criminal behavior. Some will engage with multiple prostitutes in one night. The voyeur who spies on others and the exhibitionist who enjoys exposing his genitals in public are functioning on level 3. These are illegal acts, though they bear relatively minor consequences.

Level 4: Molestation, incest, and rape. Child molestation, incest, and rape are included in the fourth level of addiction. Addicts who are arrested and convicted for these offenses will serve time in jail. Victims pay an even heavier price, and they may begin to victimize others.

Your husband exhibits all the characteristics of a sex addict. Your description of his addiction points us to level 1—however, you may be aware of only the tip of the iceberg. Even if he hasn't indulged in level 2 activities yet, you know that's just around the corner.

It's time for a major confrontation. Carefully think through and write down what changes you must have if the relationship is to continue. And do your homework before confronting him—call Sex Addicts Anonymous (see appendix) and find out what programs are available in your area for him. (While you're doing so, see what support groups they offer for you, too.) Insist that he follow through or else. If he refuses, you must follow the "or else" you've set up. There's no other way to handle this, unless you want to settle for allowing him to continue his destructive addiction.

Have you ever wondered if it's possible to be raped within a marriage? Read on.

Dear Nancy: *Can a woman be raped within a marriage? There are times when I don't want sex, and my husband literally forces me. Once I even bled and had bruises from resisting.*

Dear Confidential Friend: Yes, marital rape definitely exists. All women—even married women—have the right to control their own bodies—to make decisions about having intercourse, becoming pregnant, and having children. Rape strips these rights from them, whether or not they're married to the rapist.

"Marital rape" is a term used to describe sexual acts committed without a wife's consent or against her will. It can be defined as any unwanted intercourse or penetration perpetrated by force or threat of force. Marital rape includes sexual acts performed on a woman when she can't consent because she's under the influence of alcohol or drugs or is unconscious or disabled. In marital rape, the perpetrator is the woman's husband. A woman may have reason to fear her husband from prior experience and be afraid to resist. Many women have been hurt for not cooperating. They've been physically beaten, psychologically and emotionally abused, had money taken from them, or been threatened with abandonment for refusing their husbands. Whenever a woman submits to sex out of fear or coercion, it is rape. Although not much research on the subject exists, husband-rapists, by their own admission, rape to reinforce their power, dominance, or control over their wife or family, or to express anger.

The idea that when a woman says "No" she really means "Yes" continues to be reinforced by the media as well as by the pornography industry. And some religious ideologies give husband-rapists an excuse by teaching that sex is a "duty" for wives.

Victims of marital rape suffer all the consequences of regular rape, but they're often less likely to see what's been done to them as a violation of their rights. Some people still believe marital rape to be less harmful than rape by someone other than a husband. As recently as 1976, husbands couldn't be charged with raping their wives, but today, marital rape is a crime in all fifty states. Women can now sue their husbands in civil court for pain and suffering and for medical and other costs incurred because of sexual assault.

Marital rape often has severe and long-lasting consequences. Physically, women may suffer injuries to the vaginal and/or anal areas, lacerations, soreness, bruising, torn muscles, fatigue, and vomiting. Women who have been battered as well as raped by their husbands may also suffer broken bones, black eyes, bloody noses, and knife wounds. And it's not surprising that when someone a woman presumably once loved and trusted attacks her, she suffers long-term psychological consequences.

Women will often stay with their husbands after a rape because they do not have the resources to leave. If a woman has children, the prospect of moving and having them change schools and friends complicates the situation. Many women also are unaware that wife rape is a crime.

If you've been experiencing sex imposed upon you against your will through force, threats, or intimidation, you need to seek personal and/or legal counseling. You can find such counseling services through rape crisis centers, domestic violence services, and family service agencies. If you have been raped, you should seek immediate medical treatment at a hospital, followed by counseling. And a husband who rapes also needs to seek help, although he is unlikely to admit he's forcing sex on his wife. He needs to get into treatment with a trained specialist who works with men who are sexually aggressive.

*   *   *   *   *

Remember, a healthy sexual relationship is one in which husband and wife honor and esteem the other as separate and special individuals. Each has feelings, needs, and dreams of their own and has equal personal rights and freedom. Both should desire to cooperate and participate in making their sexual activity a positive and mutually pleasurable experience.

Husbands and wives should aim to be imaginative, creative, and willing lovers. God designed that sex—unhampered by selfishness—be exciting, enjoyable, and fulfilling. Good sex, then, comes as the result of a satisfying relationship. Should you be experiencing sex problems, including time pressures and lack of sexual energy, ask God for help in solving these problems. Pray also that you might prioritize your life in such a way that you can give the energy, time, and creativity needed to enjoy a superior sex life. Remember, good sex doesn't just happen.

Smart Advice to Singles Under Pressure

Many singles have had their share of dead-end relationships and disappointments. Why? Because they've had precious little instruction on how to choose a mate and yet are expected to make brilliant choices. Those who count only on luck, passion, and romance will end up with disappointing marriages or in divorce court. Statistics indicate how often this proves true. However, singles that adhere to carefully formulated principles can significantly increase their probability of having a great marriage.

Most unmarried people look to marriage to solve their problems and make them happy. They assume a quick trip to the altar will ensure happiness. Often, the greater their problems, the faster they rush. But weddings do not automatically change anyone nor do they ensure happiness. Romantic excitement clouds the realities involved in a long-term marriage and the sacrifices a couple must make to ensure that the relationship works. And couples certainly cannot survive if they haven't dealt with their own brokenness.

My prayer is that God will use the advice that follows to help singles who read this book learn how to build and maintain a dating relationship that may eventually lead to a mutually satisfying marriage.

Dear Nancy: *I'm a twenty-five-year-old second-year medical intern. I am an ambitious and motivated person, but above all, I seek the Lord's will in whatever I do. I'm looking for a dedicated, lifelong partner who will be not only* *a passionate lover and soul mate but also a friend and dedicated confidant. I want to have a family and raise children who grow up to honor and glorify God.*

Through providential circumstances, I made contact with a wonderful, twenty-seven-year-old gentleman with whom I communicate via email. He also is a committed Christian. Our communication over the past several months leads me to believe that he's exactly what I've been searching for. The first time we talked to each other, it seemed like we'd known each other for years. We're extremely comfortable with each other and are brutally honest, as I believe we need to be in such a relationship. We haven't met yet, but plan to soon.

I've spent hours in prayer, earnestly seeking the Lord's guidance. Please give any thoughts, ideas, cautions, or advice on how to proceed.

Dear Single Physician: Because communication through email is instant, people think they can assess a relationship more quickly and fall in love faster. Let's examine what the process of communication involves. Communication has three aspects: words, tone of voice, and other nonverbal elements. Studies have determined that words deliver 7 percent of the message; tone of voice, 38 percent; and other nonverbals, 55 percent. So, through emailed messages, you get 7 percent of the message, because tone of voice and nonverbals are missing. Over the phone, you get a little more: the spoken words, 7 percent, plus the tone of voice, 38 percent, for a total of 45 percent; but a whopping 55 percent is still missing! Only during face-to-face interaction can you put the process of communication together and judge accurately the truthfulness and honesty of the person who is communicating with you. People often say one thing while their body language is saying something else. This is why email romance is dangerous. You link up with a stranger.

Let's discuss your brutal honesty. It is impossible to judge honesty on four months of emailed messages! If this guy were a serial killer or a sadist, do you think he would email you about it? He is telling you only what he wants you to know about him. This type of game goes on all the time when boy meets girl. Both put their best self forward—particularly, early in a relationship. Making an impression is the name of the game; the Great Pretenders weave their magic spell on each other. Both put on their rose-colored glasses and rush toward marriage without taking the time to identify what's under the masks.

I recommend that people take two years to get to know each other. When a couple is "dating" via email, they must be even more careful. Their courtship is scripted via dreamy messages, whispered messages of love over the phone, and, in your case, no face-to-face evaluations. This is all wrong. When a couple becomes seriously interested in one another, one needs to move to where the other lives. (Don't tell me you can't do this. If you married, one of you would move!) The ideal would be to see each other almost daily to cut through all the masks. You need to see him after a long, hard day at work, when he's just been fired from a job, at church, in a restaurant, with his family and his friends, and in a hundred other situations.

Here's another caution. Having dealt with hundreds, perhaps thousands, of singles in similar circumstances, I've learned that singles can "hear" God say anything they want to hear God saying when they think they're in love. But our God is a patient God and will never rush you into anything. God teaches patience and frequently tells us to wait.

Am I encouraging you to end this relationship? Not at all. Make plans to meet. Then you'll be better able to make a judgment regarding whether the relationship should continue. In the meantime, make no declarations of undying affection. Email doesn't provide enough clues to make sound judgments regarding a life partner. After meeting, should you decide to pursue the relationship, continue with phone calls, emails, and occasional get-togethers. After a year of such communication, one can move near the other to test the relationship for another year. Before you make a major move like that, I suggest some compatibility testing (see appendix) rather than relying solely on what your fluttering heart tells you.

So many men out there, this next girl writes, yet so few Christians! Should she eliminate all who are not Christians from her dating agenda?

Dear Nancy: *I am very much in love with a man I met at work. We are both in our thirties and are compatible in every area but spiritually. Even though he's not a Christian, he goes to church with me, and I believe in my heart that he will convert someday. There's no one at church for me to date. Besides, this man's moral standards are higher than are those of all the other men from church whom I've dated. What do you think my chances are for converting him? I'm willing to take my chances.*

Dear Christian Single: I understand the difficulty. Looking for someone with whom you can share spiritual oneness drastically reduces the field of eligible candidates. There is a *chance* that your friend may convert. But the admonition against a relationship between a believer and an unbeliever still exists. *Never marry in hopes of someone changing.* If you fail to match in your spiritual values as well as mentally, emotionally, and physically, you are compromising your standards and beliefs. This puts you on dangerous ground.

Don't try to ignore the problem, justify the relationship, or disobey God. Instead, take a hard look at what this means for you and the one you love. Unless you do it now, in all the years to come you'll deal with the consequences of being unequally yoked.

Imagine the frustration two builders would experience trying to work on a house from two different sets of building plans. Differing designs and materials would produce such confusion and conflict that the project would fail. Even a casual observer would say, "You can't build a house from two differing blueprints."

The same advice applies to naive lovers who enter marriage with differing sets of spiritual blueprints. When one is a Christian and the other is not, they enter an arena where they can never achieve spiritual oneness. All the seminars, books, counseling, and tears in the world won't solve the problems this couple will encounter. What a difference it makes in marriage when both partners can turn to God in the midst of turmoil and together find a refuge and strength, a present help in time of need.

It's amazing how much disobedience flourishes under the rationalization that I found rampant in your letter. You need courage to end this relationship. Call it off. Make a clean break. The pain will be severe, but the peace afterwards will be even more incredible. Surround yourself with Christian friends who can support you in prayer. If you choose to disobey the biblical admonition, you are headed for certain disaster and a lonely future. If you make the hard choice now, you will soon have peace.

The same question is repeated below with a slightly different slant:

Dear Nancy: *I am twenty-eight years old and studying linguistics in a public university. I really like some of the ideas you present in* Smart Love: A Field Guide for Single Adults *(see appendix), but I'm not sure non-Christian girls are a bad influence on me. What do you think about dating outside one's faith?*

Dear Wants to Date Unbeliever: Some single adults become really uncomfortable when people quote Paul's warning: "Do not be yoked together with unbelievers" (2 Corinthians 6:14, NIV). They begin the rationalizations: "I know she's not a Christian, but she goes to church with me, and I just know she'll convert." "But there's no one at church to date!" "I know she's not a Christian, but she has higher morals than any of the other girls I've dated."

It's amazing how much disobedience flourishes under rationalization. I understand the rationalizations as well as the difficulty. Yes, she *may* convert someday. But the admonition against a relationship between a believer and an unbeliever still exists. Instead of trying to ignore the problem, justify the relationship, or rationalize, take a hard look at what this means for your future should you marry. There are scores of Christlike men and women in our churches married to unbelievers. Some became Christians *after* they married. Others married without heeding the scriptural advice. But they all carry the pain of spiritual loneliness.

Spiritual compatibility is so important because during a time of stress, two who worship together can tap into a source of strength to carry them through the tough times. No couple goes through life without being touched by adversity or tragedy. This imperfect world carries much evil—heartache, pain, disappointment, illness, emotional upheavals, financial setbacks, and death. When a couple needs to seek God in prayer, they find great strength and courage as they seek Him together, rather than singly!

"Do not be yoked together with unbelievers" is godly wisdom. Unmarried Christians must heed it or reap the consequence of living in a home where the shadows are never lifted. God didn't give this advice to keep you from finding a mate, but to protect you from pain. Don't get yourself so wrapped up romantically with someone who doesn't share your faith that you can't bear the thought of a future without that person. The safest way to protect yourself from such pain is to maintain a policy of dating only those of like faith.

When someone's in love, the future looks incredibly bright. How can one know for sure that their current love is indeed the right one?

Dear Nancy: *I am a twenty-four-year-old male who is contemplating marriage and wants to be confident about this step. I feel I need to go through a lot of counseling before finally deciding. Many of my friends who married thinking they truly loved each other are now divorced. I don't want to marry only to end up divorcing; I want to marry for keeps. I love my girlfriend very much. She is such fun to be with, but I feel like I can't move until God gives His approval. His will is the most important thing to me. Can you help someone like me?*

Dear Doubtful Groom: Your desire for counseling before entering marriage is truly commendable. Far too many couples enter marriage loving each other but end up divorced.

A recent Gallup study showed that more than one-third (38 percent) of people who have divorced reported that at the time of their marriage they were aware of the problem that caused the divorce. This proves the theory that couples tend to ignore relationship problems when dating. They view even evident problems with rose-colored optimism. When they encounter a problem, they minimize its seriousness, thinking they can correct it after marriage. Then, when the romantic glow dims, what they ignored becomes even more glaringly apparent.

Most churches or pastors require an engaged couple to have only two or three counseling sessions, during which most of the discussion focuses on planning the wedding service. If a couple wishes to be married in a month and the church and pastor are available, their wish is granted. These churches don't require a waiting period, helpful reading, training in communication skills, or compatibility testing. The pastor may direct a few general questions to the couple about some problems they may encounter, and that's it. Churches that function in this manner are little more than "blessing machines" for tomorrow's divorces.

You seek to move beyond this immature and foolish method of entering marriage. Chapter 13, "Getting Fit to Be Tied," of my book *Smart Love* will be of particular interest to you in evaluating your suitability for one another and your readiness for marriage. Perhaps the most important section involves a serious look at "divorce insurance"—it lists six things you can do to make sure you don't end up as a divorce statistic.

One thing you can do as a couple is to take a compatibility test. I recommend the premarital personal and relationship evaluation (PREPARE; see appendix). It gives an objective diagnosis of relationship strengths and weaknesses as well as an assessment of conflict-resolution ability. It predicts with 86 percent accuracy which couples will divorce and with 78 percent accuracy which couples will stay happily married. Taking such steps may sound unromantic or unappealing to some. But doing so prior to marriage prevents divorce and promotes happiness.

This next question is from a cautious young adult who wants to build a healthy relationship that lasts.

Dear Nancy: *I'm currently in what I consider a good relationship with someone I really care about. Everything between us is good. How can I tell if* *what we have is the real thing? I've had a lot of experience in dating but just never seemed to find the real thing. I'm just out of a very painful relationship. I've put myself together again, and I want never to go through what I've just been through. Is there any way to tell in advance if one has found true love?*

Dear Searching: Single adults think they should be able to discern true love because they're more mature now than when they were teens. Sometimes, because people haven't experienced the exhilaration of "love" in many years, their excitement becomes overpowering. The truth is that adult singles experience many of the same silly feelings so apparent in teen dating—the exhilaration, quickened sexual response, and rush of excitement. Often, these feelings are amplified by age because the adults may feel that time is running out. These feelings are just as likely to color and confuse the judgment of adults as that of seventeen-year-olds. A woman approaching the age of forty realizes her biological clock is ticking. Should she still desire children, she must hurry. This produces tremendous pressure.

Differentiating between love and infatuation is always complicated because both conditions share similar symptoms: passion, a desire to be close, and strange emotions. Passion may be present without genuine love. It is entirely possible for people—particularly for males—to feel passionate or to have strong sexual feelings for someone of the opposite sex whom they've never met. Passion doesn't necessarily indicate true love. And no one can maintain fierce passion for long, although people vow they will. If all a couple has going for them is passion, the relationship will likely end in three to six months.

The desire to be close can be just as overwhelming in infatuation as in love. You may wish to be together all the time and dread when you must part. You may feel empty and lonely when your loved one is not with you, but this doesn't necessarily mean that you have real love.

And strange emotions can occur just as frequently in infatuation as in real love. In fact, "funny feelings" and strange emotions are probably more indicative of infatuation than of genuine love. The latter consists of much more than excitement or sick feelings and will continue long after these strange feelings subside. Infatuation isn't bad as long as you recognize it for what it is—a brief interlude of romantic fantasy that cannot last. Given enough time, it will pass or possibly develop into a relationship that is more than a rush of emotions.

If you've analyzed your situation carefully and still can't decide whether you've found true love, allow yourself more time—two years of dating prior to marriage. This two-year time frame provides ample opportunities to find out what you need to know to make the final decision. After you've been in a relationship about a year, I recommend you take PREPARE.

Ending a satisfying relationship is never easy. What should a person do?

Dear Nancy: *My parents don't think my boyfriend, Jake, is the right one for me because to them he appears controlling. They constantly warn me about him, but I don't see this in his behavior and am tired of hearing their criticism of him. I'm twenty-seven—old enough to be making my own choice. I think Jake is near perfect.*

Dear Believer in Perfection: When people's family and close friends see that they are well suited to their partner, they usually approve. They see how well the personalities blend, whether they share many interests, and how the couple complement and motivate each other. However, when parents or friends don't approve, beware! If your parents are convinced that the one you have chosen is wrong for you, they're probably right. Family and friends are extremely interested in your future welfare and don't want you to get hurt. And because they are not as emotionally involved as you, they may be able to see certain characteristics you can't see. You may be old enough to make this decision alone, but this is one time it's smart to listen to Mom and Dad.

Here are some signs that identify controllers. They want to:

- know where you are and who you are with every minute
- decide who your friends can be or who you can spend time with
- decide where you go and what you do
- dictate how you dress, style your hair, and decorate your home
- make decisions for you without consulting with you

When all is said and done, a controller gives you the impression that your views aren't important. Controllers think their opinions and wishes are superior to yours. It takes some people a long time to wake up to controlling behavior because they have been controlled for so long that they don't recognize it as controlling. To them, it is normal.

In the end, remember that statistics show that marriages that lack the blessing of parents have a high failure rate. When parents approve, take heart—there's a good chance you have found genuine love. If parents and friends object, beware. PREPARE can settle this issue in your mind as well as for your parents. You can trust its accuracy.

This next guy promises the world. Will he deliver?

Dear Nancy: *I have been going with Carlos for six months. He is married, and this presents a slight problem. But he has promised he will leave his wife soon. We plan to get married as soon as his divorce is final. My best friend constantly warns me against dating him and thinks he is using me. I don't think so. I believe him.*

Dear Believer: You are refusing to deal with reality. A man who is dating you while still married to someone else is dishonest and is breaking his solemn marriage vow. You have idealized him to such a degree that you refuse to see him in anything but the best possible light.

During the early stages of romance, people often defend their loved one regardless of the reality of the situation. Rather than listening to the opinions of others, they blind themselves to objective evaluation. You should listen to the candid observations of your friend because it's so easy to be tricked by romance.

Furthermore, until Carlos's divorce is final, you are dating a married man. And until the final decree is signed, there's always a chance he and his wife will reconcile. In your case, Carlos hasn't even made the final break with his wife yet. Frankly, I doubt he will. When and if he does leave his wife, he won't be emotionally ready to date you or anyone else. He's already proved that he can't be trusted and can't keep a commitment to a woman. This man lacks integrity. What makes you think you can change all this?

By dating a married man, you are setting yourself up for tremendous pain. If you are a committed Christian, you must also realize that you are leading him into sin as well as sinning yourself by enticing him to break his wedding vows. Next to my two-year rule, the strongest advice I give to singles is not to begin dating too soon after a divorce and certainly not before the divorce is final! Read chapter 14 of *Smart Love,* "Second Chances."

The following gal finally faced reality!

Dear Nancy: *I am thirty-eight years old and was very much in love with a boyfriend who couldn't seem to hold down a good job. He always needed money, and I kept giving it to him, hoping he would eventually marry me. I even gave him my credit cards. But when he charged more than six thousand dollars and* *then left me and quickly married someone else, I woke up. Now I'm alone and heartbroken.*

Dear Alone and Heartbroken: What a hard way to learn that you can't buy real love! You were so desperate that you resorted to bribes to try to make a man fall in love with you. All it did was keep him around long enough to run up some large debts for you to pay off. You, like so many others, have been tricked by a Great Pretender. To protect your future, check with a counselor about possible abandonment issues that may trigger foolish reactions. Pick up the pieces of your life and carry on.

A dreamy-eyed lover wants a stamp of approval on a new romance. Can this one work?

Dear Nancy: *I've met the most wonderful woman. I knew it when I saw her. She looked just as I always pictured the girl of my dreams would. On our first date, we talked half the night, and I felt as if I'd known her all my life. I felt an incredible closeness that I've never experienced with anyone else. I'm convinced that dreams really do come true. What do you think?*

Dear Believer in Dreams: You think dreams really do come true, but your evaluation won't be valid until after a year of dating. Why? Because love grows, and growth requires time. It's infatuation that hits swiftly and suddenly. It's impossible to know the real person after only a few meetings.

What you felt when you saw her is called "chemistry." Some chemistry should be at work when boy meets girl. It quickens the heart, takes your breath away, and makes you desire closeness. I believe in chemistry. But unless you want the girl of your dreams to become a nightmare that haunts you day and night, the relationship must be tested beyond the chemistry you felt based on one date.

Early in a relationship, people wear masks while putting on their best behavior. Any unpleasant traits are closely guarded, hidden, controlled. For this reason, it takes months and even years of seeing a person under varied circumstances before you can say you know that person really well. The people who don't do this are the people who end up complaining that the person they married has become a stranger.

Don't jump into marriage. Allow your relationship to grow slowly. Maintain a friendship, and don't hurry the love stage. A leisurely beginning can be pleasurable and much safer. Eventually, such friendships can lead to ecstasy that resembles infatuation in intensity but is rooted in reality. Dreams do come true—when you obey the rules of common sense and slow things down.

Chemistry! It's powerful—but is it enough?

Dear Nancy: *I've just met someone new, interesting, and good-looking. We've had a few dates, and everything is going well. I get a good feeling every time I'm with her. There is definitely chemistry between us. I think either a relationship works or it doesn't work. Either you feel it or you don't. This relationship just feels right, and I think I'm safe in being guided by this gut reaction.*

Dear Feels Right: If only discovering genuine love were as easy as you think it is! Where did you come up with the idea that chemistry and love are the same thing? Probably from romantic love scenes portrayed in movies in which the script reads, "Her heart raced with excitement. She melted into his arms, and their bodies merged."

When you've been conditioned for this to happen and you desire it intensely, it's likely to happen. Here's a warning though: Many who marry based on chemistry alone wake up later to deal with a disastrous relationship! Relying on feelings alone to guide you toward love is dangerous. Why? Because chemistry is based mostly on physical or sexual attraction. Certainly, marriage relationships need that spark and pull that lights up your eyes and makes you feel alive. But to base a relationship on this feeling alone is ludicrous.

Although genuine love includes chemistry and physical attraction, it springs from many other factors as well, including character, personality, emotions, ideas, and attitudes. Compatible personalities, along with common interests and values, go a long way toward developing a lasting love relationship.

Don't make any quick commitments based on feelings alone that you'll regret later. Remember, true love can survive the test of time. You need to date at least two years.

Can someone be in love with two people? Read on.

Dear Nancy: *I'm in love with two men and can't seem to choose between them. Len is sensible, stable, and responsible. He's a banker; he's careful with money, and he'd provide a secure financial future for the children and me. He's also dependable—always there when I need him.*

Matt is more irresponsible and fun-loving. He drives a fancy car (that he can't afford). He's pleasant and happy all the time and easy to get along with. I love his sense of humor, although there doesn't seem to be a serious bone in his body. Life with him would be a blast. Help me choose between these two great guys!

Dear Help Me Choose: Chances are you aren't in love with either of these men. Some need in you draws you to the fun-loving spender, while another need longs for the qualities of stability and responsibility of your banker friend. Genuine love focuses on one person in whose character and personality you find the qualities you believe are most essential. Rather than tearing yourself up over which one to date, put a hold on dating either one for a while and see what happens.

A slow learner asks whether a relationship can flourish when promises aren't kept.

Dear Nancy: *My boyfriend, Eric, failed to pick me up for a job interview as he promised he would. I missed the appointment and had no chance at a great job for which I was well qualified. A year later, he was still forgetting things, making up excuses, and failing to show up even when he promised that he would. I finally broke up with him. Why was I so slow to learn?*

Dear Slow Learner: When you think you're in love, you idealize the positive qualities of your partner with complete disregard for reality. While concentrating on the positive, you ignore the negative. When you see a negative trait, you tend to excuse it by thinking, *That doesn't really matter,* or *That's not what he really meant.* Or you imagine him blossoming and growing under your love and encouragement.

Infatuation keeps you from seeing anything wrong with him, and you can't admit he has faults. You defend your love against all critics. You admire one or two qualities so much that you fool yourself into believing they can outweigh all faults or problems.

You are living in denial regarding fears about things you don't think you can handle. Put yourself in the hands of a good therapist to check out abandonment issues. I think your core belief is that you don't deserve anything better than this guy. You may be a slow learner, but here's hoping you catch on before it's too late.

Next, let's talk about strategies for successful dating.

Dear Nancy: *It's not asking a girl out that bothers me; it's where to take her. I always fall back on the same thing—something to eat and a movie. I find such dates boring, and I'm afraid the women do also. I'm a well-educated business-man who is reasonably successful. I enjoy sports and work out regularly, but I have trouble maintaining relationships over a long period. What's wrong with me?*

Dear Businessman: Nothing major, just your choice of activities. There are two kinds of dates—and I'm not talking about good ones and bad ones. Sign up for some date coaching!

There are spectator dates: going to movies, plays, concerts, and sports events, or watching TV or listening to music. Spectator dates are popular, especially early in a relationship. They're low stress because they don't involve trying to keep a conversation going. Furthermore, everyone knows how to "spectate"—just sit and watch. On the down side, spectator dates defeat the main purpose of dating, which is getting to know one another. Watching others perform allows little time for interaction. And spectator dates can be expensive.

A second type of date, the participation date, involves activities: playing miniature golf or tennis, canoeing, sailing, hiking, visiting a museum or a zoo, or doing crafts projects together. Participating together in an activity encourages the expression of creative abilities, affirms feelings and worth, usually costs less, and allows a couple to explore likes and dislikes. Each can develop skills and abilities as well as gain insights into the other. Such dates are seldom boring.

However, participation dates require creativity and initiative. For many, planning an activity requires more effort than they're willing to give. Some people are too self-conscious to participate in such dates because they fear they don't have what it takes to make themselves look good.

Your date life appeared boring because it *was* boring. You can spend money to make a date unforgettable, but you don't have to do that. Design some creative dates with a personal touch. Here are some ideas. Play table tennis, croquet, or horseshoes, or go rollerblading, bike riding, jogging, or hiking. Make ice cream, bake homemade bread, or plan and cook a gourmet dinner. Or explore a new town, go picture taking, collect shells on a beach, pass out Christian literature, or visit a nursing home.

So spice up your dating life with some participation dates. You'll have more fun and get to know your date better. Then let me hear from you after you're married!

Does snagging a quality person to date require an inner radar?

Dear Nancy: *I feel just like Leo, the cat you described in* Smart Love—*the cat who got locked in a dryer and came out bruised, ruffled, and cross-eyed, who doesn't purr but just sits and stares. I've been in and out of so many relationships that dead-end in disappointment. I'm trying not to give up on finding true love someday, but I'm really hurt and lonely.*

And the only guys I date are real losers. I think I'd have more success if I had a list of danger signals—clues to warn me in advance that the guy is a loser. I come from a very dysfunctional family with multiple divorces and abuse. I don't think I'm destined to have dysfunctional relationships just because I came from that background, but I lack the "radar" other women seem to have. I want to avoid trouble.

Dear Radarless: Here goes. Beware of guys who show fear and anxiety when faced with a new social situation that holds no threat; express guilt when there's no reason for guilt; frequently exhibit intense emotion and excitement inappropriate to the situation; have phobias toward certain objects, situations, or ideas; are ritual ridden; have uncontrollable impulses; have a hypochondriacal obsession regarding their health; have moods of depression.

If a guy doesn't have a job, an apartment, a car, goals, good manners, and good grooming habits, his marriageability is marginal. If he shows extreme shyness, hostility toward the police or others, expresses suspicion over people he meets, makes a conspicuous display of clothing or possessions to impress others, shows arrogance around friends, behaves in a boisterous manner, is preoccupied with sex or shows a strong aversion to sex, has an insatiable desire for adventure and excitement, makes tactless and embarrassing public displays of affection, lies, or distorts facts, he is not a good risk.

If a guy doesn't get along with other people, doesn't keep his word, blames others for his bad luck, or makes scenes, he's a loser. If he doesn't pay his bills, has a poor credit rating, has been in trouble with the law, won't introduce you to his friends or family, has been married and divorced multiple times, doesn't see or support his kids, he's a big-time loser. Any guy who hates his job, women, the government, or people of other ethnic groups is a loser. A guy who always feels sorry for himself, makes fun of other people, borrows money, or mooches off you or others is a loser. A guy with low self-esteem is the biggest risk of all, especially if he expects you to "fix" him. And alcohol problems and drug habits are other distinguishing traits of losers. This list is only for starters. You and your friends can add to it.

I think you have a co-dependency issue. Read Carol Cannon's book *Never Good Enough* (see appendix).

If you are having trouble getting dates, you can commiserate with this next despairing single.

Dear Nancy: *I am reasonably good looking and have a good job and a wide circle of friends. I am active at church and have my world pretty much together, except for one thing—no dates. There haven't been any for several years. This was OK for a while. I was finishing my education and building my career; there wasn't much time for romance. But now I'm ready for romance, and it eludes me.*

I'm not interested in the women who pursue me, and when I find someone I'm interested in, the feelings aren't mutual. Am I too picky? Many of the prospects within my world are either too old or too young. Some seem too nice, and others act like jerks. Some try to control my life, and others don't want a commitment. I've made a real effort to stay in circulation. I signed up for a class at the university and took up a new hobby. I go to lots of parties and am involved in my church's singles activities. Yet I often spend my evenings alone. I'm getting desperate.

Dear Desperate: You're in the same boat as thousands of other intelligent, successful single adults who can't seem to find the right partner. Many singles think that being alone is worse than a prison sentence. They think that being alone makes them abnormal, and they feel desperate to find a life partner. Being single doesn't brand or label you. You're not a social misfit. However, if you continue to give in to feelings of desperation, you'll make bad choices. Feelings of desperation will lead you into patterns of destructive behavior.

It's important that you come to terms with being single. It's OK to be single. Then you must deal with your loneliness. Loneliness is a feeling that both marrieds and singles can experience. To chase after anything or anyone desperately to avoid loneliness is a big mistake. There are things worse than loneliness.

Reach out to others rather than expecting them to reach out to you. You might prefer to spend Saturday night with a significant other. But since most singles meet their dating partners through friends, you can enjoy your friends and increase your odds of meeting someone at the same time. Then you'll find that your lonely times are bearable, and aloneness isn't so bad after all. (See appendix for Christian dating services.)

It's quite evident from the following question that this couple will encounter major problems.

Dear Nancy: *My girlfriend and I have been going together for a little over a year and are talking marriage in a couple months. I'm twenty-seven and have never been married. I own my own business and have done well financially. I've given her a Rolex watch as a pre-engagement gift.*

Before we make it official, however, I want to settle a couple concerns. Although our relationship started out really well, lately we've been doing a lot of arguing and have had many disagreements. We always settle these disagreements eventually, but sometimes we go through long periods of the silent treatment before it happens. My girlfriend says she loves me a lot, but she isn't very affectionate with me and says she feels "smothered" by my affection for her. What does that mean?

She was brought up in church. She talks about her family a lot, yet I've never met her parents, and she seems to resist the idea that I do meet them. She's twenty-five and twice divorced but has no children. I've been raised with no religion and never went to church until I started going to her church. I have strong moral convictions, so although we sleep together, we're refraining from having sex until we get married.

Sometimes my girlfriend is terribly irritable, touchy, depressed, and so moody that I can't stand to be around her. Other times she is great, and we get along fine. I don't understand her mood swings.

Other than these small matters, she's gorgeous, and I think she'll make a great wife. What's your take?

Dear Talking About Marriage: Being gorgeous won't cut it in the face of "many disagreements," "long periods of the silent treatment," "feeling smothered," religious differences, mood swings, and two divorces! Can't you see the red flags here? I have a real problem with people blindly jumping into marriage in spite of evident problems. With two divorces behind her at age twenty-five, either she is making very poor choices or she doesn't have the capacity to sustain a long-term relationship. And something is very wrong when she avoids introducing you to her family.

Any couple who can't deal effectively with their differences shouldn't even consider marriage. Some arguing during an ongoing relationship is normal. If a couple never disagrees, they're not really being themselves and have probably not learned to interact honestly with each other. But there is such a thing as too many disagreements, especially if they're loud or long. People fight about three main issues: abandonment, significance, and control. What do your fights center on? Even a well-matched couple may have a series of misunderstandings, but, when your fights outnumber the periods of peace, you should be worried.

Her mood swings and irritability may be due to premenstrual syndrome (PMS). The symptoms occur monthly, generally seven to fourteen days prior to menstruation, and they worsen as menstruation approaches. They subside at the onset or after several days of menstruation. A symptom-free phase usually follows. She should seek a medical opinion to solve this problem. And before marriage, you should accompany her to this appointment for a fuller understanding of PMS. Also, find out whether she might have a more serious problem, such as depression, disthymia, or bipolar disorder. You need to know before you commit.

Sleeping together while trying to remain pure for marriage doesn't make sense. Whenever an unmarried couple remove their clothing, caress each other's bodies, and sleep together, they've gone too far, whether or not intercourse has occurred. Such intimacy should be reserved for marriage only. Technically, it is only a breath or two away from intercourse (see *Smart Love* chapter 10). Such sexual encounters present several hazards. Research shows that many women who cannot respond freely to sexual stimulation in marriage can trace this back to sex play before marriage. Their bodies became programmed to stop short of intercourse, and even after marriage, this programming still governs their response. So, they can't enjoy intercourse. Much premature ejaculation and impotence in males can be traced to the same cause.

Be smart. Slow your courtship down. Refrain from sleeping together. Find out what you are really dealing with by taking PREPARE. And don't rush into marriage—I feel trouble ahead.

The rest of the story: This couple never made it to the altar. They ended up with a pregnancy on their hands, she had an abortion, and the relationship died. I never learned what happened to the Rolex watch!

Rather than be alone, some get caught in a sexual trap. Read on.

Dear Nancy: *My boyfriend and I are both single adults who have previously been married. We are both committed Christians. We struck up a friendship at a singles' meeting at our church. We've been having an intense sexual affair, and I feel somewhat guilty about it. We've discussed stopping the sexual portion of our relationship but get stymied on how to carry out our resolution. We used to go places and be involved in many activities, but now most of our time together revolves around being alone and our sexual relationship. We don't talk like we used to. I long for more depth to this relationship, but I'm terrified that if I cut him off sexually, he'll leave me for someone else.*

Dear Terrified: When a couple gets this involved physically, other areas of their relationship fail to grow. If he won't stick around if you take away the sexual side of your relationship, then you know what he wants. If he won't respect and support your request to end physical intimacies, he likely won't respect or support anything else you want or need after marriage.

Remember, it's easier to become sexually intimate than conversationally or emotionally intimate. When a couple isn't married and sex or other deep physical intimacies dominate the relationship, it's time to break up. Begin fresh with someone with whom you can balance the relationship's emotional, physical, and spiritual development.

Developing a relationship minus sex is the ideal. Few couples today wait until marriage to become intimate. The ones that do are to be commended.

Dear Nancy: *I just attended your Smart Love seminar. I thought you needed to hear from one couple who made the decision not to have sex before they are married. I'm not saying it's always easy, but we've followed the steps you outline in your book to make sure we don't go too far too soon. I just wanted you to know that some people out there are taking your advice. You are making a difference in the world. I'm proud to be a virgin.*

Dear Proud: I'm proud of you too. It's gratifying to know that my books and seminars have made a difference in people's lives. One study showed that those who abstain from sex until after marriage score 31 percent higher on sexual satisfaction than do unmarried people who think sex outside of marriage is OK. Another study reports that those entering marriage with the fewest sexual experiences are most likely to report their marriage as "always warm and supportive." And yet another study shows that if a couple abstains from sex prior to marriage, they are 29 to 47 percent more likely to enjoy sex after marriage.

A chance at this kind of happiness is worth waiting for. You've made a wise choice!

The person writing the next letter needs to make a hard choice, soon!

Dear Nancy: *I'm so confused. I've been to your seminars and know your stand on sex before marriage. But if I don't do something fast, we're going to land in bed. It hasn't gone that far yet, but we're headed that direction. I'm crazy over this man, but he can't keep his hands off me. He lives out of town and visits on weekends. He has his own room in my two-bedroom apartment. But before we go to bed, we have passionate sessions that are getting too tough to handle. If I don't get help soon, it'll be too late.*

Dear Confused: First, *have him stay elsewhere!* I'm constantly amazed at those who take daring risks with their sexual behavior. Adults who live in apartments or own their own homes must lay down strict guidelines regarding deportment when entertaining persons of the opposite sex. Periods of cuddling and cooing in front of a cozy fire can lead to sexual intimacy. Others think they can travel together and share a motel room or go camping and share a tent. Such game playing is foolish. No one can play with sexual fire for long without being burned! God would have us flee the "*appearance* of evil" (l Thessalonians 5:22, KJV, emphasis supplied). We're not to flirt with temptation.

Take time for a thoughtful self-inventory and decide what limits to put on your sexual behavior. At what point in the pair-bonding steps will you stop? (See chapter ten in *Smart Love.*) After setting your standards, plan how to maintain them. Develop a specific plan to follow that you can continue to allow your love to grow without compromising your standards.

Be up front with your boyfriend. Openly communicate your sexual ideals and values. You can be both forthright and tactful in letting him know your limits. This is an excellent way to prevent touchy situations. Next, get an accountability partner—someone to whom you report your behavior. Then stick to your guns.

Responsible behavior does not include living together before marriage. Does the next situation have a familiar ring?

Dear Nancy: *My boyfriend and I have been living together for more than a year. Recently we've come back to church, and we realize that if we're going to be* *faithful to God's Word, we can't continue with our present living arrangements. We dearly love each other and want to get married, but for certain reasons, we can't do that right now. What can we do to save our relationship even though we know we've started out wrong?*

Dear Started Out Wrong: Your desire to make this right is admirable. First, you must find separate living quarters. You can never be "right" with God until you obey His commands. Then you're ready to ask God for forgiveness. How blessed to have a Savior who knows all and yet forgives all. We serve a God who will totally and completely forgive our sins when we truly repent. Ask for divine forgiveness, and then accept it.

Next comes the hard part. Stop seeing each other for at least six months. Vowing not to have sex and continuing to see each other as before won't work. Once a couple becomes sexually active, it is next to impossible to be together without indulging in sex. It's similar to being addicted to a hard drug—during a sane moment you pledge you will never touch the stuff again, but when the craving hits, you can't control yourself.

During this time you may phone and write each other. If you are in a formal engagement, you may see each other on occasion, but only with a third party present. The only way to find out what you have going for you is to isolate the sexual factor. In any scientific experiment, the variable must be isolated. In this case, the variable is sex. After discontinuing sex and not seeing each other for six months, you'll be in a better position to determine if what you have is real love or infatuation.

Should your partner be unwilling to forgo sex for this period, a couple things become crystal clear. First, he considers fulfilling his sexual desires more important than establishing a long-term, emotionally healthy relationship. Second, he doesn't respect your wishes. And if he doesn't respect your wishes now, likely he never will.

In the following case, she permitted a guy to go further than she should have. Now he's out of her life, and there's a new problem.

Dear Nancy: *Jack and I went together for nine months. We really thought we were in love and did a lot of hugging, kissing, and intense petting—what you'd call step nine. I permitted this because I really loved Jack and thought we were going to get married. I was shocked when he suddenly broke off our relationship and immediately started going with another woman. I've heard via the grapevine that they're already sleeping together. I was so lonely and hurt that I* *began dating a fellow I don't even like that well. He's very timid and shy and acts almost like he's scared of me. Once he held my hand, but that's it. What's with this guy? I need more than this.*

Dear Needs More: When you and Jack broke up, he went to another woman and moved her immediately to a higher level of physical involvement. You moved into a relationship with someone who wants to take his time to get to know you and attempts no sexual liberties. You want more and are probably encouraging and maybe even pushing him up the pair-bonding scale. Neither you nor Jack is taking time in your new relationships to get to know your partners as you should. If either of you were to marry, you'd likely find yourselves in very troubled relationships and never fully understand why until it is too late.

People who've been involved with someone face a challenge. In subsequent relationships, they're tempted to rush or sometimes skip entirely the pair-bonding steps. Every progression of physical affection establishes a new plateau from which it's extremely difficult to retreat. People become conditioned to the progressive nature of petting. Each step demands the next one, right up the pair-bonding scale. Each level of sexual excitement is so immediately rewarding that it becomes nearly impossible to be satisfied with lower levels. This is what has happened in the relationship with your new boyfriend. You became "conditioned" to the sexual liberties of step nine in order to prove love. And now you expect your new boyfriend to express his caring through step nine. If he doesn't, you think he doesn't care.

Rethink what you want: Do you want a guy whose main interest is your body and who will go to any length to get access to it? Or do you want a guy who is interested in taking his time, who wants to get to know you in a nonphysical way before turning on sexual motors? Once you turn on the sexual motors, sexual urgency dominates, clouding other relationship issues.

Can a person who's been sexually active or previously married develop abstinence?

Dear Nancy: *I've just finished reading* Smart Love *and got some excellent help. The break-up chapter was great. But I disagree with what you have to say about sex before marriage. I've been married and divorced twice and am single now. I'm used to sex on a regular basis, and now you're trying to sell me on celibacy? I'm no monk. Everybody is doing it. Seriously—in my crowd, I don't* *know of anyone who practices abstinence. What's wrong with two consenting adults who have been previously married having a little recreational sex?*

Dear No Monk: You're right on one point. It is very difficult for a previously married person who is used to proceeding through the twelve steps of sexual arousal without stopping to slow the process to stop at steps seven, eight, or nine. Married people aren't accustomed to stopping. They achieve sexual intercourse without thinking through levels or steps.

When a marriage ends and a person returns to the dating scene, the steps become a blur. Many start dating immediately and become sexually involved, thinking it is just the normal thing to do. For some, years have elapsed since they were part of the singles scene and had to think through sexual issues—what's right and what's wrong and how far to go. For those who are carrying painful baggage either from the death of a spouse or from a divorce, the excitement of being with someone who finds them sexually desirable may be overwhelming. Without thinking about the consequences of blindly building a new relationship, they may slide into sexual involvement with only a twinge of conscience.

The rush into sexual intimacy after a marriage ends is one good explanation for the higher divorce rates in second and third marriages. The fact that your crowd doesn't believe in or practice abstinence doesn't excuse you. If you don't want to end up adding to the statistics for a higher divorce rate for second marriages and beyond, you'll re-evaluate your sexual values.

Does abstinence before marriage really contribute to happiness?

Dear Nancy: *I already know what the Bible says about sex before marriage, but there must be other reasons for abstaining. Give me a couple of straight answers on why it's better to wait. No mumbo jumbo!*

Dear No Mumbo Jumbo: There are many benefits to total and complete abstinence before marriage. In *Smart Love,* I list fifteen. Here, I'll give you two:

1. Abstinence before marriage helps prevent divorce. According to various studies, women who are sexually active before marriage are more likely to divorce than those who abstain.[1] Nonvirgins have a divorce rate 53 to 71 percent higher than do virgins. Those who embrace and practice biblical standards can increase their odds of a lasting marriage. Conversely, those who are not virgins at the time of marriage increase their odds of divorce by 60 percent.

2. Abstinence prior to marriage eliminates the risk of contracting a sexually transmitted disease (STD). If you are having sex outside the marriage bed, you are a prime candidate for STDs. Unmarried partners simply do not know one another's sexual histories. Studies reveal that such people are very uncomfortable discussing STDs, contraception, and condom use. They think they can sense whether a partner is or isn't safe. No one can know that intuitively.

One study showed that 20 percent of men (though just 4 percent of the women) said they wouldn't tell a potential partner that they had tested positive for HIV. Forty-seven percent of men and 42 percent of women said they would understate the number of previous sex partners. In a new national survey, men reported an average of fifteen sex partners; women reported eight.

Women are more vulnerable to AIDS than men are because the vagina is highly susceptible to cuts or tearing during intercourse. Women are at higher risk also because the virus is more concentrated in semen than in vaginal fluid, and susceptible cells of the vagina are exposed to semen for a prolonged period.

"Safe sex" isn't safe. The failure rate in preventing pregnancy for couples using condoms is at least 15.7 percent annually. Among young unmarried minority women, the failure rate for preventing pregnancy is 36.3 percent annually. The *British Medical Journal* reported the failure rate in preventing pregnancy due to slippage and tearing of the condom to be 26 percent. Obviously, anyone who relies on condoms for birth control can be called a parent! If condoms have such a super-high failure rate at preventing pregnancies when women can conceive only one to two days per month, we can only guess their failure rate at preventing STDs, which can be transmitted 365 days per year! And we can't accurately test condoms for AIDS protection. The AIDS virus is 450 times smaller than sperm and can easily pass through the smallest hole.

When a person has sexual relations, he or she is potentially exposed to all the diseases carried by all the people with whom that sexual partner has had sex. Now, note the following progression, which assumes that all the people involved have the same sexual history: one partner per year. In the first year, each person would have had sex with one other person. In the second year, that person would, in effect, have had sex with three people—last year's partner, the current partner, and the person the current partner had sex with last year. The third year, seven people. The fourth year, fifteen people. The fifth year, thirty-one people. The sixth year, sixty-three people. By the seventh year that person would, in effect, have had sex with 127 people!

The only way to be sure you won't get an STD is to be in a monogamous relationship with someone who is also monogamous. Otherwise, you must examine not only your current sex partner but also all of your partner's partners for the past fifteen years. Someone can be a carrier of an STD like AIDS for fifteen years and not know it. If you've had two to three sex partners and your partner has had two to three sex partners, you're nearly certain to catch an STD.

A good way to help maintain your sexual boundaries is to picture what you want your honeymoon to be like. Picture the entire scene: the place, the mood, the attitude, the process. It's powerful!

Temptation, temptation, temptation. What's a single person to do about sex?

Dear Nancy: *I'm a thirty-seven-year-old, never-married man. I lead a busy life—I own my own business and have a successful career, plenty of friends, and a full social schedule. I'm reasonably good looking and intelligent. I've done a lot of dating but haven't yet found that special someone. I'll get right to the point: Do you have any suggestions on how an unmarried person is supposed to handle their sexual urges? Married people have access to sex when they need it, but what is a single person supposed to do? Lately I've come close to burning in hell!*

Dear Burning in Hell: No one needs to give in to sexual urges just because they have them. Both males and females can deny expression to the sex drive for months or even years or permanently with no ill effects. Many men and women never marry or have intercourse, and they lead normal, happy, and productive lives.

What we're talking about is "sublimation." This means that a person transfers his or her sexual drives to acceptable outlets. It means that when you cannot or will not indulge your sexual urges, you look for another form of expression. Singles can find an outlet for sexual tension by becoming registered nurses and using their energy up in caring for their patients. Or they might develop a passion for writing or gardening or for working with the mentally handicapped or recovering addicts. They might pursue an occupation that will absorb their interest and much of their time. They can become involved in an active sport, community service, hobbies, service clubs, or church work. To sublimate sexual energy means that you discover and develop interests and activities that give you enough personal satisfaction so that you can *redirect* your sexual energies. You substitute other forms of expression for your sexual urges.

Sublimation is more beneficial than repression. If you repress your sexual desires, you ignore them or pretend they don't exist. Repression only delays the time when you must face the issue. In sublimation, you recognize your drive and deal with it constructively. Sublimation of the sex drive doesn't mean that you reject sex, but rather, it means that you accept it by taking charge of your sex urges.

From time to time, we all have to control our sexual desires. Even married people must do so. A physician may recommend that a pregnant woman avoid intercourse for several weeks prior to the birth of a baby and for several weeks following delivery. A husband may take an extended business trip that separates him from his wife. They must exercise self-control during such times.

Sex desires are very real, but they are more urgent when you sit around doing nothing. So take your mind off the subject and plunge into an absorbing activity. You'll find it nearly impossible to concentrate on sex if you get out of the house and attend night school to learn a foreign language. But if you sit around the house surfing the Net or watching sexually stimulating sitcoms or titillating HBO or the openly sexual MTV, you'll soon feel like you're burning in hell all over again.

God has promised, "No temptation has seized you except what is common to man. And God is faithful; he will not let you be tempted beyond what you can bear. But when you are tempted, he will also provide a way out so that you can stand up under it" (1 Corinthians 10:13, NIV).

This couple almost learned the hard way that being a Christian isn't enough.

Dear Nancy: *Paul and I met at church, where we were both youth leaders. Leadership meetings threw us together, and we began dating. We both had high standards and felt secure in the fact that we're Christians and members of the same faith. Sexual involvement wasn't even an issue for us.*

However, one night, while watching a video at my place, we went further than either of us believed possible. We were so carried away that we were on the very threshold of intercourse. We were brought up to believe that sex belongs exclusively in marriage, and our church confirms this. Paul promised me after that night that he loved me more than ever and would never leave me. We promised each other that it would never happen again. It was an accident. But it has happened again, and I'm afraid unless something changes soon, we're doomed.

Dear Doomed: "Petting," or body fondling, is a powerful force. It's a step beyond hugging and kissing and yet not as sexually intimate as intercourse. Those who do it tend to make up rules as they move along because they don't know the rules in the first place. This leaves a wide range of body-exploring activities open to question, guess, and negotiation, as you discovered. To clarify this dilemma, I have divided it into three stages. Stage one, a preparatory stage, includes light hugging and kissing without caressing or fondling of bodies. Stage two includes deep kissing and caressing each other's bodies inside and outside of clothing above the waist. Stage three, a more intense and intimate stage, includes caressing each other's bodies below the waist—frequently to orgasm, but without penetration.

When an unmarried couple engages in body fondling with the intention of not having intercourse, they must constantly be on guard to stop lest it go too far. Body fondling, or foreplay, was not designed to stop on command. God's plan for us is that sexual relations with our mate should be fulfilling. Starting and stopping, however, leaves one very unsatisfied and frustrated. Eventually, what may have been exciting makes you want to go further.

Secular philosophy tries to sell the idea that we should see how close to the edge of the cliff we can get without falling off. God would have us walk as uprightly as possible, avoiding potential danger.

Someone inquires, "Is sexual touching OK for a man, but not for a woman?"

Dear Nancy: *I am a single woman in a steady relationship who recently attended one of your seminars. I have grown up with strong beliefs about abstinence from sex until marriage, as is taught in the Bible. Since I'm not going to have sex until marriage, I've never let a man touch me below the waist, although I have touched some of them in an effort to relieve sexual pressure and make them sexually happy. I've always prided myself on holding out and keeping myself pure until marriage. Your seminar has made me question my virginity when I still hope to be a virgin.*

Dear Hope to Be a Virgin: In my estimation, any couple who has proceeded this far has gone further than God would have them go physically prior to marriage. And why is it acceptable for you to touch your boyfriends below the waist, but not for your boyfriends to touch you below the waist? If it is wrong for males, why is it not wrong for females? I believe God is speaking to you through your conscience by prompting questions in your mind severe enough for you to write me. I believe you need to seek forgiveness and to live closer to His will.

More and more singles are asking the following question:

Dear Nancy: *I attended your recent dating seminar and enjoyed it very much. But there are some things that are so personal that it is difficult to ask them out loud. I hate to be so blunt, but I need to know what you think of oral sex. Is it the same as intercourse? Where does it fit in the steps to pair bonding?*

Dear Questioning Saint: Oral sex is a few degrees beyond mutual masturbation in the hierarchy of sexual experimentation. I was conducting a question-and-answer session with a large group of young men on a college campus after presenting pair bonding and was questioned about a pair-bonding number for oral sex. "I'd place it at eleven," I said. (That's on a scale of twelve.) A young man from the group called out, "I'd place it at thirteen!"

Actually, oral sex wasn't considered in the original research. But whatever the number, people must overcome inhibitions to expose themselves to such nudity and sexual openness. I neither condemn nor condone oral sex within marriage, believing it is up to the couple to decide if it is right and desirable for them. But it should have no place during courtship. Both mutual masturbation and oral sex require a nakedness of body and soul that should be saved for marriage only. The dictionary definition for the word "virgin" means "purity" or "chastity." It means "untouched." In my estimation, this definition excludes both of these activities. Just because someone avoids penetration doesn't mean that person has avoided fornication.

Another single inquires about questionable activities.

Dear Nancy: *I am forty-four years old and in love with a wonderful man whom I met two months ago. He is so kind—he treats me better than I've ever been treated in my life. We truly love each other and plan to get married in five months.*

We've been sleeping together, and I feel really guilty about this. I told Jim how I felt, and he doesn't want to hurt me in any way. So sometimes we sleep together in the same bed but refrain from having sex. Please forgive me for being so blunt, but sometimes I relieve his sexual drives though oral sex. Is this OK for a couple who is going to get married in five months? I really love this man and know he loves me. He isn't the same religion I am, but he is a Christian and we both want to obey God.

My divorce will be final in five months. Then I can finally be free of my past. My last husband sexually abused our daughter and physically abused me. I am so happy I found Jim and want to marry him just as soon as possible. I don't want to miss one month of the happiness I know he will bring into my life. I deserve it, because I've had such a miserable past. Jim will make my life wonderful!

Dear Feeling Guilty: You are breaking every rule of good sense in this relationship with someone you've known only two months. To name a few of the mistakes you're making:

- You made the decision to marry way too soon.
- You're viewing marriage as an answer to your miserable past.
- You have unrealistic expectations for your future happiness.
- You haven't had sufficient time to observe whether Jim has personality or behavioral problems.
- You're sexually involved, which clouds the development of the emotional bond between Jim and you.
- You're dating before bringing closure to your marriage.
- You're doing all this while still suffering from emotional trauma due to the abuse you experienced.

You look to marriage to take away the pain from your very troubled past and to make you happy. You think a quick trip to the altar with someone who meets your needs of the moment will solve your problems and ensure a happier future. But weddings don't automatically change anyone, nor do they ensure happiness.

The flush of excitement from a new love relationship drives you now. You are allowing this new romance to cloud the realities involved in establishing a healthy relationship. There's little possibility it will survive if you don't deal with your own brokenness.

When you've been abused and are fearful, you're vulnerable to being swayed by the attentions of anyone who woos or flatters you. People who lack self-worth and fear being abandoned will cling in desperation to any relationship, even one that brings pain. To avoid becoming trapped in another destructive relationship, you must be ruthlessly honest about your own brokenness. You need to deal with the hurt and pain from the past—all the unfinished business from your previous marriage. You need to heal before getting involved with any man. Dating is beyond your capabilities for now. Back off from emotional involvements of any kind, and seek help. Al Anon or a twelve-step program or cognitive behavioral therapy (CBT; see appendix for chapter 1) could give you the help you need before you endanger your future and Jim's.

Sex before marriage has many consequences. The woman in the following letter discovered this too late.

Dear Nancy: *Approximately two years ago, I contracted syphilis and genital herpes. The syphilis was cured with penicillin. Unfortunately, I will have recurrences of herpes for the rest of my life. Until now, I've told no one.*

I've begun dating a man who's attending a medical school located about six hundred miles from where I live. We've known each other for two years, but began dating only recently. Our interest in each other is escalating, and we manage to see each other about once a month. We phone and email often. I am finding him to be the kind of person I hope to marry someday.

Here's my question: Do I have to tell him I have herpes? If so, when? We haven't talked about marriage yet. Am I guilty of deception if I continue to let our relationship escalate without mentioning my STD? Suppose he's not the man I eventually marry? How many men will I have told before I do get married? I want to be open and honest, but I don't want to have my business all over the streets. I want this to remain between God, my husband, and me. What shall I do?

Dear Questioning Friend: You must tell your boyfriend you have genital herpes prior to getting married. That point is clear. The crucial question is *when* to tell him. You should do so before a formal engagement. There's a stage (stage five of the dating game) when you're "engaged-to-be-engaged 'someday' "—when you're talking seriously about marriage. At this stage, relationships are much more easily broken than when you're formally engaged. I recommend that you tell him at some point toward the later part of this stage—before your engagement becomes formal. This way you can both back out gracefully should it come to that.

Prior to the time you tell him, talk to your physician about the possibility of health risks or other problems that could be passed on to your own children and the risk your fiancé will assume by having intercourse with you. Since he's a medical student, he'll likely be aware of the risks.

You've learned a difficult lesson about the consequences of sin. Now experience God's unconditional forgiveness so you'll never have to face that guilt again. Hold your head high. You are a child of the King!

All of God's children are precious in His sight. Sometimes, it's hard to remember that fact, as the following letter shows.

Dear Nancy: *I am a thirty-year-old man. I graduated at the top of my university class and am now professionally employed. To make a long story short, my social life is in the garbage can, and I am extremely lonely. It seems that every time I'm attracted to someone, she either is taken or isn't interested in me. I am beginning to wonder if I'm just not attractive to the opposite sex. This causes me great pain and agony, because I want so much to have a companion.*

I've prayed until I'm sick of praying for God to send me a Christian woman to marry. I'm beginning to wonder if there is even one sympathetic bone in God's body, because He hasn't answered my prayers. Very few people can ever fully comprehend the destructive power of loneliness. I'm overwhelmed with despair.

Dear Overwhelmed: I can empathize, but this is one problem I can't solve. Only you can. Are you active in social and spiritual groups in your church? Can you volunteer to help with projects where you can lend some expertise? Are you investing yourself in service to others? What organizations and clubs do you belong to?

Love relationships should come as the natural result of friendships. Even if none of those friendships results in a romance, every one of those friends has other friends, which increases your chances of meeting someone compatible. You don't want to depend on your friends for dates, but having a wide circle of friends increases your odds of finding someone to date. Throw a party for your friends. Ask them to bring their friends.

Anglers wouldn't go to a neighbor's swimming pool to reel in the Big One. They'd go to a lake or river where fish are plentiful. The same holds true in the dating game. Go where the fish are, and use the right lure. Unfortunately, once most singles have achieved their educational goals, they go where the fish aren't. A man should try aerobics, swimming classes, gourmet cooking classes, or church. The biggest "sin" of the dateless is to wait for the phone to ring while they bemoan the fact that they never meet anyone interesting.

People tend to date the most attractive and popular persons. That's only natural. But many people make great companions even though they wear glasses, are short, overweight, quiet, or not beauty-contest material. Sometimes these "finds" just haven't blossomed yet. Avoid the shallowness of searching for only the most attractive people. You could be overlooking someone with great potential. Look around again!

* * * * *

Through the mass media and other forums, society programs us to believe that love will solve all personal problems. Such a concept leads people down a dangerous path, because they expect romance to offer what only Jesus can supply.

Rather than securing all your hopes and dreams to a human being, why not secure them to Someone who will never change? Jesus is always the same—yesterday, today, and forever. He keeps all the promises He makes. You can count on it. And His love is completely unconditional. He'll always love you regardless of your appearance, failures, and mistakes. When others fail you, He'll be there to love and care about you. He's the only One who loves perfectly.

Jesus is the only One who can supply all your needs, fulfill all your desires, and meet all your expectations. Anchor yourself to Him. Then you will be less likely to be disappointed in love—more likely to find a satisfying love for your sojourn on this earth.

---

[1]See Nancy Van Pelt, *Smart Love: A Field Guide for Single Adults* (Grand Rapids, Mich.: Fleming H. Revell, 1997), 196.

CHAPTER FOUR

Systems
Gone Wrong

One of the key factors to achieving a highly effective marriage is remaining committed to one partner. That's called fidelity. Confining one's sexual expression exclusively to one's partner for a lifetime is the only way to build an emotionally healthy, stable marriage. It's also basic to character building, and your character defines who you are. Paul wrote, "Each one of you should know how to possess [control or manage] his own body (in purity, separated from things profane, and) in consecration and honor" (1 Thessalonians 4:4, Amplified).

Dear Nancy: *I found out my husband had been having an affair with my best friend for five years. I left him immediately, but he talked me into coming back after a separation of a year. Recently I've been diagnosed with gonorrhea, and one of my friends tells me my husband has had sex with several women in our church since I've taken him back. Now I'm devastated.*

Dear Devastated: If you were 100 percent faithful to your husband before your separation and since your reconciliation, you must have contracted the gonorrhea from him because of his continued infidelity. Obviously, this man doesn't understand commitment and the exclusivity that belongs to the marriage bed.

First, get yourself treated for the gonorrhea. Second, set boundaries to protect yourself from further disease. Tell your husband you will not have sexual relations with him until you are satisfied that your sexual relationship is exclusive. You must also be assured that you are both disease-free. Even then, you may want your husband to use condoms to help protect yourself from dormant viruses such as herpes and HIV. Third, armed with prayer, you need a confrontation with him of major proportion. If you make him only "uncomfortable," he will likely not accept responsibility for change. It's highly probable that he'll be motivated to make necessary changes only when he is faced with the imminent loss of his home, wife, children, and reputation. You provide that strong motivation to do the right thing.

In your confrontation, make it clear that he cannot have both his family and another woman too. Stand up for your rights as the woman married to him. Once you do this, you'll gain back some of the respect that you've lost through his affairs.

Throughout this confrontation, remain confident and calm. Convey that you believe in what you are doing and that you are not afraid. You and God can cope regardless of the outcome. Refrain from talking too much. And please do not cry, gnash your teeth, or beg him to come back to you. Your purpose is to convey that he has now been caught in a whirlpool of ugly events that may take him in a direction he had not anticipated. It may be necessary to separate from him for a time to let him know you're serious. During the separation, do not phone him except for urgent business. When the business is complete, hang up with quiet confidence. When you exert this new attitude of confidence, he may recognize that you have changed and wonder what's going on. Should he ask, reveal nothing. You want him to wonder about the future.

At some point during this crisis, he's going to wonder if he's doing the right thing. A virtual tug of war will be going on in his head. He'll feel guilty about breaking up the marriage and what's happening to his kids. On the other hand, the lure of the other woman and the excitement of the forbidden affair will hammer on his consciousness. The pros and cons will continue to go round and round. This is what you want.

When the time comes for another face-to-face encounter, don't go into the battle unprepared. Plan carefully what you'll say. You might even role-play this encounter with a counselor or a trusted friend.

During this encounter, tell your husband that you were incredibly stupid to let him come back the first time without setting boundaries to monitor his faithfulness. Because of your foolishness, you had to be treated for a sexually transmitted disease and you had to deal with his unfaithfulness all over again. Tell him that he has violated your trust not once but twice, and state that you are through making foolish mistakes or playing games with him. Let him know that although you once pledged your love to him, you are pursuing a course to remove yourself from emotional enmeshment and dependency on him so that you never again have to suffer the pain that he's put you through. Set him free to chase other women if he chooses. Say all of this with no more emotion than if you were reciting a recipe for a friend. Wish him well and walk away with a clear conscience.

Your husband will likely be shocked at your confident approach. He's been trying to get you off his back, and here you jump off all by yourself. He no longer has to escape your clutches. From this time on, ask for nothing and look bored every time he calls or approaches you. He'll likely begin to wonder what's going on—if maybe you've found someone else.

You may not be able to salvage your marriage with this approach. But if you want your relationship to have even a ghost of a chance of succeeding, these steps are necessary. Pulling back often produces immediate and dramatic results. Quiet confrontation with an aura of self-worth is the most effective way of bringing back a wandering husband if he retains even a spark of decency.

Make certain that you're not spouting idle threats when you tell him you're setting boundaries. Be prepared to follow through with consequences. Boundaries have no impact if you don't enforce them. Get support through prayer partners and your own prayers for strength. I also recommend that you get the help of a counselor as you attempt to find reconciliation and the restoration of your marriage.

What does the future hold for the two of you? Only God knows. However, one thing it doesn't hold is a spot in your husband's life for both you and another woman. Let him know he can't have her and expect to have his home, wife, and children too.

This next wife can't seem to let go of her past.

Dear Nancy: *My husband and I are both thirty. We've been married for ten years and have two children. We're dealing with some big stuff that is really bothering me. We had to get married because I was pregnant. I considered not telling him I was pregnant and raising the child alone, but I finally did tell him.*

He assured me he loved me and wanted to marry me. Now I wonder if he would have married me if I hadn't been pregnant.

My husband is the strong, silent type; he cuts me out of his thoughts and life most of the time. We don't talk or have fun together—we're too busy with the kids, our business, and our church, and I homeschool the kids. Two years ago, I became really friendly with another man—he and his wife were our best friends. Although we didn't end up in bed together, we went too far, and I have terrible guilt feelings. I told my husband about it, and he has forgiven me and wants to pick up the pieces of our marriage and go on. But the wife of this man doesn't know. We live in a small town, and we run into them everywhere we go, even at church.

I can't seem to forgive myself for what I've done. I don't know why my husband wants me anyway because I could live without sex and in ten years of marriage have never initiated it. And I don't think I've ever had an orgasm. Is it possible to get my life back on track, or have I committed so many unpardonable sins that there's no turning back?

Dear Guilty Wife: No, you haven't committed the unpardonable sin, and yes, you can get your life back on track. First, however, you must clear the deck. What's clouding your mind is your guilt. Seek repentance from our Lord, who is the only One in the entire universe who can offer you the forgiveness and peace you want. When you're suffering under a load of guilt, it's a wonderful relief to be a Christian. You have a Savior who waits with outstretched arms to hear you say, "Lord, I've sinned. Forgive me." And when you sincerely seek His forgiveness, He'll not only forgive your sins, but He'll also cleanse you from all unrighteousness (see 1 John 1:9). What a promise! *Forgiveness* we must ask for. *Grace* He extends to us freely without our asking!

You might try writing a letter to God listing all the sins and the trauma from the past. Pour it all out—the pain you've brought upon yourself and others—starting from before you were married. Take your time writing this letter, and be very specific. When you feel ready, take your letter in hand, and, in a ceremony between only you and God, light a match and burn your letter. While watching the edges char, ask Jesus to take the guilt and pain from your life and set you free. He can and will do that for you—and His healing is available to all who simply ask. Just as gold is purified by fire, burning the letter helps purify the sins from your heart and mind. Painful, yes, but the results are brilliant.

Now you are ready to change your behaviors. When people try this kind of change, they tend to go in all directions at once, which usually creates more problems than it solves. It is much more effective to work on one area at a time. Start with a problem that offers the possibility of experiencing success relatively easily. You might cut out one activity this week, put the children to bed early, and spend time with your husband.

Let me suggest a communication exercise to get you talking to and appreciating one another again. Grab a watch with a timer or a kitchen timer. Sit in chairs facing each other with your knees between your husband's. Your knees will touch the front edge of his chair. Your hands are to rest relaxed in your laps, not folded across your chest. After assuming this position, look into each other's eyes for two minutes. No talking. Then one partner completes the following open-ended sentence and talks on this subject for three minutes: "One thing you bring to this relationship that I really appreciate is . . ." The other partner responds, "Thank you for caring enough to share your feelings with me. I will consider everything you said carefully."

Next, the first partner says, "Something you have achieved that makes me really proud that I'm married to you is . . ." The other partner responds as before. The first partner then goes to a third topic, which is: "One way I have failed to be the partner you really need is by . . ." The other partner responds as before. Then you reverse roles, and the second partner works through the three topics. At the close of this exercise, enjoy a hug for thirty seconds, timing it on the clock.

Even a simple exercise like this can make a big difference in your relationship. The important thing is not to give up. It has taken you years to get where you are now, and it may take time to get to where you want to be. Look for signs of improvement along the way. Count the victories and receive the blessings!

After all this, if you still feel the wife of the other man needs to know what happened, give him the opportunity to tell her. Set a deadline. If he chooses not to tell his wife, let him know that you're not willing to live in guilt any longer and that under the direction of the Holy Spirit you will confess and ask for his wife's forgiveness. Then you and your husband can let God heal your hearts and work on theirs. God can and will heal both marriages if you allow Him to.

Through Christ, you can find hope for the future if you can gain the courage to risk starting over. You can get your life back on track again.

Unfaithfulness, laziness, abuse, despair! Read this heart-rending saga of a couple trying to salvage their marriage.

Dear Nancy: *My husband, Bob, and I have been married for fourteen years and have two children. Bob loves chasing women. I've kicked him out of the house twice because of adulterous affairs. Right now, we are back together, and I am trying to pull myself together emotionally and spiritually. I have never recovered from the pain of his philandering.*

Following his first affair, he was on one of his "highs," telling me he loves me like never before and will never be unfaithful again. These "highs" last only a few months, and then he is off chasing skirts again. His "great love" makes little difference when he's panting after another female.

All the counselors and pastors that we've counseled with imply that it's my fault. "What did you do to cause him to do what he's done? If you'd done such and such, it wouldn't have happened." They listen to a man who is an absolute expert at making excuses for his behavior, believe his lies, and play right into his game. For ten years, I've lived in this frame of mind. If I could change, do more of this or that, he would be happy with me and stop his philandering.

You are probably used to counseling women who get fat, don't dress or do their hair, have a half a dozen kids, never look at their husbands as men, keep a dirty house, and know only one position for sex. But I haven't spent the past fourteen years in a convent. I've paid for exotic vacations to Florida, Jamaica, Puerto Vallarta—anywhere Bob wanted to go. I spent eighteen hours a day at a computer to pay for those trips. Then he would tell everyone that I cared more for my job than for him. I've gotten drunk enough to participate in oral sex, anal sex, and anything else he could think up to keep him home. I've had sex by the road, in the ocean, on the beach, on the floor, in the car, with the kids "asleep" beside us, and on a river bank in a foreign country (with, I found out later, bandits on a ridge above us).

Bob isn't a bored husband and never was. He's an empty person who's been promiscuous in every aspect of his life since he was thirteen years old. His whole life has been built on the empty foundation of instant gratification, no matter the pain or humiliation to others. We're going down the same path we've been down before. What's wrong with this man?

Dear Wife of Philandering Husband: Nothing is wrong with this man that you as a wife can fix by having sex by the road, in the ocean, on the beach, on the floor, in the car, etc. You are married to a sex addict. And nothing is wrong with you that caused him to be a sex addict. The sex addict uses sex to lift his mood in the same way a drug addict uses drugs. To him, the sexual experience can become as addictive as a drug-induced high. The sex addict begins to rely on the endorphin-induced "high" that his sexual behavior produces. When he experiences an unpleasant emotion, his brain signals that he needs his "fix," and he can't rest until he gets it. This pattern becomes ingrained after years of repetition. Due to years of acting out sexually, a man cannot simply stop because he "just says no." To stop, he needs outside help.

Almost all sex addicts have deep, unmet needs from childhood that they're trying to manage. They're often intensely lonely people who have searched unsuccessfully for years for the unconditional love of a father or mother. These legitimate, God-given needs for affection and nurture have gone unsatisfied, and they now try to satisfy them by acting out sexually.

The addict feels a sense of relief and euphoria when he nurtures himself sexually, but guilt and shame soon replace the good feelings. This is especially true for the Christian who knows what Scripture says about healthy sexuality and violates it anyway. His morals are not enough to prevent him from seeking relief when the unresolved pain at the core of his being rises up again. So, the cycle is replayed repeatedly. Each time he swears that he will never do it again, but the combination of unmet needs and the out-of-control compulsion are too much for him.

Your husband, along with many other sex addicts, is unknowingly practicing a counterfeit repentance. When caught in their addiction, they feel deep remorse, heap mounds of guilt on themselves, and promise never to do it again. Though deep emotion may accompany true repentance, it need not. True repentance is demonstrated by obedience. Repentance is not about feeling an emotion and making all kinds of promises; it is about following through on what God tells you to do.

It is unreasonable for either you or your husband to expect that the addiction he has spent years feeding and acting on will suddenly disappear because he repents. Through ongoing accountability, a refusal to entertain fantasies, and reaching out to others in times of weakness, he can begin to change. No quick and easy repentance exists. True repentance is a bloody battle carried out over a lifetime.

You've been through a bloody battle of your own with this unfaithful man. You would certainly be within your rights to seek a divorce from him. If you have the energy or inclination to fight one more battle along with him, positive help for sex addicts is only a stone's throw away. Contact

Exodus International (see appendix). This organization not only provides addicts the help they need to deal with their addiction and restore them to wholeness but also provides ongoing support to wives—women like you who are hurting, lonely, confused, and angry. There are also books that you would find helpful (see appendix).

Affairs affect not only the innocent, but also the guilty. Read on.

Dear Nancy: *I met my husband when I was fifteen, and we married when I was seventeen. My husband was twenty-five and was divorced after three years of marriage to another woman. I didn't think his age or the fact that he'd been married before mattered. Two months after we married, I was pregnant, and my life began to fall apart. My husband didn't want to do anything for me or go anywhere with me. He said he cared, but he was careless. He taught me to "harden up" and told me "don't take anything off of anyone" and "don't trust anybody." He constantly accused me of things I never did or would push me toward other men with snide remarks.*

One time I found myself alone with a really good-looking, married friend. I was at my lowest emotionally and high as a kite on joints. He fed me the words and affection I ached to hear and seemed to be really understanding. All I wanted was a few hugs and a kiss or two, nothing else. I tried to stop things from going too far, but he called me a tease. I gave in and hated it. Then my marriage got worse. I had a second son and cheated on my husband again. Finally, I moved out.

Now, I realize I love the Lord and want to live totally for Him. He's been my only true Friend through all of this, and I've done nothing but hurt Him. I've reunited with my husband, and things are going well between us except when I mention religion. He wants me never to mention anything to do with religion when he's around. When I did once, he made a horrible scene. I want to confess my affairs to my husband; the guilt is eating my insides. But I don't want to tear apart our home or the lives of my two sons again. I feel like I'm trapped in a terrible prison.

Dear Trapped: Before you rush off to relieve yourself of the guilt by telling your husband about your affairs, you should answer some questions. Why do you feel this tremendous urge to tell him everything? What is the possibility of discovery if you don't tell him? What is the possibility of your repeating this kind of behavior? How long ago did the incidents occur? What is your attitude toward the incidents now? What has taken place since the incidents? What will be gained if you do tell him? What will the outcome be?

If your only reason for telling your husband is to relieve your own guilt, I recommend that you hold off. There are other ways to handle guilt. Seek the help of a Christian professional marital therapist, preferably one trained in cognitive behavioral therapy (CBT), before making any decisions relative to the future.

Selfish choices by a husband have severely affected the emotions of the next letter writer.

Dear Nancy: *During our entire twelve years of marriage, my husband has gone to bed with anything and everything in a skirt. On top of this, he also has a problem with alcohol. We've separated twice, he has been "converted" three times in the past four years, and he's been rebaptized twice in the past two years. These so-called conversions usually last a month or two; then he's at it again.*

I've read everything in print on marriage and infidelity ad nauseam! I've tried all the tricks of the trade and been through the whole maze—from guilt straight through to self-righteousness. I've been to counselors and pastors until I'm sick of both. I'm exhausted and know I've failed. But I refuse to spend the rest of my life beating my head against a brick wall and punishing myself for what I didn't do. I know he has talked personally with you and that he reports one more reconversion and promises it won't happen again. At this point, I'm not sure it's wise or if I'm willing to give him another chance.

Dear Exhausted Wife: No wonder you're exhausted! Twelve years of trying to solve your husband's problem! You haven't failed; he has. The only thing you haven't understood is that you are married to a sex addict. None of the "tricks of the trade" will help when dealing with sexual addiction.

Sexual addiction is never about the wife. It's about the husband. This is not to say that you have no influence on your husband's behavior. Rather, it's an issue of sexual brokenness on his part. As a sex addict, he's dealing with issues that predate you. You are not the cause, nor can you be the cure.

Understanding this brings both comfort and pain. Comfort because you finally understand it's not about you, and pain because you also understand that you can't fix him. Understanding that your husband's sexual brokenness is not about you will bring some initial relief, but it will do little to soothe the profound ache in your soul. You feel deeply violated, betrayed, and devastated.

Many sex addicts unknowingly practice a counterfeit repentance. When caught acting out, they often promise never to do it again, exhibit deep remorse, and heap mountains of guilt on themselves. Repentance can certainly include deep emotion, but not necessarily. True repentance is shown through obedience. Repentance is not about feeling an emotion and making promises. It is about following through on what God tells the sinner to do.

The continued presence of sexual addiction doesn't mean the addicts haven't really repented. It only means that they're broken and fallen. Repentance doesn't take the addiction away; instead, it gives addicts a means of consistently being able to make another choice. Sex addicts must learn that repentance is not an event but a process. It's not a matter of finally getting serious about religion and getting over their "problem." It becomes a matter of choosing not to act on the impulses that will continue to torment them.

It is unreasonable for you to expect that your husband's way of thinking and behaving will suddenly disappear because he repents. It is only through ongoing accountability and a refusal to entertain fantasies that the sexually addicted person can make changes. True repentance is a fierce battle carried out over a lifetime.

Sex addicts can find healing only if they develop relationships that hold them accountable, if they deal with their past, and if they experience true repentance. They can't find wholeness without doing all three. If your husband is willing to confront all three of these issues honestly, healing is possible. He'll have to let others in. He'll have to face the hurting little boy inside. And he'll have to develop a vibrant relationship with the Lord.

Get your husband into an Exodus International group (see appendix). To handle your own emotions, join a support group for wives. And I highly recommend that you and your husband read Russell Willingham's book *Breaking Free* (see appendix). With these things in place, your relationship just might have a chance.

Is there a chance the husband described next is addicted to porn?

Dear Nancy: *Something is really wrong in our marriage, and I'm not sure just what. My husband isn't as interested in sex as he used to be. I've gotten new nightgowns and made myself available and seriously tried to entice him, but he doesn't act like he used to. I'd suspect another woman, but he's home at night and during the day he's at work.*

Often at night, he doesn't come to bed until late. He's on the computer. I'll get up in the middle of the night to look for him, and again he's on the computer. I've discovered him watching porn on our computer. What do you think is going on here? I'm getting frantic for an answer.

Dear Frantic Wife: My guess is that your husband is into Internet pornography. Many people don't see anything wrong with porn. They think that as long as they don't physically consummate a relationship, it can't be considered adultery. But I, along with others, maintain that infidelity begins at the point of making a strong emotional connection. When people respond with a heightened emotional and or sexual awareness and have a sexual longing for a person who isn't their mate, infidelity has occurred.

The Internet has made pornography readily accessible. People don't have to sneak out of the house and fear that friends, colleagues, or fellow church members will see what they're doing. From the privacy of their homes, they have easy access to every type of sexual fantasy. Sometimes it pops up without even an attempt to access it.

The big lie at the base of most pornography is that it offers people some super-sensational sexual experience that they haven't known about or tried. Pornography is billed as a sexual stimulant when it is actually a sexual de-sensitizer. Initially, people begin with light forms of porn, and they experience tremendous sexual stimulation. But over time, they need increasing amounts or deeper forms of pornography to produce the same stimulation. Pornography desensitizes people's response to the very things that God created us to respond to sexually.

People who become hooked on porn are deluding themselves that porn can compensate for a lack in their relationships. Actually, it just makes fantasy relationships more convenient. Your husband is actually stealing time and energy away from you—time and energy that he could and should be investing in strengthening your marriage.

A few simple guidelines would prevent the tragedy of marital breakups due to porn addiction. For example, put the computer in an open area of your home where others pass by. Avoid using the Internet when feeling tired, lonely, or misunderstood. Install a service that filters or blocks so-called adult sites from your computer (see appendix). Remove your personal profile from online services to minimize your chances of attracting pornographic advertising. If these suggestions don't solve the problem, cancel your Internet access. If your husband is addicted, he should contact Exodus International (see appendix).

To get your husband to go along with these suggestions, you may have to employ "the ultimate ultimatum" described in my book *Smart Listening for Couples* (see appendix). This problem will not go away by itself; it will only get worse over time. Act now.

Just how should a wife act when she discovers that her husband has been unfaithful?

Dear Nancy: *I've just discovered that my husband has been having an affair with a woman twenty years younger than he is. He is a well-known businessman and a leader in our church. Our children are all away at college, but they are going to be devastated when they hear about this. I simply do not know which way to turn or whom to go to for advice. I am numb with shock. Please help me soon!*

Dear Numb Wife: When a wife first discovers that her husband is having an affair, her emotional life comes crashing down around her. She experiences overwhelming feelings of shock, betrayal, sadness, fear, and anger. She desperately needs to talk to somebody about what is happening, but a deep sense of shame makes that difficult. She questions why her husband has to go to another woman to have his needs met and why she is not good enough. These are painful questions because she almost always assumes that some fault of hers has caused her husband's behavior. "If I were only more interested in sex or if I lost some weight, he wouldn't be doing this," she reasons.

There is no magic formula that will remove the pain in your heart. Instead, you need to allow yourself to feel in order to work through it. You need to take two steps in order for healing to occur. First, give yourself permission to mourn. God understands your need to grieve. Second, surround yourself with people in the body of Christ who will give you a place to mourn and heal. The last thing you need to hear from well-meaning Christians is insensitive platitudes, quick fixes, or a guilt trip that obligates you to forgive your husband prematurely. You need women to surround you with love and acceptance and allow you to experience your emotions.

As you work through the grief process honestly, you will experience deep despair. This is when you embrace the pain of losing your dream of a perfect marriage based on trust and faithfulness. This may not be pleasant, but it is necessary, so you can progress to accepting the reality of your losses, which can then give way to true acceptance and the ability to forgive. What you need most is a support network that will give you the space to grieve while loving you enough to prevent you from getting stuck in any of the stages of grief.

As you work through your grief, you'll also need to set boundaries on your husband's behavior—a nonnegotiable line that lets your husband know you will not tolerate more adultery. An unwillingness to set such a boundary will result in co-dependent and enabling behavior. A good place to start is to insist that he get help through an organization that deals with sexual brokenness. I highly recommend Exodus International. Issue a strong statement to the effect that if he doesn't choose to seek help immediately, then you will have to make some choices of your own.

Next, I recommend that you discontinue all sex relations with him. This will protect you from getting a sexually transmitted disease or HIV. He may accuse you of controlling and manipulating him, but his choices have forced you to make some choices of your own. For you to submit sexually to someone who is engaged in a promiscuous lifestyle would be to encourage him to continue his sinful lifestyle. When he begins taking responsibility for his actions and there is no threat of STDs or HIV, then you can resume the sexual relationship.

You can experience a healthy marriage once again. Before you do, however, you must do your grief work and insist that your husband get into a program that deals with sex addicts. Then let God and others love you and your husband back to wholeness. It won't happen overnight, but it can happen.

This man has a past. Now, what about the present and future?

Dear Nancy: *My best friend had an affair with a young woman three years ago. Since that time, he has come to the Lord, and now he and his wife and three children are active in our church. Although they're not baptized members, they are earnestly seeking to know Jesus. The man has confessed his sin to the Lord and knows he has been forgiven. But he's afraid to talk with his wife about his adultery since he is certain that she will seek divorce immediately. According to him, his wife will never find out about it if he doesn't tell her. Should he tell his wife and clear the deck once and for all—knowing full well that his marriage will collapse?*

Dear Best Friend: What should a person do in such a situation? The Bible contains no "Thus saith the Lord" regarding it, so we must look to scriptures that apply. First John 1:9 tells us that if we confess our sins, Christ will forgive us and cleanse us from all unrighteousness. This indicates that one must confess to Christ, not necessarily to one's mate. This man has broken his wedding vows and sinned against God and his mate. But if he has asked God for forgiveness and received it, either he is forgiven or he isn't. This verse doesn't say anything about going to the other person and confessing.

So, I think we're left with two options. The first is that this man doesn't tell his wife what happened. This means that he will have to bear the burden of this secret sin for a lifetime. Can he do this? And can he forgive himself—or will this secret haunt him and their marriage forever? Withholding it from his wife might raise a barrier between them and leave her wondering why she can't "get through" to him at times.

The second option is to tell her and risk the consequences, which might include divorce. What would be the purpose of telling her? Doing so would relieve this man's conscience and roll the burden of guilt off his shoulders. He might feel relief, but the news would greatly complicate her life, increase her burdens, and possibly destroy their marriage.

If he chooses to follow this route, I highly suggest he do this in the presence of a third party—perhaps his pastor, to whom he has already confessed, or perhaps even you. His wife will likely be in shock for a time. No one should press her for an immediate decision. If she orders him from the house, he must go. If she needs time to think it over, he must give her this time. Should she forgive him and wish to rebuild their relationship, they will need follow-up counseling and ongoing support in order to strengthen their marriage.

These are the two options as I see it. This man must decide which route he should follow. He will have to make the final decision. I suggest that he fast and pray while deciding.

PHYSICAL AND EMOTIONAL ABUSE

The problem of physical abuse is reaching epidemic proportions in today's families. The violence that has become so evident in society around us has invaded the husband-wife relationship as well as parent-child interactions. Embarrassment and shame sometimes keep people from sharing their crisis with anyone. But crime should not be kept a secret. People in the church often say nothing for fear of not knowing what to say or maybe because they don't want to cause any more distress. While other factors may also trigger violence in a family, abuse begets abuse, perpetrators beget perpetrators, and this sin becomes a generational sin. However, with healing, the chains of abuse can be broken.

Dear Nancy: *I am a twenty-year-old university sophomore who has already been through three abusive relationships. The first guy was a star athlete, senior class president, and Mr. Personality. Everybody loved him. When he wanted me to be his girl, I was in seventh heaven. After nine months of dating, he gave me a cell phone and began calling me thirty times a day to check on where I was. Then he began following me to my classes to see where I was sitting and whom I was sitting by. He cut me off from all my friends. I soon learned he had a terrible temper and that I'd better not cross him. He would pound his fist into the car seat inches from where I was sitting and kick the tires on his truck so hard that he hurt his foot. It took me eight months to escape from this dangerous relationship.*

Then I began dating Dale, another seemingly nice guy who also had a terrible temper. I tried to break up with him when, after we'd been dating a few months, I found him with another girl. He went into a rage. When I tried to run from him, he grabbed me and left bruises all over me. Then he began following me everywhere I went. I finally got away from this guy.

My third boyfriend didn't exhibit any temper to start with, and I thought that at last I had a winner. But eventually I learned that he too went into terrible fits of anger. When I tried to break up with him, he held a knife to my throat for three and a half hours, threatening to kill me. This ended only when I promised him that I would stay with him forever. This time I got my dad involved, and this guy never came around again.

However, the violence I've experienced has so traumatized me that I no longer trust men and am almost afraid to date. What am I doing wrong?

Dear Traumatized Student: National statistics show that about 12 percent of high-school students experience physical violence—slapping, hitting, or punching—during a dating relationship. The likelihood of violence increases to 20 to 25 percent by the time they're in college. A St. Louis study of 885 teenagers showed that 33 percent had been threatened with physical violence when dating. A mere 4 percent ever told their parents or an authority figure about it.

What you and many other girls don't understand is that abuse or violence rarely begins with hitting. It starts with control. Girls who don't have a lot of experience with dating often think this control is evidence of love. The difference between the boundaries of love and control are foreign to them. Guys often give pagers or cell phones to their girlfriends—not as a token of affection, as the girls think, but as a means of knowing and controlling at all times where their girlfriends are and whom they are with. No boy should treat you as if he owns you. You are beginning to catch on, but some girls never get it.

Here are some danger signals to watch for the next time you're in a relationship. You're on dangerous ground when your boyfriend

- wants to know where you are and whom you are with every minute
- attempts to stop you from seeing or talking to certain people
- always tells you where to go and what to do
- embarrasses you by calling you bad names or puts you down
- does things to scare you
- shoves, kicks, or punches you or threatens to do so
- threatens to kill you or himself if you leave him

These are all problems bigger than you can solve. If the person you're dating does any of these things, inform your parents or another authority figure and get away from the guy now and totally!

Other people play mind games that relegate their boyfriend or girlfriend to the land of nerds. The same St. Louis study showed that 52 percent of the subjects had experienced one or more of the following forms of emotional abuse while dating: constant criticism, blame for all problems, threats of physical harm, isolation, repeated insults, destruction of possessions, and being completely ignored. Intentional public humiliation that makes one look and feel like a fool in front of others is also a form of emotional abuse.

After three such relationships, your self-worth has likely been damaged and needs rebuilding. Work through the steps to building self-worth as outlined in chapter one of my book *Smart Love: Straight Talk to Young Adults About Dating, Love, and Sex.* You also need to slow down when moving into a relationship. The first thing you should do is to get to know the guy as a friend. See how he responds with a group of friends when he gets angry. Introduce prospective boyfriends to your dad. Fathers have a way of looking into a guy's eyes and figuring out what he has on his brain. If you work on your self-worth, slow down the dating game, and have your dad check out your boyfriends, you'll be able to go into a relationship and regain the trust in men you've lost because of your past abusive relationships. Should you have more difficulty than anticipated, you may need therapy to help you get over the trauma you've experienced.

You should maintain any future relationship for at least one year before allowing them to become serious. Do so to determine whether your boyfriend is wearing a mask. Because of your history with abusive men, you need a year not only to uncover a man's masks but also to see your own pattern of rationalizing, justifying, and minimizing his behavior. Let your father observe him for a year, and listen to his advice.

The big thing is to risk loving again. After being hurt, people tend to insulate themselves so no one can ever hurt them again. You may need some protection during the healing process, but the time comes when you must risk entering a new relationship. Withdrawing into a shell cuts you off from loving again. The greatest hazard in life is to risk nothing. By risking nothing, you may avoid getting hurt, but you can't grow, change, learn to live, or relate well with others. No one is chained to the heartbreak of a broken romance. Peace comes as you let go of the hurt and risk loving again.

A loving and kind husband would not do what the husband of the next letter writer has done.

Dear Nancy: *Even though my husband and I have been married for eighteen years, we've never communicated well. Recently he took my name off our joint checking account without telling me, and this is upsetting me terribly. I shouldn't be surprised, because both incomes have always been his money. Everything is always his way or no way at all.*

We have three children, all of whom are terrified of their father. Our lives are headed in a downward spiral. I do realize that if anyone's going to change, it'll have to be me. But I would just as soon have a divorce and live singly for the rest of my life. I seek only peace. I feel like I am totally controlled.

Dear Controlled Wife: You are living with a control freak that has no concept of equality within your marriage. Whenever one spouse attempts to control or dominate the other; disregards the other's opinions, desires, activities, and lifestyle; or attempts to force the other to do something against his or her will; that spouse is demonstrating a lack of equality. Unless there are extenuating circumstances because of things you've done, this is evidence of unreasonable control.

While your husband isn't violent or physically abusive toward you, he's emotionally abusive through his control. A clear example of control includes making decisions without consulting the other. Removing your name from a checking account without your knowledge or agreement demonstrates a gross lack of consideration for your feelings.

Controllers attempt to force other people into line through fear and intimidation. Your husband is obviously fearful of losing his power and authority. He fears opening up and becoming vulnerable. You fear being attacked and overwhelmed by his control. Such attitudes totally block intimacy. The more he acts alone, the more isolated and alienated you feel. This leaves you more starved for closeness and intimacy. His continued controlling nature will kill any love you have for him. Acts of love remain meaningless because you feel he doesn't really care about you. You feel used.

You crave freedom to operate within your sphere of responsibility. Eventually, you may develop headaches, ulcers, or sleeplessness or go into depression. You need the support of a husband who will encourage you in your role as wife, mother, and homemaker.

Breaking out of the tenacious grip of a controller isn't easy. But it becomes possible with third-party intervention. Seek help from a counselor who understands control freaks.

Your statement that you realize you're the one who will have to change is remarkable. It is a giant step forward. As long as you sit back and say, "He is the one who needs to do all the changing," your relationship won't change.

Eileen had a similar problem. Her husband wouldn't talk with her enough to meet her needs. She prodded, nagged, and complained. She read all the books, dragged him to marriage seminars, and scheduled time together. In the end, when her time, energy, and patience were exhausted, he talked no more than he ever had.

Eventually, she realized that she wasn't responsible for her husband's behavior nor could she change it. The only person whom she could change was herself. When this truth finally penetrated her gray matter, she decided to make a big change in herself. She stopped begging him to talk. She no longer complained or nagged him, but she did begin making herself less available for conversation and actually began cutting conversations with him short. When she wished to converse, she talked, regardless of his two-syllable replies. To fill her time, she joined a women's bowling team and began taking a night-school course.

At first, her husband appeared relieved to have her go her own way. After several weeks, however, he became curious about his wife's new behavior. Where was she going? What was she doing? Who was she with? When he questioned her, she responded briefly and went about her business. Eventually, he appeared to get a little jealous of all the time she spent elsewhere. One day, he confronted her with an amazing request. "Honey," he said, "I think we need to start spending more time together, don't you?"

Mission accomplished. But not when she tried to change him, only when she changed her own behavior. The moral? Work on changing your reaction to your husband's controlling ways.

Hang tough—and work on getting that third-party help you need.

Hanging tough is sometimes difficult when a spouse hurls angry words and becomes extremely hostile. When fits of temper are exposed, the person receiving the abuse can feel almost hopeless.

Dear Nancy: *I married Dan when I was sixteen and he was eighteen. We've been married for twelve years and have three children. When I got married, I dreamed of a peaceful home because my parents bickered a lot when I was growing up. But now there's so much bickering and fighting in our house that I just can't stand it anymore. I know what triggers my husband's anger and try not to arouse it, but regardless of what I say or do, the anger in him boils up.*

Now I'm getting afraid of my husband. He's never actually hit me, but he has slapped me around some, shoved me down on the couch or bed, and grabbed my arm so forcefully that I've been black and blue for days. When he was growing up, he was forced to sit and watch while his father beat his mother nearly every week. Do you think this has anything to do with all the problems in our home now?

Dear Fearful Wife: Yes, the home in which your husband grew up may very well have influenced his behavior. Some 80 percent of men who abuse their wives grew up in homes where they observed abuse. It's a learned behavior that abusers have seen modeled—most often in the family they grew up in. They've seen and experienced the power and control that abusive behavior offers them. This goes beyond experiencing stressful circumstances. Abusers *choose* to exert power and control over another person through their behavior, and they pick their victims carefully. And while your husband may never have punched you, you are a victim of family violence. Physical assault includes behaviors such as shoving, pushing, and kicking along with hitting. And slapping is a form of hitting.

You need to ask yourself why you are still married to this man. Can't you see that his anger is increasing and that if his present behavior continues, you'll soon end up so battered that you'll be lucky if all you need is hospital care? Maybe you are staying because you need the bits of love and affection he doles out to you. Or maybe you are terrified that he will become more violent if you leave, as he may already have threatened. Perhaps you fear for your life or that he will take the children away from you or that you can't support yourself and the children alone. Or maybe you are just too embarrassed and ashamed to admit that you are a battered wife.

Then again, maybe you reached out for help in the past but some well-meaning church leader or friend told you to be a good wife, to pray more, to have faith in God and things would get better. Or maybe they even told you that it was your Christian duty to remain in your marriage. Maybe they said you needed to do so for the sake of your children.

Perhaps now you believe you have no hope and no escape from the problem that haunts your marriage. Or maybe you've been tolerating the situation because you believe your situation will improve. Only rarely does that happen without intervention.

The cycle of abuse has three phases. In phase one, the wife tries very hard to avoid any behavior she knows will upset her husband. She learns to coax, cater, and defer. She becomes adept at reading the signs of building rage and carefully picks her way through daily contacts. The batterer watches her with mounting tension, looking for reasons to blame her for his rage.

Phase two is dominated by battering. Realizing his rage is out of control, the batterer finds reasons to blame his wife, to teach her a lesson. Any small incident, either external or internal, can trigger his actions. This reign of terror can last for hours or sometimes for days. The wife rarely seeks help because she knows that would increase his anger.

Phase three usually consists of a period during which the batterer exhibits kindness, contrition, and loving behavior. Often he'll beg for forgiveness and make tearful promises. Many times the wife feels it's her responsibility to hold the family together and to give him another chance to improve. She wants so desperately to believe he'll change. But when she assumes that his kindness or his promises constitute a long-term change in attitude and behavior, she is being unrealistically optimistic.

What you may really need is a deeper understanding from a Christian standpoint of suffering, mutual submission in marriage, repentance that includes a change in behavior, forgiveness as a process, and the discernment that will enable you to know whether your relationship can be treated and restored or whether to grieve its loss. But you also need to understand that the abuse is not your fault and that you do not need to stand alone through it. You need protection, and help is available (see appendix).

Your husband also needs help so that he can begin taking responsibility for the physical and emotional pain he is bringing to you and your children, all of whom should be able to count on him for love and support. He needs to be held accountable for his actions and encouraged to seek the professional intervention necessary to bring about the change in behavior that must happen if your relationship is to be restored.

This next wife is living in a nightmare with a pastor/husband.

Dear Nancy: *I have been married five years to a man who I thought was the answer to my dreams. But this is no dream; it has become a nightmare. He takes great pleasure in criticizing me. He often follows me from one room to another, seeing if he can top the last ugly thing he said to me. And he's physically abusive as well as verbally abusive. His anger seems to build up, and then he hits me. I run from one room to another to get away from him. I try to find a place to hide so I can get my shaken body together. I want children so badly, yet I don't want to bring them into a home like this. What makes our situation even worse is that my husband is a pastor. Help me or I'm leaving.*

Dear Abused Wife: You have practiced acceptance, patience, kindness, long-suffering, and forgiveness to a fault. But the more you give, the worse things get, and the more selfish, demanding, and controlling your husband becomes. Your husband has a personality disorder that doesn't respond to ordinary interaction. He needs professional treatment. You indicated that he refuses to go. "The ultimate ultimatum" might save your life and your marriage at this point.

Make a list of all the behaviors you will no longer tolerate. State precisely what changes you must have if your marriage is to continue. Write this out in a letter and make copies for yourself and a trusted supporter. Then pack a suitcase, just in case, and put it in the trunk of your car or leave it with a good friend or at a safe place.

Leave a copy of your letter where your husband will find it. If after reading it, he berates you, go to another room where you do not have to listen to his attack. If he follows you or threatens you with physical violence, leave the house immediately. If he calls you on the phone ranting and raving about the stupidity of your demands, hang up. Forget how scared you are, how weak your knees are, how badly you are shaking.

After a few hours or nights away, you may return home. But every time he challenges one of the changes you asked for, your response is always the same: you leave the house or hang up on him. Don't fail to do this even once. Continue responding in this manner until he recognizes that you're serious. When you begin to take yourself seriously, stand up for your rights, and demand respect, he is much more likely to take you seriously too. One of the changes you must demand is professional counseling for him and marriage counseling for both of you.

One woman asked her abusive husband to sit down while she stood (so she had the advantage of being above him) and talked to him. She demanded that they seek counseling. He refused, insisting that he didn't need any help. He said she could go if she liked. She had her suitcase packed and by the door. She informed him she was leaving him and would be staying at her parents' house for a week. If he changed his mind during that week, he could call her. She prayed every day while sticking to her guns. Within the week, he called and agreed to go for counseling. Their marriage now had a chance.

There's a very small chance that the next marriage can survive.

Dear Nancy: *I have a son from a previous marriage who visits from time to time. My problem is that my husband becomes angry when this child comes home. Last week while my son was home alone, he did some cooking using new kettles that still had the tags on. When my husband found this out, he became furious. He got so mad that he knocked my son to the floor. (My husband is a large man—over six feet tall with a heavy build. My son is slight of build and probably weighs around 130 pounds.)*

My husband beat my son around his head with his fists until my son was bleeding profusely. I called the police and if my son presses charges, my husband could be charged with assault and battery. My son was taken to the hospital, treated, and released, but he may have residual problems from this. I am terribly upset about this attack.

My husband keeps excusing his behavior, saying that my son raised his hand and he thought he was going to attack him. I'm scared. The week before this happened, my husband became angry with me and threw me across the room onto the floor. A couple of months before that he tried to choke me. What shall I do now? I might add that I do have a good job and earn a respectable salary.

Dear Battered Wife: You are living with a time bomb, and it is only a matter of time until you're the one who will end up in the hospital (if you're lucky) or the morgue (if you aren't so lucky). Your husband's vicious attack on your son is a major signal that he's not a safe person. When you add that he has recently tried to choke you and has thrown you to the floor, we both know that he's not safe to live with. The next time he becomes upset, it could be all over for you or someone you love.

You have a good job and earn a good income. One day real soon while he is at work, move your belongings to an apartment and get a restraining order against him so that he can't come near you. If you can't move immediately to your own apartment, get yourself under the protection of a women's shelter. They will help you through the difficult transition.

There is little you can do to help this man until he wants to help himself. Many women's shelters also offer programs for abusers, but this man must be willing to admit he is an abuser and seek the help that is necessary if he wishes to continue a relationship with you. You don't need a relationship with an abuser. The marriage that God ordained didn't include such treatment. Love doesn't act this way under any circumstances. Arrange to visit your son away from your husband.

My heart aches for the couple in this next scary situation.

Dear Nancy: *I am in a second marriage to a man who is scaring me. When he becomes angry, he grabs me around the throat and shakes me. He often does this in front of my eighteen-year-old daughter. He is very controlling, and I no longer know what he is doing with any of our money.*

Although I work full time, he berates me for not making more money and blames me for all our financial problems. On payday, he comes to my office and takes the check from me. His behavior is getting more secretive. He has a cell phone but won't tell me the number. He has very bad credit, so he's had me open numerous charge accounts in my name. But he won't let me charge anything on any account.

Recently, he took out two insurance policies that total $275,000 on my life. He also forced me to sign a second mortgage on our home for $125,000. When I asked why we need that kind of money, he told me it's because I don't make enough money to pay our bills. He's taken my name off the phone bill. He has an ATM card but doesn't allow me to use it.

I know that my husband does some gambling, but recent behaviors have raised my suspicions that perhaps he is gambling more than I thought. His best friend, a lawyer, once told me that my husband was a nice guy with one big problem—gambling. I am not allowed to go into one room of our home. He keeps his desk, files, and a briefcase there under lock and key. I'm not allowed to see any bills. My husband tells me he wants a gun for Christmas. I'm scared.

Dear Scared: When a woman cannot trust her husband implicitly to give her accurate information about what he is doing with his time and money as well as everything else, she has no basis for a relationship with him. Trust is foundational to marriage. And if I had a husband who kept all his secrets under lock and key, who wouldn't discuss finances with me and constantly berated me for not earning enough money, who forced me to sign a large second mortgage against my will, who has tried to choke me, and who took out $275,000 in life insurance on me, I'd be more than suspicious. Add to this that he gambles, and I'd be running scared.

You need more facts to substantiate your suspicions. Do your homework. Get copies of phone bills, bank statements, and credit card accounts to substantiate where your money is going. Call the credit bureau and check on his credit as well as yours.

If your worst suspicions are confirmed and he has accumulated massive debt, you have three choices: (1) You can put up with the situation, continuing to work so that he has enough money to support his gambling addiction, and hope he'll get help someday. (2) You can confront him with what you know and lay down boundaries. He must admit that he has a problem and voluntarily seek help. (See the appendix for contact information on Gamblers Anonymous.) You must also enroll in the program for spouses of gamblers as well as take control of the finances. Unless he agrees to these boundaries, you leave. Or (3) you can seek a separation. In this case, you need advice from a good lawyer. In community property states, what's his is yours and what's yours is his. This means that you incur half of his debts. Find ways to protect yourself financially should the marriage end.

Your options are limited. Protect yourself as best you can from this point on. A marriage can survive many setbacks and struggles, but the one thing a marriage cannot survive is a lack of honesty. So, unless he wants to come clean with what he's doing with his time and money, you have no future.

SEXUAL ABUSE

The sexually abused don't just grow up and forget the horrors of their childhood. Sexual abuse leaves scars that people carry throughout life. Without detection, reporting, intervention, and treatment, many will remain victims for the rest of their lives. Breaking the cycle of sexual abuse will not only protect our children but reduce crime now and in the future.

Dear Nancy: *Recently, my twelve-year-old daughter came to me crying and told me that her father has been coming into her bedroom at night for several years and has taught her how to "have sex." I am so shocked and stunned over this revelation that I absolutely do not know what to do or where to turn. To compound the problem, my husband is a highly successful and respected pastor. I'm afraid if I told people, they wouldn't believe me. I did take my daughter to the doctor to be examined, and he confirmed that her story is true. I don't know where to turn.*

Dear Pastor's Wife: This is why incest is called "the sin people don't talk about." The very word is so frightening that most of us prefer not to discuss it, let alone face it in the family. Since the doctor has confirmed that abuse has taken place, the situation demands immediate intervention. You must call Child Protective Services immediately, unless the doctor has already done so—which the laws in most states require. Don't question whether you should or shouldn't. It is your duty as a mother to protect your child from all harm. This supercedes your duty to your husband.

When your husband is confronted, be prepared for what you may hear. He may admit that he approached your daughter once or twice but only because she was seductive and enticed him. Sometimes men do confess that it occurred, but say that it was only because they were so drunk and now they have no recollection of it happening. Your husband will likely swear it will never happen again. He may promise to make it up to you and beg for forgiveness. He may ask you to pray with him and then lay the entire matter aside. He may remind you that if he goes to jail, he'll lose his job, and you'll lose your home, and the family will be separated. Be prepared for all these arguments.

Your duty as a mother is to support your daughter through this and to protect her in the future. You are doing so right now, but within a few weeks your concern may begin to change focus from protection to survival. You may feel that you can't make it on your own and that you need the financial as well as the emotional support of your husband. You may want to put all of this behind you and be a family again. You may want this so badly that you may actually begin to deny or minimize the situation. "Maybe she did seduce him." "Maybe she made up the whole story and lied just to get back at her father because he put some limits on her."

Should your mind continue with this fantasy, you might be tempted to suggest that your daughter change her story. Or you might want to tell her that Dad has admitted the problem but has promised it will never happen again. Or you may act depressed and talk of all the calamities that have befallen the family—the job loss, creditors at the door, "we'll soon be on the street"—putting tremendous pressure on your daughter to do whatever it takes to make it go away. Guard against laying this burden on your daughter, who has told the truth. The doctor confirmed it, remember?

Think of what your daughter is going through. If she doesn't change her story, she's likely to assume responsibility for all that has happened to the family. She'll think it's happened because she told rather than because of what her father did. She'll believe that everything people say about her father applies to her as well. Her guilt and depression will increase, although she'll become skilled at hiding it. She has already learned how to hide her feelings and keep secrets. She'll think she's let the family down. At this point, she may say anything to try to put the family together again. In this case, she'll be vulnerable to being abused again.

Unless you get your daughter the help she needs now, she will continue to have confused sexual identity, feelings of shame, and low self-esteem. Such feelings will lead her to partners who feel the same way about themselves, although they may look great on the outside. And the cycle of abuse continues.

Your daughter will need counseling from someone who can lead her to the healing power of Christ. Since parents stand in the place of Christ, at least to the age of accountability, she's had her capacity to enter into a healthy relationship with God undermined. Since she hasn't been able to trust her earthly father, she'll now have trouble trusting her heavenly Father. She needs a counselor, preferably female, who understands that her emotional and spiritual natures both need to be healed. You can find counselors who don't charge a lot through the health department or a similar source, but they can't heal the spiritual wounds. A skilled Christian counselor will eventually be able to help your daughter pull the tattered edges of her soul together and eventually move into the forgiveness phase.

Matthew 6:14, 15 tells us that we must forgive just as Christ has forgiven us. This applies even to the perpetrator of incest. Unless your daughter completes this phase, she won't experience lasting healing because bitterness and hatred will keep her wounds open. You ask how such a thing can be forgiven. Without excusing the sin or minimizing its enormity, we must recognize that the perpetrator too is a soul who needs the cleansing of the blood of Christ. In the future, he can be led to face his sin and be forgiven. Only Christ Himself can provide that kind of forgiveness.

Now we'll look at healing for you. Generally, when such an offense occurs, a family will turn to their pastor for guidance. In your case, the pastor is the perpetrator. So you may have to turn to the pastor of another congregation for spiritual guidance during this difficult time. You too will need to put yourself in the hands of a capable counselor to work through all the issues that need resolution. In addition, tell your prayer partner or members of a support system you trust about your husband's sin and then, together with at least two or three of these supporters, confront him. Matthew 18:20 lends support to this idea: "Where two or three come together in my name, there am I with them" (NIV; see also the preceding verses).

It is criminal that so many women are raped. This tragedy often has far-reaching consequences.

Dear Nancy: *When I was a junior at a Christian college, I was raped and became pregnant. Against the wishes of my parents, I decided to keep my daughter. I reported the rape, and now the courts are making me look like a slut. I am very concerned that my child be in a loving, stable home. I am under so much stress and don't know whether or not I made a mistake.*

Dear Concerned: You need all the help you can get in rearing your new baby daughter for the Lord. During the early months, you will likely be concerned regarding her physical needs, which are difficult to decipher when she can communicate with you in no other way than crying. Do remember her emotional and spiritual needs as well, even though they do not evidence themselves at this time. You are laying a foundation now on which you will build all the good things later on. You *can* provide a loving, stable home. Be confident!

I encourage you to get one of my books, either *Train Up a Child* or *The Compleat Parent,* and study the book carefully for further help. Of special importance is the area of self-worth and character building. Other books can be of help as well.

I am proud that you reported this rape. Yes, some defense attorney may attempt to make you appear to be a slut, but you can depend on the fact that God looks on the inside. He knows your heart. Submit your will to Him.

We hear much about sexual abuse to women. But what happens when a man is sexually abused?

Dear Nancy: *My husband is a physician who grew up in a rural area with immigrant parents and several siblings. They were very poor but worked hard to have the necessities of life. This created traits of self-reliance and fierce independence. The boys in the family shared one bedroom, and the girls shared the other. The hired hand who helped work the farm had his own quarters.*

When my husband was six years old, the hired hand was instrumental in saving him from a burning barn. My husband was always the hired hand's favorite, and this event increased the bond between them. Then the hired hand asked my husband to sleep in his quarters. This led to three years of sexual abuse by the hired hand. To this day, my husband uses this to distance me, to distrust me. To top it off, he had mumps as a child and became sterile. He calls all of this his "handicap."

I was sympathetic when I first heard all this. Not anymore. Now I'm sick of hearing about it. Prior to our marriage, my husband had three other dysfunctional marriages. The women left for their own sanity because of control issues and their desire for someone to fulfill their sexual needs. I was unaware of this until after we married. At first, I felt pity for him and figured he'd been dealt a poor hand. But after twelve years with this man, I'm tired of his pity party and lack of trust in me. I can see now why his previous wives divorced him. What help is there for a man like this?

Dear Physician's Wife: If your story of your husband's background is accurate, it probably explains his control issues, sexual problems, and lack of trust in you. But to stay on a pity party for forty years and four marriages because of a "handicap" about which he's done nothing is another matter. A few years ago, people knew little about sexual abuse. It was discussed only behind closed doors, and there was little or no help for victims. Now there is help for men who have been sexually abused. But your husband has to want it, and there's little you can do to get him there.

Much has been offered to female survivors of sexual abuse, but the needs of male victims differ from those of females. For example, most male survivors exhibit anger. The good news is that males can find help too. Exodus International deals with this problem. I recommend reading *Victims No Longer*, by Mike Lew (see appendix).

During a marriage seminar that I was conducting, a woman in her mid-forties approached me cautiously after the lesson on sex. Her health was deteriorating rapidly, yet her doctors could find no physical reason for the diverse symptoms she exhibited. With difficulty, she told me her sordid history of physical and sexual abuse at the hands of her brothers. For nearly forty years she kept this childhood pain locked up inside, never hinting of her agony even to her husband. Here's her story in her own words.

"All my life I felt like 'that dirty little girl.' My parents were good people, but we never talked in depth. I was the fifth child and craved acceptance but never got it. I always felt ugly and wore hand-me-down clothes. I learned to get by with very few material things, even though my sister had nicer clothes than I did.

"My brothers began abusing me sexually when I was six or seven. Two brothers experimented only once, but my other brother made a practice of it. My world crashed simply because I idolized him. I was no longer that carefree, happy little girl. Life became very serious.

"I quickly learned to stay out of the hay, where I had loved to go as a small girl to listen to the quiet meows of the newborn kittens and let puppies climb into my lap. I stayed close to my mother, helping her around the home, but dared not tell her about the sexual abuse. I was deathly afraid of men and would have bad dreams that an 'icky' old man would come through my bedroom window and sexually abuse me. I feared our preacher, who would pick me up and toss me in the air. I was afraid he was just trying to see under my dress. Uncles would come to our house and give big hugs and kisses. I hated it.

"All of this was blocked out of my mind until I married and had a little girl. As I watched my daughter grow up, I experienced unbearable fear. I guarded her with my life, because she had four older brothers. I was very open in our home about sex. This was the only way I could deal with my past. Then things began coming to a head when I developed many physical problems, yet the doctors found nothing wrong with me. I was a wreck, couldn't sleep, kept going to the doctor, and was afraid of everyone and everything. My husband knew something was wrong but didn't know what. I wanted to curl up in a ball and scream to everyone, 'Please help me before it's too late!'

"I had a hard time hugging our boys. I could tell my husband that I loved him, but not the boys. Our oldest boy broke the ice, however. He always hugged me and said, 'I love you, Mom!' I had never heard this as a child, and I'm sure my parents never heard it from their parents either.

"To think of going to a counselor or talking with my husband about my past was like being slugged all over again."

As this woman told me this, her tears flowed freely. I could see that she was at the breaking point. For nearly forty years she had kept this childhood pain locked up inside, never even hinting to her husband about her agony. In order for her to achieve release from the torment that gripped her, she needed to confide in him. My suggestion brought on immediate panic. After much prevailing and prayer, she finally allowed me to bring him to the room where we had locked ourselves. Then she unfolded her story to him for the first time.

I stayed in the background as a most poignant drama unfolded. Lovingly, her husband encouraged her to tell him everything, to get it all out. When the whole sordid tale was exhausted, he displayed uncanny sensitivity. Gently he picked her up off the chair where she was sitting and placed her on his lap, where he held and caressed her soothingly. Then he uttered the words she needed to hear more than anything else: "Honey, I would have married you anyway." And healing was on its way!

A year later I received another letter:

"When I attended your marriage seminar a year ago, I was still 'that dirty little girl.' I didn't realize that I was a victim. Thank you for helping me tell my husband. I thought I could never let him know that terrible part of my life. As we reflect now on that painful day, he feels it was God's perfect timing—the best time I could have told him.

"The Lord directed us to a specialist in the field of sexual abuse. My healing has been slow but steady. Forgiveness is the key. I have taken Jesus by the hand down that long pathway of my childhood. We have stopped at each little place of hurt, and He has said, 'It's OK, My child. I love you.' He was with me every step and wiped the tears away.

"It has been a long and painful recovery. Healing is definitely a process. Sometimes I almost feel like my past never happened to me. Jesus has even given me love for the brother who abused me for years. I have forgiven him and gotten rid of the resentments I've had for him all these years."

Some of those reading this book may be experiencing problems due to unfinished business from the past. Unresolved problems and painful memories seem to follow us and hamper the here and now. They resurface at the most unwanted times. Burying wounds from the past doesn't allow healing. Rather, it prevents healing, because the injuries fester and eventually an infection develops. If the wound was deep, it can cause the patient and those around her or him much suffering.

Can a person do anything to alleviate hurts, unfairness, or bitter resentments that lie in the recesses of the mind? Yes! Two things will aid you in putting the past behind you. First, do not expect the person who hurt you to change. You may secretly be hoping that person will suddenly become what he or she has never been and fill all your needs. Let go of such hope. You're not responsible for what that person did to hurt you, but you *are* responsible for how you allow your memories to affect your life today. The ideal is to grow to the place where you can say, "I had these painful experiences, but that was yesterday. Today is today. I don't have to be bound by my past. I'm now free to grow in a new direction if I so choose." Rather than constantly hoping for a miraculous change in the other, determine to love and accept that person in spite of what has happened.

Second, recognize that the person who hurt you is probably also coping with negative memories. Many problems are perpetuated for generations—not intentionally but because no one broke the cycle. The following biblical advice is needed at this point: "Brethren, I do not consider that I have made it my own; but one thing I do, forgetting what lies behind and straining forward to what lies ahead, I press on toward the goal for the prize of the upward call of God in Christ Jesus" (Philippians 3:13, 14, RSV).

This can be the day your life changes!

Raising Sane Kids in an Insane World

Nature is a little careless about whom it allows to become mamas and papas. Producing a child in or out of wedlock doesn't require a license or a test. Couples find themselves saddled with children without training in how to parent, discipline, or build character. Parents bravely battle toy-strewed rooms and furious cries. Although the problems change, they never end, and parents plunge on, doing their best. And despite all their good intentions, some parents are disappointed in their youngsters' behaviors. Their children may fail their classes, sass, or disobey.

She may whine, throw temper tantrums, wet the bed, or argue. He may be lazy, uncooperative, or disrespectful. They may demand attention, fight with each other, or try patience to the limit.

Parents with good intentions may rightfully ask, "How can my children be so disobedient when I've tried so hard?" or "Am I doing as good a job as I think I am?" Rearing a child can be devastating, head splitting, and nerve shredding at times. Days may come when you feel like trading your children at a swap meet! There may be days when you feel as though you have failed miserably and have done everything wrong; when despair rushes in like a flood. This is when parents write, searching for an answer to some dilemma they face. Some need only a little encouragement. Others need information. Still others face serious problems.

Dear Nancy: *I am pregnant with my first child and am wondering if it would be OK if I put her in day care. I love my job and don't want to give it up.*

Also, I'm not sure we could live adequately on my husband's salary if I were to quit work. Yet I can't bear the thought of having someone else raise my child. What should I do?

Dear Pregnant Mother: I'm unalterably opposed to day care unless it is absolutely necessary, and I've formed my opinion based on factual research, not on mere personal preference. Let's look at what some research reports conclude.

One report says that when parents place a child in day care during the first three years of life, there tends to be less positive interaction between mother and child.[1] This same study concluded that children who spend most of their time in day care were three times as likely to exhibit behavioral problems in kindergarten as were children whose mothers raised them. Traits such as aggression, defiance, and disobedience were also directly correlated to the amount of time spent in day care. And another study concluded that children who spent more than thirty hours a week in settings outside the home were more demanding, less compliant, and more aggressive. These children got into more fights, were crueler, exhibited more bullying behavior, talked too much, and were mean.[2]

There's just no one quite like good ole mom to nurture children. Research into the development of the brain confirms this. The crucial years for the development of the brain are those from birth to kindergarten. During these years, children need positive, nurturing stimulation from their mother and other caregivers. When this stimulation is lacking or replaced by negative or stressful stimulation, the developing brain is disabled or damaged. After children are five, correcting the quality of the environment may make no difference. In other words, by age five, children's brains are wired to think, learn, trust, relate, communicate, compute, analyze, and explore. This new brain research confirms what we've known for years, that children's first and most important teacher should be their mother.

It's next to impossible for youngsters to get the vital, positive, nurturing mental stimulation their brains need from television, videos, or day-care workers. Only a parent or other family member who talks to them tenderly, holds and corrects them lovingly, and teaches them about everything from their belly button to the butterflies and stars provides this kind of nurture.

You think you have to work for economic reasons, doubting your family can live on your husband's salary alone. Although you didn't supply me salary information, let's say you and your husband each earn thirty thousand dollars a year, for a total of sixty thousand dollars. Starting with this figure, let's look at whether one needs a second income to survive.

An annual salary of thirty thousand dollars means a monthly salary of twenty-five hundred dollars. Most people spend $250 a month in commuting costs, for such things as public transportation or gas, oil, parking fees, and vehicle maintenance. And if you don't own your car outright, add to this the cost of monthly payments on your car. You'll likely spend an average of $125 a month on work clothes—office workers need suits, silk blouses, and pantyhose. You'll likely spend an additional $120 a month on lunches, office gifts, and obligatory donations. And don't forget your day-care expenses, at about eight hundred dollars per month for one child. Add in the taxes that are taken out of your check, and figure your forty hours a week plus an hour or two for dressing and commuting each day, you'll be earning, in effect, a dollar or two an hour.

By the time you pay for all this, working outside the home turns into one expensive hobby! And think of all the time you spend away from your child, the stress on the family due to your absence, and the housework you'll need to do evenings and weekends.

A sensible alternative is to start your own at-home business. It could be anything from clothing repair and alterations to a beauty salon, medical transcription, Internet services, or desktop publishing. Do your homework by going to the library and researching what you can find on business in that area. Look up articles on the Internet. Talk to others who are in similar businesses. Subscribe to publications for more information. Join clubs that can teach you more about your field. Setting up a small, at-home business can be stressful, but at least you'll be home with your child, so you'll have the best of both worlds.

For parents who have no choice but to leave their infants, the main concern should be to find a loving individual to provide the care. The best choice is to have that occur in your home. The second best choice is care in someone else's home. The least desirable situation, especially for infants, is day care. If that is the only solution, find a place where there's no more than one to three infants or small children per adult caregiver.

Many parents have experienced the following problem with their children.

Dear Nancy: *I'm having a hard time training my two-year-old to be quiet in church. In the parents' room, the other mothers and fathers are usually talk-*

ing and laughing and the children are playing—not at all an atmosphere for teaching reverence. How would you handle this situation?

Dear Concerned Parent: Thank goodness there still are a few parents who are interested in *training*—a key word here—their children to be quiet in church. I've witnessed an increase in parental laxness in quieting crying children. Recently, I was present in a church service where a child began screaming. At first, the parent made no effort to take the child out. When the screams reached epic proportions, the parent finally did so, still making no effort to silence the screams.

And as you noted, parents' rooms have become noisy play areas for children and chat rooms for sociable parents. In my opinion, parents' rooms are for emergency use. I recommend instead that, whenever possible, you sit with your children in the sanctuary near a door. When a child misbehaves in a way that disrupts the service, take him out, discipline as necessary, and as soon as his behavior is under control again, bring him back into the sanctuary. Should the child be screaming when you're removing him from the sanctuary, cover his mouth with your hand while you're walking out. Unless you follow this plan, your child will act up during every service to escape having to sit through it.

One of my most popular seminars over the years has been "The Art of Making Sabbath Special" (see appendix). In this seminar, I suggest ways to keep young children occupied during the church service. Since most church services are not designed for children, they need some spiritual entertainment to occupy their busy hands and minds. That doesn't mean Mutant Ninja Turtles or Spiderman!

I suggest that you prepare a church bag for your child. This bag should contain items appropriate to your child's age. Mine includes a coloring book of Bible scenes and color crayons, stencil patterns that the child can trace, a press-and-peel board with magnetic figures of Noah and the ark, a magic drawing pad, a picture book, and a felt "quiet book" that contains a number of quiet activities. Don't let the child get into the church bag too early, however, or he'll have it all used up and be bored by the time the sermon begins. Teach your child to participate in the worship service by standing to sing, kneeling to pray, and giving offerings.

I believe that by the time children are twelve or so, they're old enough to sit through a worship service without "entertainment." By conducting worship at home, you can teach young children how to sit still. Begin with short periods, like one minute while you tell a story. When they've mastered that, try two minutes. Keep increasing the length of the worship, and by the time the children are older, they'll be able to sit for relatively long periods.

After the church service, you should keep one eye on your children even while you're greeting your friends. Unless you do, you may find them running down the aisles of the sanctuary or playing leapfrog over the pews. Teach your children that the sanctuary is the place where we meet with God, and because of this, it's a holy place. When we enter a holy place, we behave differently than we do in other places.

Little minds wander with the wonder of life, so you must teach these lessons consistently over time. When you do this while your children are young, you'll be able to relax more when they're older. So, continue to work on your child's behavior now!

Can children learn in an atmosphere of arbitrary restraint and harshness? Read on.

Dear Nancy: *My wife and I have three children, one of whom is beginning first grade, while the others are preschool age. We've worked hard on obedience, but at times we've disagreed regarding methods of discipline. I tend to have more of an authoritarian style of parenting, and she can be quite permissive and lax. How can we reconcile the two? And which is better for kids?*

Dear Authoritarian Parent: You and your wife have opposite parenting styles, and neither extreme is good. Both extremes hinder children's development. Researchers have found a third style of parenting, "authoritative parenting," to be the most beneficial. In the authoritative approach, parents set clear boundaries and rules. They enforce these rules firmly, using commands and corrections, while they also encourage the children's growing independence and individuality. Authoritative parenting encourages open communication between child and parent, with verbal give-and-take. Parents and children both recognize that they have rights.

Children raised in this parenting style tend to be more competent, industrious, self-reliant, persistent, and determined. They tend to have a stronger sense of their own abilities and are less susceptible to feelings of depression and anxiety. Children raised by authoritative parents generally have better academic achievement and social adjustment.

While permissive or authoritarian parenting styles are less than ideal, there's something even worse. Opposing each other in the presence of your children—objecting to some disciplinary action taken by your spouse—has even more devastating results. It can be difficult to step aside when you feel your wife isn't handling a disciplinary situation correctly. But stepping aside is exactly what you should do. You damage your children when they observe you disagreeing over how you should handle them. If you do oppose what your wife is saying or doing, *speak your piece in private, never in front of the children.*

You and your wife differ in temperament, methods, and response. Your children will rapidly learn how to respond to each of you. They already know who is strict and who is the softie, and they'll adjust their behavior accordingly. Despite these differences, your children will likely mature normally—as long as they know their parents work together on major issues. But if they ever learn they can divide and conquer, they're likely to use that technique against you both. Each of your children needs to feel secure, and this security grows in the garden of consistency. It will be deeply threatened if they see one parent trying to make up for the lack of the other or if they see one contradict, argue with, or undermine a stand the other has taken. As parents, you and your wife should remember this motto when attempting to work together: "United we stand, divided we fall."

Your children need discipline in an atmosphere of love. Competent parents avoid extremes in both permissiveness and punishment. If you love your children with a nurturing love, then you and your wife can discipline them with a proper balance between love and control even though you have opposing disciplinary styles. Your overall goal as parents, however, should be to adopt a parenting style that encourages your children to become all they can become—even if that means changing deeply ingrained habits.

What about habits formed and influenced by the media?

Dear Nancy: *I worry about the influence of television, rock music, video games, and novels on my children: a boy, thirteen, and a girl, sixteen. Should I allow them to choose their own entertainment? Most of their friends attend the theater. My kids say they're the only ones whose parents are so strict. I'm about to cave in to their demands because I don't want to be a dictatorial parent who regulates everything my children do.*

Dear Worried Parent: You *should* be worried about what the secular media are trying to pump into your children's minds. Television and the media are filled with sex and violence, and their underlying purpose is to shape each generation of adolescents. But the rock-music industry takes the prize for producing the most dangerous material for kids. Mom and Dad dare not get too busy to monitor all of their kids' entertainment, since new predators lurk near them on a daily basis.

Above all, get the TVs, video players, and computers out of your children's bedrooms and into the family room, where you can monitor and regulate what they're engaging in and how much time they're spending with these activities. Make every effort to screen out filth and violence, remembering King David's words: "I will set no wicked thing before mine eyes" (Psalm 101:3, KJV).

When caught in the "everybody's doing it" bind, explain that families don't do everything alike and that you have little concern about what other parents are doing, simply because you are committed Christians. You have not only the right but also the responsibility of monitoring the type of music, television, movies, and computer games kids play in your home. Notice the word *monitor*.

However, if you try to restrict teenagers entirely from listening to or watching what's currently "in," they'll likely rebel. Please note that even if you can control what your teens listen to or watch at home, you can't control what they do outside your home. You must trust that you have instilled proper values during the early years and that these will carry your teenagers through this difficult time when peer pressure remains heavy. Few teens will be strong enough to reject entirely the music and entertainment of their age. Once again, you will need to offer subtle guidance without sounding totally arbitrary. Naturally, you needn't allow teens to force their taste in music on other members of the family, and you can put controls on the volume of the music played in your house.

Make every effort to protect those you love. The secular world is bearing down on families everywhere, threatening the welfare of our children. It has placed parents in a difficult position. They must either close their eyes and go with the flow, ignoring the harmful influences threatening their children, or figure out how to defend them. Your task as parents is to build such satisfying and affirming relationships with your teens that they want to maintain the values that your family stands for.

The next problem is becoming more and more frequent as parents are increasingly homeschooling their children.

Dear Nancy: *My husband and I have decided that we do not want to send our son to school when he is five years old. We want to keep him home until he* *is seven or eight. Our neighbors have been trying to convince us that we are harming our child if we don't let him attend kindergarten with his friends. At what age do you think children should begin school?*

Dear Undecided: Your decision gets my vote, and for good reason. Dr. Raymond Moore (you'll read more about his research and work in the next letter) confirms that it is risky and unwise to place young children in a formal educational setting. He especially warns against doing so with immature boys. He conclusively demonstrates how parents can effectively teach their children in informal ways at home until the ages of eight, nine, and ten or even older! At that time, parents can place them in a formal school setting, and they'll quickly catch up with their age-mates. Not only do they catch up quickly, but they also tend to be leaders in their classes. (See the appendix for information on his book *Better Late Than Early*.)

When children are thrown together in classroom settings, they become vulnerable to the wrong type of socialization. The tendency is for the stronger, more aggressive kids to take over and to intimidate the weaker ones. The most immature in the crowd suffer most in this situation. When this happens to a boy in kindergarten, he becomes fearful and unable to cope—not a good way to begin life. To quote Dr. James Dobson, "Research shows that if immature boys in particular can be kept at home for a few more years and shielded from the impact of social pressure, they tend to be more confident, more independent, and often emerge as leaders three or four years later."[3] You are right. Stick to your guns!

Read on for more on homeschooling and the development of children during the early, formative years.

Dear Nancy: *What is your perspective on homeschooling? We are considering this for our four children, ages two, four, five, and six. We want to provide the best learning environment for our children, but we don't want to deprive them of socialization. My husband and I have hashed and rehashed this subject, and we just can't agree on what to do. Can you help?*

Dear Unsettled: The advantages of homeschooling are clear in my mind even though it was not available when Harry and I educated our three children. We chose the next best environment at the time—private Christian schools. But if given the opportunity today, I would probably homeschool my own.

Homeschooling is now the fastest-growing educational movement in the country; it continues to grow at a rate of 15 percent per year. Why is it growing so rapidly? Because government education is failing. When you compare our children with those of other industrialized nations, you can see this.

According to the reports, U.S. third-graders score near the top in math and science when compared to other industrialized nations. By the eighth grade, they rank near the middle, and by grade twelve, they rank at the bottom. Kids in public schools rank at the fiftieth percentile on academic tests, while homeschooled kids rank at the eighty-seventh percentile for one-sixth the cost! Furthermore, homeschooled kids are "joiners." They are active in civic and political activities, which shoots holes in the theory that homeschooled kids are social misfits. They have an aura of confidence and respect about them that is rare in public school kids. And perhaps most important, homeschooling allows parents to transmit their values in a highly effective learning environment—their home.

To learn more about the reasons for homeschooling your kids, read Dr. Raymond Moore's books. Dr. Moore is one of the foremost researchers on the subject of homeschooling. Two of his books, *Better Late Than Early* and a companion text titled *School Can Wait* (see appendix), are considered classics in the field.

Not all parents are cut out to homeschool their children. But for those who want and need this type of time with their children to form bonds of trust, respect, and love, I highly recommend it. Several online curriculums are available for children in grades K-12 (see appendix).

Parents in this culture have many concerns regarding purity, as the next mother does.

Dear Nancy: *My beautiful, well-developed daughter will soon be sixteen. Boys call her constantly on the telephone, and she seems to be in great demand for dates. I am a single mother and am terribly worried that she will become sexually active before she is married. I know she craves male companionship; her father hardly ever comes to see her. How can I ensure that she will remain pure and stay out of trouble until she is married?*

Dear Mother of Teen: Face it, you can't. If she wants to become sexually active, there is little you can do to stop her. Naturally, you'll want to supervise her activities and monitor her behavior to the best of your ability without overdoing it. But the fact remains that teenagers today have multiple opportunities to engage in sex when and if they want to. No parent, teacher, or pastor can follow a teen around day and night to prevent misconduct.

The ultimate choice about remaining chaste until she marries remains with your daughter and will be determined by what she thinks about herself and what she desires for her future. Your job as a parent is to prepare her to make that choice. Before you can prepare her, however, you must prepare yourself. I highly recommend you read *Smart Love—Straight Talk to Young Adults About Dating, Love, and Sex.* I've also prepared another resource for concerned parents like you, titled *Smart Love Sexual Values Discussion Guide for Parents and Teachers* (see appendix). This guide will lead you and your teen through six lessons and prepare her to pledge herself to sexual purity until marriage.

During early teen years, dating standards should be a frequent topic during informal times, such as when the two of you are watching TV or riding in the car, as well as during family worships and family conferences. Your daughter should feel free to make any statement or ask any question, as shocking or adverse as it might be. You should avoid responding with lectures, put-downs, or any form of retribution. Wouldn't you prefer that your daughter get information from you rather than just from her peers? Remember also that during the teen years your daughter's opinions and perspectives may differ from yours. Remember also that they will change. She may overstate her views in an effort to meet your objections or to break loose from your values. An overreaction from you at this point may well ensure that she will some day attempt the very things you more or less forced her into defending.

Does this plan of action come with any guarantees about her purity until marriage? No. But this option is making a powerful impact on teens the world over. It's your best option and worth a try.

Satan works while parents sleep. This next parent is wisely suspicious.

Dear Nancy: *I suspect that our seventeen-year-old son is using drugs. He runs around with a wild crowd at school. Many of his friends have long hair and pierced ears, and this crowd dresses very sloppily and is generally lazy and defiant. My son's grades are dropping, and because of this he was dropped from the basketball team. I try to track his whereabouts, which isn't always easy to do. I caught him in some lies, which increases my suspicions. How can I find out if he is using drugs, and what can I do to help him if he is?*

Dear Suspicious Mother: I always advocate respecting teenagers' privacy. This means staying out of their bedrooms, personal letters, emails, diaries, and phone calls. Parents who search through a teenager's room and personal effects seeking evidence of clandestine activity are usually violating their teen's right to privacy. However, when you suspect that a child is involved with drugs, search and seizure is in order.

An enormous number of teenagers admit to being "stoned" in front of their parents, who didn't even realize it. You need to be alert for the clear and unmistakable warning signs of drug use. Kids experimenting with or addicted to drugs may exhibit the following signs: needle marks on arms or legs; red, watery eyes; small pupils in the eyes; furtive glances; chronic drowsiness; marked restlessness, with body spasms and a tendency to walk fast; easily upset stomach; ulcerous sores on their arms, legs, and body; uncontrollable giddiness; a strong body odor; habitual scratching or rubbing of the nose; frequent dizziness; obvious mental and physical deterioration; depression and despondency; persecution complexes; chronic sleepiness; loss of interest in school; inability to concentrate on studies; lack of interest in athletics or any other forms of exercise; irritability; telling of stupid lies; and refusal to talk because of preoccupation with self.

Your son exhibits several of the symptoms listed here. A thorough search of his room may provide more clues. Once you obtain a little more information, you need to act. This may have been going on under your nose for some time, and his addiction will only intensify. One option would be to contact *TOUGH*LOVE and work with other *TOUGH*LOVE parents, who draw a hard line on drugs. The other option is to get him into a drug-treatment program of some kind. See the appendix for two that I recommend because they follow principles I find consistent with the Christian lifestyle. Several residential programs are also available.

Act soon. You have no time to lose. Your son is seventeen; he'll be treated differently by the authorities and by rehabilitation programs once he is eighteen.

Throughout your son's rehabilitation, continue to love him. And remember, the most effective weapon in keeping a young person from drug addiction is the security of a well-adjusted, rewarding home life, with family ties made strong by love. Make certain that you and your husband stand together on issues. If there are any inconsistencies in your life that could contribute to your son's addiction, get help now.

A wild child's choices cause concern for this next father.

Dear Nancy: *My wife and I have been married twenty-two years and have three teenagers. The oldest and youngest are model kids who have been honor students and have won numerous awards for deportment and academic and sports achievements. But our middle child, our fifteen-year-old daughter, concerns us.*

Without permission, she crawls out of her window at night and doesn't return until three in the morning or later. The first time it happened, we learned she went to her boyfriend's house. My wife and I gave her a very severe warning and restricted her privileges. Within a few weeks she did it again. We've taken away her driving permit and her spending money, but her attitude tells us she's going to continue to do it. She dresses in tight tee tops and in general won't listen to anything we have to say. Our oldest boy didn't give us these kinds of problems.

We are a highly respected family in our church and community and need an answer fast in order to bring this critical situation under control.

Dear Needs an Answer Fast: Parents often assume too much credit for their children's good behavior and too much guilt for their children's bad behavior. I read in your letter the pride you rightly feel over your oldest and youngest children. But I also read the guilt and shame you carry over the behavior of your daughter. Whereas your oldest and youngest children have brought you pride, your daughter's behavior has threatened your status professionally as well as in your church and community.

Guilt over what she has or has not done or what you should have or should not have done only makes matters worse. Fear of failure often clouds our thinking so that we can no longer distinguish between valid guilt and irrational guilt. Each new problem encountered presents new fear of inadequacy until the oppressing guilt paralyzes us. If we cannot deal with guilt openly and honestly, it will corrupt our relationships with our mate, other children in the family, and others. Guilt is a thief. It robs us of joyful living.

Your worth and identity are not dependent on what you have or have not accomplished as a parent. You have disciplined your daughter appropriately for her misdemeanors. Appreciate your own worth! Only then will you be able to deal with your guilt and help your daughter through her traumatic teen years. She also is a person of worth, even though she may be choosing values different from those you want her to choose. You must allow her to develop her own values and live life as she sees fit.

The choices your daughter is making could lead to sexual misconduct, which could end in pregnancy, abortion, or sexually transmitted diseases. This makes it more serious than some other offenses. Should she on one more occasion defy the rules of the house by sneaking out to see her boyfriend or for any other reason, I would strongly urge you to consider family counseling. Family systems theory suggests that when one member of a family is acting out, that person is sending a message that something is awry in the whole family system. The best method of fixing the system is to have all members of the family own the problem and go to a therapist as a family. This requires the services of a Christian family therapist. Getting this therapy could be an eye-opening experience for all of you. And it could save your middle child from being the scapegoat.

If these efforts fail, you might enroll her in Project Patch Ranch, located in Idaho, or in Miracle Meadows School in West Virginia. Both schools offer parents an alternative for teens who are making inappropriate choices at home. Under the guidance of a trained staff, behavior modification inspires a change in attitude (see appendix).

Only our children can hurt us as this daughter is hurting you. You may not be able to make the pain disappear, but you can choose to focus on hope for the future. During the trying periods of your daughter's behavior, you'll find great comfort in leaning on a higher Power. But never forget that it isn't the number of prayers that makes the difference to a teenager; it's how praying works in your life that will speak to her heart.

Intervention is a must for a family with an uncontrollable son.

Dear Nancy: *My wife and I have a son whom we love so much that it hurts us. He's only twelve, but his behavior is out of control, and we don't know what to do next. He lies about everything. Can a boy of twelve be a pathological liar? And whether or not he needs something or even wants it, he'll steal it. Our home is in the mountains. Although he is well aware that fires are very dangerous in this area, he has lit two fires in the grass behind our house. He also lights fires at school. And at the dinner table, he acts out bizarrely.*

We took him to our physician, and he diagnosed him with ADHD and put him on medications, which have helped to a degree. But last week he pulled the pin of the hitch of the utility trailer that I pull with my pickup. If the safety chains hadn't been on, this could have been fatal. This is the fourth time he's done this.

We are prisoners of our own son and don't know where to turn. We can't live this way any longer. My wife and I are afraid of him and think we need to act before he pulls a knife on us. As much as we love him, we can't handle him in our home any longer. By the way, this boy is adopted. What suggestions do you have?

Dear Parent of Adopted Boy: During a normal rebellious phase, you might expect your son to challenge your authority in a number of areas: He might talk back to you, argue with you, test rules and curfews, question your religion, and reject long-established family values. However, your son's behavior has taken him out of the mainstream of life. He is exhibiting a seething anger and hatred that is forcing him into a narrow detour. You definitely need outside intervention.

Before you do anything else, I suggest that you arrange an inpatient stay for him in a psychiatric facility for children and adolescents. The evaluation you'll get from this institution will be extremely helpful in finding a place where he can get the help he desperately needs. There are several options open to parents who want their child in a Christian environment. There are also residential homes and challenge programs that take in and school defiant and unmanageable children.

Advent Home is a licensed residential group home that accepts twelve- to sixteen-year-old boys with special learning disabilities like ADD, ADHD, and other learning and behavioral dysfunctions. This home provides boys with individual and group counseling, accelerated schooling, work skills, play therapy, spiritual growth, and wellness. Parents visit the students and participate in the counseling. In the country setting of this home, work and play, fresh air and sunshine, adequate sleep, minimal negative peer pressure, a healthy and wholesome diet, and trust in God all contribute to the healing process.

Although some boys need more time than others need, the average length of stay is eighteen months. Research shows that 90 percent of those who complete the program return home well adjusted. One year after completing the program, these students are getting along at home, attending school, working, and experiencing minimal problems. (See the appendix for contact information regarding this home and for information on Solid Rock Ranch in Grass Valley, California—a new private school for teen boys with ADD, ADHD, or ODD.)

Another alternative is to resort to "tough love." The organization *TOUGH*LOVE is an international network of support groups of parents who draw a tough line for problem kids. Members of *TOUGHLOVE* tell their kids to straighten up or else. *TOUGHLOVE* forces kids to choose between living as a decent human being at home with their family or leaving home. Parents then give their youngster the choice of living with friends, relatives, or other *TOUGHLOVE* parents (see appendix).

Such measures are the last resort for parents who haven't been able to handle problems such as defiant behavior, lying, stealing, sneaking, truancy, failing grades, hostility toward God and others, alcohol and drug abuse, poor social skills, self-image problems, or irresponsible and undisciplined or destructive and aggressive behavior, as well as those who have been dismissed from other schools. Such steps sound radical, but they are effective.

An obviously troubled mother seeks help for her child.

Dear Nancy: *I am the mother of an eight-year-old girl who masturbates heavily and has since she was about three years old. When she sits on her rocking chair and rocks back and forth, she becomes almost glassy eyed, and I am sure she is experiencing orgasm. She will rub against objects in our home and in her bed. Whenever I catch her, she stops.*

I've tried every approach imaginable to get her to control this. I've threatened, punished, spanked, and called what she's doing a sin. I've even prayed with her about it. At one point, I lost control and screamed that if she didn't stop, I would take her to a psychiatrist. She asked if the psychiatrist would operate on her or give her an injection. When I said No, she told me to take her to a psychiatrist!

My daughter is very withdrawn and has no friends her own age. But she identifies well with older people. My husband and I have vast marriage problems. He's a heavy masturbator and into pornography. He's extremely hostile to police when he gets a ticket. He has refused to join us for family devotions, and I believe he is bitter against God. He's an accountant with a large firm and has embezzled funds from it.

In spite of these problems, I have a positive attitude towards life. I am a happy person and will not consider separation or divorce. I can cope with the marriage problems, but my daughter's problem with masturbation is getting me down.

Dear Mother: For generations, the very word *masturbation* brought fear and shame to thousands. Just a few years ago, people thought masturbation caused insanity, deafness, blindness, epilepsy, baldness, weight loss, weakness, and sterility. Often children caught "in the act" were beaten and sternly warned that they would go to hell because of it.

To prevent their children from masturbating, parents tied their hands and legs to the bedposts or used other physical restraints, such as handcuffs or even metal devices over the genitals—some of which even had sharp points that would dig into the flesh of the penis if it became erect. One device would ring in the parents' bedroom to indicate when a boy had an erection so that the father could rush in and save the boy from himself! Occasionally, parents resorted to such extremes as surgically removing a girl's clitoris or suturing the labia, and operations were also performed on boys.

Nowadays, medical authorities insist that masturbation is a normal part of growing up. Almost all boys and at least 75 percent of girls masturbate at one time or another, especially once they have discovered the pleasant sensations that come from pressing against, rubbing, or handling the genitals. Many times masturbation merely reflects children's search for knowledge about their own bodies, but some children resort to masturbation to compensate for a lack of love and attention at home.

It is unlikely that occasional masturbation causes many of the feared diseases for which it was blamed years ago. But it can destroy self-worth, character, and morals and may result in feelings of melancholy, irritability, and jealousy. As in your daughter's case, children may suffer from deep feelings of guilt and remorse and feel degraded. Masturbation can also become a habit, which is what I think has happened in your daughter's case.

A child who masturbates a great deal is usually a troubled, unhappy child. She may have few friends (which you indicated in your letter) and may not enjoy a normal amount of childhood fun. In such a child, masturbation is not the cause of the problem but a symptom that something in the child's life is not right. You should make a concerted effort to create good play situations. Your daughter needs plenty of physical exercise—time when she can climb, run, and expend energy. She should have hobbies and interesting and challenging tasks at home. Compliment her on tasks well done and the effort she expends toward getting her tasks done. Plan more family fun and projects with her in mind.

The problem evidencing itself through masturbation may even go deeper. Your daughter's behavior may even be symptomatic of molestation. Could someone in your family be molesting her—someone you might not suspect? To check this out, I highly recommend that you get a medical examination for signs of such abuse. The exam should include tests for semen and STDs and even vaginal tears, etc. (See appendix for information on the Childhelp USA National Child Abuse Hotline.)

When you discover your daughter masturbating, don't threaten punishment or embarrass her. Doing these things will only motivate her to become more clever in hiding her habit from you. Rather than making a big deal of it, downplay the fact that she is masturbating. Use a positive approach—talk quietly with her about it, giving information and answering questions as you talk. You can require that her hands be on the table while you're talking. Check her clothing to see that it fits properly. Tight clothing may cause excess pressure on the genitals, increasing the problem. Check also for any rash, irritation, or urinary tract infection that could be causing her to rub or scratch her genitals.

If the problem persists, seek professional help from a licensed clinical social worker with training in this area. Very troubled children seek masturbation as a consolation for their feelings. And I really must ask why you continue with a relationship as dysfunctional as you describe. Your marriage problems may be spilling onto your child and could be the root of her problems.

In this next letter, a mother tells of finding some shocking things.

Dear Nancy: *I have a problem that I am embarrassed to talk to anyone about. My son, who is fourteen and is six feet tall, is into some bizarre sex things that I don't know how to handle. I went into his room unannounced the other day and found him dressed in my underclothes—bra, pantyhose, and slip. I was so shocked that I'm afraid I overreacted and handled it badly. I find wads of toilet paper in his bed, so I suspect he is masturbating into this as well as into pieces of my underclothing. I've also found pictures of nude girls under his mattress. Maybe it's a good thing I don't know what else he's into. I have talked openly with this kid about masturbation. I can't tie him to a bedpost—he's too big! How much of this is normal?*

Dear Embarrassed Mom: For the most part, masturbation during the teen years takes on a different meaning from what it carries during earlier years. No longer a matter of curiosity or a simple childish pleasure, it has a deeper sexual meaning. Your son has lived with his body for fourteen years but now feels new urges, moods, and physical sensations as his sexual responses and capacities awaken. All of this is normal. The most serious damage resulting from masturbation is the guilt connected with it. Young people have committed suicide because they felt too weak and evil to go on living.

Your son needs to understand that, as he grows into manhood, his sexual concepts can become more meaningful. He must learn that genuine sexual satisfaction comes from giving rather than receiving. He needs to grasp the concept that real fulfillment can be found only in a love relationship that involves another person and not in solitary physical pleasure. That is why God created man, woman, and marriage.

Realize also that although teenagers are deeply concerned about the subject of masturbation, it remains one of the most difficult areas for parents to discuss. You can help your son by assuring him there is nothing wrong with what is happening to his body. Please make sure you do not burden him with feelings of guilt, self-hatred, or degradation. At the same time, it is your duty as a parent to emphasize that people need to guide and control their sexual expression. If he does not learn self-control, he will grow up to be a selfish, greedy, undisciplined adult. The great danger is that some parents, in a desperate attempt to help their children control sexual urges, go either to the extreme of overcontrol or to the opposite extreme of not teaching enough control.

One author offers this advice to parents who encounter the problem of pornography: "When you discover a copy of a lurid book, a girly magazine, a dirty joke book concealed in your teenager's room or notebook, do not act with emotion or embarrassment. He is not some strange monster, nor are his interests unnatural. He is fascinated by this material because he has heard about it from friends. He wants to find out for himself. Making a scene, destroying the material, and/or accusing him of shameful desires will not necessarily decrease his interest. It may only make him more clever in hiding it from you and plant the notion in his mind that he is twisted and perverted." Instead, point out to your son that pornography depicts genital contact only, and that it promotes relationships devoid of affection, love, and commitment. The use of such material to stimulate erotic fantasy flies in the face of what the Bible teaches God intends that sex can and should be.

Most of what you encountered is a normal part of growing up for a teen boy. He's experimenting with various activities to learn about sex. Keep talking openly with him about all sexual topics so that when he has a question he feels comfortable in turning to you. When a young person's natural curiosity isn't satisfied in an intelligent way, he or she may turn to pornography to find answers. Pornography offers the wrong answers—misleading information and unwholesome views that separate sex from love and marriage.

What can be done for children born handicapped?

Dear Nancy: *I have an eight-year old son whose brain was damaged at birth. He is in therapy to help him learn life skills and is being mainstreamed at school. A year ago, he had an epileptic seizure and was put on medication to control the seizures. He hasn't had one since.*

In spite of my son's brain damage, he is a charming boy. I love him so much, and it hurts me to see him like this. Are there any advances in medicine that might help him?

Dear Hurting Mother: If a physician has confirmed your son's brain damage, little can be done to correct his condition. You have him in therapy, which is good. A physician should also monitor his health in case of a recurrence of epileptic seizures. It is also a positive step to mainstream him in school as long as possible. There he will learn skills and appropriate behavior, and his classmates will learn how to adapt to and accept a handicapped child.

I have a little personal knowledge about handicapped children because one of my grandchildren, Matthew, is physically and mentally handicapped. In addition to the speech and physical therapy necessary to build his skills, my daughter, Carlene, worked diligently to build his self-esteem and have him fit into normal family life. Although Matthew cocks his head to one side when he looks at people and walks with staggering, jerky movements, he is skilled on the computer and reads well; he can interact with others, swim, play ball, ride a bike, and do a multiplicity of other things. I don't think he views himself as handicapped, and sometimes the family forgets he is! In addition to his other attributes, he has a very tender spirit toward God and spiritual matters. Although Matthew is severely handicapped in certain ways, he has been a blessing to our family.

When a mother learns that her child is brain damaged, one of her fondest dreams turns into a nightmare. Her life is disrupted in ways others could never imagine. Some insensitive people may even suggest or imply that she is responsible for the child's problems. The gravity of the situation may begin to affect her health. In time, she may find that her marriage is headed for a total breakdown. She may find herself devoting so much time to her handicapped child that she neglects her other children, if she has any.

So, my most important advice to you is to maintain emotional balance. Arrange your time and circumstances so that once a week you can get away from your son, your home, and all the responsibilities connected with being the force that makes everything in the family function. Go out to lunch with friends. Laugh, giggle, and have some fun. Take up a hobby in which you can use your creative abilities. Exercise daily. Take time for personal devotions and prayer. You and your husband should also take time away from the family to nurture your relationship.

You need to do more for yourself than just exist. You need to give yourself permission to break away from your endless childcare tasks and enjoy leisure activities. Recognize that taking time for yourself is not something you should be doing only when it's convenient. You can find the time to work it into your schedule and to afford it. You must begin thinking of time for yourself as a priority, not a luxury. If you don't take care of your needs, you won't be much help to your son or others. Taking time for yourself will refresh you, energize your spirit, lessen your stress, and make your efforts at handling your multiple priorities more successful.

The public school system can be very helpful in providing all types of therapy as well as behavior management. It also frees parents to have time for themselves. Services begin for three-year-olds onsite, with home services at younger ages. All services are free and include many specialized communication devices as well as special chairs and tables.

You may find it difficult to accept the fact that no doctor, treatment, or medication can "fix" your brain-damaged child. However, God does not leave us without hope. He's promised us that at Christ's second coming the blind shall see and the lame shall walk. God will transform all of us in the twinkling of an eye, giving us new bodies. He will make us new. One day, your son will be perfect. One day, my grandson will no longer stagger or cock his head in order to see me. Neither child will suffer the effects of sin any longer. Live with this hope in your heart.

A single parent asks the following question:

Dear Nancy: *I am a single mother with four children, all boys, ages fourteen, twelve, eight, and six. I need counsel on how to raise them properly* *without a father. They are all good-looking boys, popular at school, and obey me quite well. I want to head off trouble if I can. Do you have any advice for me?*

Dear Single Mother: When God instituted the family, He meant it to have two parents—a mother and a father. Today we live in a society that reaps the results of sin. When a family breaks up, the children suffer. Research confirms that boys experience extreme stresses when their father is absent. Let's take a brief look at some of the findings.

Researchers in the National Longitudinal Survey of Youth tracked 6,403 boys for twenty years. They found that sons of single mothers are at greater risk for violence and that whether or not the mother received child support made no difference to the child's outcome; the key factor was the absence of the father. Surprisingly, boys who lived with their single fathers were no more likely to commit crimes than were boys from intact families. The reason? Probably that fathers who don't marry but who commit themselves to raising their children are uniquely devoted.

The research also says that a new husband/stepfather won't solve the problem. In fact, it confirms that this often makes things worse for boys. According to this study, males living in stepparent families were almost three times as likely to face prison as those from intact families. Blending families produces some unique stresses. It is typical for a child to see the new parent as a usurper. Their loyalty to the absent parent can be intense. Such children rarely welcome a new parent.

There is no way you as a woman can model for your boys an endless number of male tasks—things like shaving or thinking and talking like a man. Therefore, it is your task as a single mother to direct your boys to a father substitute. It might be a youth group with a male leader, a prayer group, a Bible study class, or a soccer team. Check the library for biographies on great men. Rent videos that focus on the accomplishments of males with integrity. Read *Bringing Up Boys* and subscribe to Focus on the Family's magazine for single parents (see appendix).

As a single mom, you can provide a successful environment for your boys. Doing so will take time, energy, and creativity; but so does everything else worth pursuing in this life. You can do it. Whether you do so depends on your priorities. Success in relating to your boys in positive ways is directly correlated with positive feelings you have about yourself and with finding support from others outside the home. It may seem difficult and almost unfair that you have to take the initiative and shoulder all this responsibility, but this is crucial.

nts:

and pregnant. She is an attorney and
ny child that would be born, but her
? she should give her baby up for adop-
wo-parent home. What do you think?

, your new grandchild would be bet-
ive in an imperfect world, and now
he future of both mother *and* child.
iously a respectable and responsible
in on her shoulders even if her brain

but it is also first and foremost your
She is the one who must make the
ences. Granted, her decision affects
you as grandparents. But because she carries this baby inside her, she should have primary say. I'm sure you wouldn't want her to accede to your wishes and then come to regret her decision and blame you for the rest of your days. She may not feel able to deal with the confused emotions that can haunt a woman in all the years to come when she surrenders a baby for adoption.

Back off and let her make her own decision, and then support her decision any way you can. She's going to have a tough road ahead of her as a single parent even if she earns a respectable living as an attorney. There's much more to raising a responsible child than providing material pleasantries. You can be a great asset in helping her face the realities as they appear day after day.

Living in our culture where people idolize youth and beauty has caused emotional pain for a deformed child.

Dear Nancy: *We have two girls, ten and twelve years of age. We are a happy, Christian family, and our girls attend a Christian school. However, while our ten-year-old is extremely pretty and outgoing, our twelve-year-old is shy and not good-looking. She was born with a harelip, and she wears very thick glasses. The other day I found her crying because the other children tease her, call her names,* *and don't always include her in group activities. She is a sweet and loving child, but I fear her appearance and her retiring personality are damaging her self-esteem. How can I help her?*

Dear Happy Parent: You need to correct this problem right away. Your daughter's shy and retiring personality is likely a reaction to how others are treating her at school. Fear of ridicule and criticism can soon begin to dominate her emotions and cause her to question the point of living. Such fear and uncertainty will exhaust your daughter emotionally.

As girls are growing up, they place enormous value on their physical appearance and personality. She draws conclusions about herself partly from comparing herself with others and partly from how others respond to her. The feeling that she doesn't measure up affects how a girl feels about herself. Such a conclusion subtracts from her feelings of worth. Once your daughter becomes convinced that she is homely, she will ignore all other messages and believe she is ugly even though she has many other attractive features. The longer a child lives with these negative feelings, the deeper the roots of self-hatred extend and the more difficult the task becomes of changing those feelings.

So, first, take your daughter to a plastic surgeon to see what can be done about her harelip. Next, schedule an appointment with an ophthalmologist to investigate the possibility of contact lenses. Contacts come in many different styles and are much easier to use than they once were. When your daughter is closer to the age of eighteen, she may be able to have laser surgery so that she won't have to wear glasses at all.

In addition to doing what you can to improve her appearance, you also need to help her develop some special skill. It can be anything that she can do well to compensate for those times when her peer group calls her names or ridicules her. She might be able to excel in swimming, sewing, drawing, writing, or working with handicapped children. You can also help her build solid friendships with other girls. Then, should she receive rejection from some kids, she can compensate by saying to herself, "OK, you don't accept me. You're laughing at me and making fun of me. But I can do something you can't do." Read Dr. Dobson's book *Hide or Seek* and chapter two of my book *The Compleat Parent* (see appendix).

For any of us, happiness involves feeling good about ourselves. One of the greatest gifts you can give your child is a healthy self-respect. Then she'll be able to understand the word love more fully.

A grandmother's dilemma brought me the next question.

Dear Nancy: *We have a precious grandson whose mother became pregnant before she was married. The father abandoned our daughter and never accepted responsibility for this wonderful child. We have tried to help this little family as much as possible, and the child is now six years old. He is becoming increasingly inquisitive about who and where his dad is. He particularly asks questions after attending Sabbath School and church, where he sees complete families together.*

My daughter has never gotten any support from this man, and a Christian attorney has counseled her to avoid ever involving the father in the boy's life because of the father's mean spirit and complete denial of parenthood. Our daughter has come to us for advice as to how she should answer her child's questions, and we just don't know what to tell her. Can you help?

Dear Grandmother: Congratulations! You are doing just what you should be doing at this time—providing emotional and financial support for both your daughter and grandson. Your daughter has likely already learned how difficult it is to raise a boy by herself. You and your husband can be a valuable influence in your grandson's life. And your husband can provide the male role model that the boy desperately needs. Just continue to do what grandparents do best—love your grandchild, gently criticize when you must, listen lots, and enjoy this little lad whom you obviously adore. If you wish to enrich your already evident grandparenting skills, let me recommend a resource called *The Gift of Grandparenting* (see appendix).

Now to the heart of your question. How can you tell a six-year-old who has no knowledge of his daddy that his daddy wants no part of him? You can't. Bite your tongue if necessary. Regardless of what a bum this character is, it would be detrimental to tear down respect for the jerk in the eyes of your grandson. When he asks about his daddy, he needs to know that he has one and that at one time his daddy and mommy thought they were very much in love and that's why he was born.

Tell him that something happened to Daddy after that. He just wasn't ready at that time to be a daddy. It doesn't mean that he didn't love his son. This was a problem Daddy had in his own mind with himself. You might add that you very much want his daddy to be saved in God's kingdom and encourage him to pray for his daddy. Explain that his daddy is a good person in many other ways; he just wasn't ready to be a daddy.

You might take this a step further. Explain that someday he may have another daddy, if mommy remarries (and she will at some point, I'd predict).

Then he'll be part of a family with a mommy and a daddy. Emphasize that even though there is no daddy in his family right now, that they are still a family. There is a mommy in his family, a grandma and a grandpa, and perhaps even aunts, uncles, and cousins. This is his family. Explain that families come in all different sizes and configurations. Let him know how important he is in the family because he is the only one growing up in it right now. That makes him very important. And tell him that everyone in the family wants the very best for him.

You'll probably need to say all of this over and over again in different ways to reassure his little mind that everything in his world is normal and as it is supposed to be right now. This will give him the security he needs to feel.

I want to emphasize again that your role as grandparents is even more important than the role of most grandparents since your grandson doesn't currently have an intact home. Maintain your regular interaction with this little guy. And thank God every time you enjoy his presence that your daughter didn't choose abortion!

Bullies can traumatize, and the next mother needs help.

Dear Nancy: *My daughter Melissa, who is eleven and in the fifth grade, has always been an "A" student and very social. Now she comes home crying every day, doesn't want to go to school, and her grades are slipping—all because of a bully named Nicole. This beast terrorizes anyone who is not part of her little clique. If anyone makes her mad or goes against her rules, she puts them on "suspension." No one can talk to or interact with the one she has put on suspension. She's a real Saddam. If the girls are playing a game, and Nicole is "out," the other girls will try to take her place to keep her from getting mad.*

Until now, I've told Melissa to be like Jesus and set a good example so that Nicole could learn how to behave from her. Now I'm to the point where I'm telling her to stand up to Nicole. If Nicole bites her, she should bite her back as she does with her sister. But Melissa won't do it. I'm at the point of considering homeschooling or moving Melissa to another school. How should bullies be handled?

Dear Mother Hen: People bully because they want to intimidate others. Bullies want to drag others down to a level of powerlessness so that they can control them through fear. Other children often reward and even admire bullying behavior, making the bully popular. When bullying occurs in a school environment, it affects learning ability; children who live in fear have difficulty learning.

While I believe parents generally should allow their children to cope with the basic challenges of life, no one should force a child to endure the torture Melissa is going through under Nicole's regime. Every classroom should have an environment of safety in which children can learn. If the teacher were skilled in protecting the self-esteem and worth of every child under her care, you would have no worries. In this case, the teacher lacks the skills or motivation to learn this, and obviously the principal does also. So you as a parent are going to have to take the steps necessary to protect the welfare of your child.

Your first line of defense might to be talk to Nicole herself. Invite her to your home and make an effort to befriend her. In other cases, this has brought good results. Or you might confront her yourself and work her over just as a protective mother hen might do. This could either end the problem or create more problems for Melissa.

If this fails, you might talk to Nicole's mother. Rather than attacking Nicole in any way, which would invite instant retaliation and perhaps even greater trouble than Melissa faces now, simply explain that you have a problem and would appreciate any input she could provide in solving the problem. Then lay it out before her in as nonjudgmental a manner as you can and see how she reacts and what solutions the two of you might devise. Nicole's mother may become a little defensive during this consultation. Overlook that and see what the result might be. If the bullying stops, then you have it made without taking further steps.

Whatever choice you make, you must protect Melissa from undue torture. I too might encourage a child under such extreme pressure to stand up to the bully. If she were strong enough to do so just one time, this might end her torture.

*   *   *   *   *

The time has come for parents to rethink their values and, in most cases, to slow the pace of their lives. Forget the new car, moving to a larger home, or furniture for your redecorating project. Put into second or third place all the materialistic advantages you want to provide for your children. They don't need *things* as much as they need *you*. They need that personal investment of precious time that only *you* can provide.

Take time for a hand-in-hand walk through the woods and answer her questions about God's creation. Take time to build a kite and savor the delight on your child's face as he watches it race and dance on the wings of the wind. Take time for a romp and tussle on the family room floor, where all can chime in with musical giggles. Take time to listen to your children now, for tomorrow they may not wish to talk with you. Take time for all this *now*—tomorrow carries no guarantees.

I'm not suggesting that you invest 100 percent of your energies in your children. But the urgent matters of life always seem to take precedence, while important matters lie neglected. Sort out your priorities so that you understand the difference between the urgent and the important.

There will be times when you feel as though you've failed miserably and have done everything wrong. Despair may rush in like a flood. But one of life's greatest rewards is watching your children mature and begin to return the investment you have put into them. One day you will discover that you must have done more right than wrong because before you stands a wonderful human being whose character reveals the qualities you worked hard to instill.

The world as a whole will probably never fully appreciate the effort expended in good parenting. But in the final judgment, we'll see everything as God views it. He'll openly reward parents who have prepared their children for His kingdom. Overseeing the development of your children may cost tears, anxiety, and sleepless nights, but each parent who has worked wisely unto salvation will hear God say, "Well done, thou good and faithful servant."

1. James Dobson, *Bringing Up Boys* (Wheaton, Ill.: Tyndale House, 2001), 86.
2. Ibid.
3. Dobson, 196.

CHAPTER SIX

When Your Spouse Says Goodbye

Someone has said that divorce is emotional surgery given without anesthesia. It certainly is painfully destructive, and as a cure, it's often worse than the disease itself. Maybe you are suffering from a state of brokenness or grief over something that has already occurred in your family. Even though you may not find an instant cure, I'm hoping that you can find comfort for your hurting emotions as you identify with others in crisis.

Dear Nancy: *My husband and I are contemplating divorce. We've been married almost fourteen years and have three kids, ages seven, nine, and eleven. We've tried counseling, but nothing seems to get better. We live from one battle to the next, and the battles now outweigh the periods of peace. I seriously doubt that there's any life left in this relationship, yet I don't want to hurt my kids. Everyone talks about the effect of divorce on kids, but what about the effect of battling parents? Should we stay married just because of the kids? I'm a bottom-line person: What are the facts regarding the effects of divorce on children?*

Dear Bottom-Line Mom: Divorce will always have a damaging effect on children, and parents need to stop playing the game of denial. Yes, children are resilient, but this does not mean that the breakup of their home doesn't seriously affect them. Even children who show no outward symptoms during or after the divorce can be affected.

According to researchers, children whose parents are going through a divorce experience the same stages of grief that they would if a parent died. Furthermore, about 80 percent of children are not warned in advance that a divorce is about to take place. Even when the news is broken gently, they experience shock, depression, denial, anger, fear, and a haunting obsession that they might have been responsible.

Children respond differently at various ages. Toddlers (two to four years of age) frequently regress to more babyish behavior. Potty-trained youngsters need diapers once again. Some want to be fed. This age group tends to suffer from irritability, whining, crying, fearfulness, sleep problems, confusion, aggressiveness, and tantrums. This age group is the most seriously affected by divorce. Young children (five to eight years old) also regress in their behavior—to bed-wetting, loss of sleep, nail-biting, fears of being abandoned, and a deep sense of sadness.

Older children (nine to twelve years old) primarily experience anger—however, not necessarily anger at the parent who initiated the divorce. They may focus their anger on some scapegoat outside the family. Children who are this age when their parents divorce are the most likely to suffer problems in their spiritual development. They are likely to reject spiritual values. They may say, in essence, "I don't want anything to do with a God or religion that can't help my parents solve their problems."

Teenagers seem somewhat less affected than younger children are—probably because they can more easily understand the reasons for divorce and can detach themselves from the stress by getting away. Even then, they can be deeply traumatized. The more distant and removed teens are from the divorce proceedings, the better they can handle the situation.

According to studies, children of divorce have shorter life spans and more illness than do children from intact homes. They also drop out of school earlier. Some studies show that two out of three suicides among adolescents occur in teens from broken homes. And boys seem to suffer more from divorce than girls do, probably because boys have been taught not to express their emotions.

When a divorce is hotly contested, when there are custody battles and parents use children as pawns or go-betweens, the effects can be worse. And the effects are not always short lived. As long as five years later, over a third of children of divorce still suffer from depression. They manifest behaviors such as chronic unhappiness, sexual promiscuity, drug abuse, stealing, alcoholism, vandalism, poor learning, intense anger, apathy, and restlessness.

Another third were making appropriate progress but exhibited continued symptoms of sadness and resentment toward one or both parents.

In most cases, say the experts, it takes three to four years before children can pull themselves together. This means that children who are seven at the time of the divorce will be eleven before the effects subside. They'll have lived one-third of their life in the awful aftermath of divorce.

Some parents (like you) feel they are doing their children a favor by providing a more peaceful atmosphere. But few children report feelings of relief. Even children from homes in which the parents fight have difficulty adjusting to divorce. Most children, even those from very troubled homes, would go to almost any length to get their divorced parents together again. Many of these children share the fantasy that their parents will reunite. This fantasy often lives on for years.

Do I think a very troubled family should stay together just for the sake of the children? In some extreme situations, such as in cases of physical or sexual abuse, the effects of staying would be as detrimental as the effects of divorce. In most cases, however, *it is preferable to save the existing family whenever possible rather than to opt for divorce.* It is far preferable for all parties concerned to search for ways of solving troubled relationships.

There. You have the facts. Now, go do the right thing.

A divorcée sought my advice for the following problem.

Dear Nancy: *It's been almost a year since my divorce. I'm doing better now than I was a year ago, but I can't understand what's going on in my head. I couldn't wait to get away from my husband, and now that I have, I feel like I'm still connected to him. I knew I would still be connected through the children, but it's more than that. My mind often drifts to him. I wonder if he ever thinks of reconciliation. I still call him every time I run into a problem I can't handle. Is all this normal, or is something seriously wrong with me?*

Dear Divorcée: Most people agree that divorce is more painful than the death of a loved one. When a spouse dies, the relationship is finished; only memories linger. But when two people divorce, a relationship still exists—especially when there are children. Many couples have said to me, "If children are involved, divorce is never over!"

Try as they may, most people can't escape their former partner. More than half of all divorcées admit that their ex-partner is the first person they call in cases of emergency. Holidays can become the most psychologically torturous time of the year, with Thanksgiving and Christmas bringing on major migraines. Every continuing encounter is a reminder of the failure and rejection you have suffered.

Then there are the lingering questions about whether the ex-partner might return. Former in-laws and friends further complicate the issue. And when those who divorced enjoyed a regular sexual relationship within the bounds of holy matrimony, what are they to do now? Twelve percent of all divorced persons continue their sexual contact with each other during the first two months after their divorce!

In a study that followed divorcing partners for a five-year period after the divorce, only 25 percent appeared capable of coping adequately with life. Fifty percent muddled along in a "barely coping" capacity. The remaining 25 percent failed to recover or looked back with intense longing to times before the divorce, wishing it had never occurred.

It takes two to four years—and for some people, longer—to move through the stages of grief following a divorce. You are on your way to recovery. Let go gradually. The toughest part of the divorce journey is behind you. Continue to press forward toward full recovery and personal growth. Just don't embrace a quick remarriage as an antidote for your broken past!

Pressing forward is what the next person would like to do, but she's having a hard time. Read on.

Dear Nancy: *My husband and I were divorced last year, after thirty-five years of disaster. Now that I'm getting my life on track again, he has emailed me that he has arranged for us to attend a marriage enrichment seminar. Why would a divorced couple go to this? He didn't consult me before he made the arrangements. I begged for years for us to go to a marriage enrichment weekend, but he was always too busy. Now that we are divorced, he wants to attend. Why should our sham of a marriage be on parade at a weekend designed to promote healthy marriages? It would be a disservice to the other couples. He wants to counsel with the leaders while we are there. What would two hours do for thirty-five years of disaster? I consider this a ploy to make others think he is doing everything to work toward reconciliation.*

My counselor says my ex has antisocial personality disorder. I'm not sure that's fixable. He thinks trying to do people in with every business deal is good business. I've always disagreed. I just learned he was fired from his job—for the sixteenth time in thirty years. Now he has no place to lay his head and is living with his mother, who is eighty-six and failing. He will persuade her to give him all her property, which she signed over to the church. And he has decided that he gave me way too much and wants to open up the divorce settlement and take his rightful half. You can see why I am a little bit leery about his latest proposal.

After a year of healing, I am peaceful, full of energy, and happy. Sometimes I get lonely for the good times and still question what it will be like to get old alone. I just want all the bad to go away. I want to stay peaceful and healed, and I want to get back to being of service to others. I need your input because I may be missing something that I'm too close to see since I spent all those years in denial or trying to make this work for the kids, the church, and all the usual excuses women use for staying in bad marriages.

Dear Peaceful Divorcée: Think through why your ex is willing to go to marriage enrichment now when he never was before. If he had made this offer prior to the completion of the divorce, I would have said, "It won't hurt anything to give it one last try. God's will for your life is to stay married." But you're no longer married to this man. The divorce is final. You're in the rebuilding phase of your life. You've seen no evidence that he has changed for the better so that the two of you could rebuild and live harmoniously.

The fact that your ex has been fired from yet another job is a big clue. When he was younger, he could always get another job. But the older a person gets, the harder that becomes. Through the years, your earning power has allowed him to purchase his "toys" and live a life of relative financial freedom. He's found it isn't so easy on one salary, and he won't be able to manage on unemployment and eventually no salary. Are you willing to take that on again? And why should you?

Your divorce is final. How can he open it up again? Beware of playing into his hands. Don't allow him to know anything about your affairs. Don't play games with him. There are people in life who are toxic to us—people whom we must leave alone for our own sanity. I believe this is necessary in your case. Respond to no messages from him, or you will go back to square one in your recovery. I see dollar signs throughout everything you have told me.

You're doing a good job—keep rebuilding your life. Yes, you may be lonely. And living in an isolated area as you do makes it worse for you. But once you get your home paid off and you retire, you could always get another small place in the sunshine and travel. And you have your kids.

Keep remembering how "blessed" you are—your words. You weren't talking like that when your ex was under your roof. You are almost a debt-free woman. Think what you'll deal with the minute he's back under your roof.

My best advice: *Don't even consider taking him back.* I repeat: *Don't even consider taking him back!*

The husband you'll read about in the next question needs a miracle.

Dear Nancy: *My wife left me a week ago after a big argument. We've been married for seven years and have a six-year-old boy who is the pride and joy of my life. She's taken the child and gone to her mother's home. Her mother has never approved of me. Her entire family has wanted her to go back to her first husband because of the child she had from that marriage. Two months ago, my in-laws invited my wife for a visit—but they didn't invite me. When she got there, her ex-husband and his mother were also there, begging her to return to him. She chose not to. All of this has been very confusing to her and to me. Now that she's gone, I don't know what to do.*

Dear Confused: God established something beautiful when He created the marriage relationship, and it is exciting when I see someone taking marriage seriously now, when people all around us are mocking it. Fight for your marriage. You'll never regret the fight you put into it now. Make sure, however, that you fight with the right weapons, at the right time, and in the right way.

I recommended that you read Dr. James Dobson's book *Love Must Be Tough.* This will give you step-by-step guidance in your behavior while waiting for her return. Dr. Dobson says sometimes people are like birds in a cage. They think they want freedom. He advises that rather than attempting to lock your wife up in a cage, you should let her go. Now is the time for you to work on yourself and evaluate what you can do to enhance the quality of the relationship should she return. If you want to give your marriage a chance to succeed—slight as that chance may be, I recommend that you follow Dr. Dobson's advice and not deviate from it. Deviations could cost you your marriage and your self-respect. You don't want to lose either!

I believe in miracles. Families are made up of people and personalities, and change is always possible—especially when you lean on divine power.

It would take a miracle to repair the damage done by the years of neglect evidenced in the following letter.

Dear Nancy: *My wife left me, and I'll do anything to get her back. We lived together for four years and have been married for four years. I thought everything was great between us, but now that she's moved out, she tells me she was miserable. Yes, I know I was working long hours in our business, but only to provide a good living for our future. There was no time to romance her or to enjoy life. She worked full time as a police officer and also helped me in my business by doing the accounting and making deliveries. In addition, she poured a lot of money into the business. I know that I didn't tell her how much I appreciated what she was doing, and now I want to correct all this, give her stock in the company, and make it right. I clearly see where I went wrong, but she tells me there's no hope and she's had enough. Please help me win my wife back. I'm devastated.*

Dear Devastated Husband: I hear your desperation and sympathize with you and all other men who have contacted me after it was too late. Women have a tremendous capacity for putting up with neglect while yearning for a closer relationship with their partners. Then one day something snaps within these patient women. They can take no more. When that happens, no one but the Holy Spirit can reach them.

Having a successful marriage requires work. We might compare it to feeding fuel into a full-sized luxury car. If you want to drive that powerful, shiny automobile anywhere, you have to keep the tank full. In the same way, you must keep your marriage full of romance, kind and loving deeds, and intimacy. If you let that auto sit in the driveway for a time, it will gather dust and begin to rust, and the gas will evaporate. You can clean and polish cars, replace rusty parts, and refill the gas tank. Marriages aren't so easy to fix— especially after a wife has moved out. Many men just like you agree to work on their marriages once their wives are gone. They're willing to make changes, read any book, listen to cassettes, or go for counseling. *But it's too late!*

While praying for reconciliation, work on your life and get your priorities straight. Read *Highly Effective Marriage.* Learn how to nurture a marriage, what a woman wants from her husband, and how to meet her needs. When she sees, even from a distance, that you've changed your focus in life, your marriage just might have another chance. You'll never regret the effort you put into salvaging your marriage. You will reap rich rewards in all the years to come.

Reaping rich rewards sometimes takes hard work. Read on.

Dear Nancy: *When I married for the first time, I was young, innocent, and unlearned about the disciplines of married life. Marriage number one went down the tubes. I was devastated, but I survived and launched into another "perfect" relationship. This one couldn't survive the trauma of cancer—my already uncommunicative husband withdrew into silence when I was diagnosed with breast cancer. I survived a mastectomy, but he moved into another room and withdrew from me physically. I faced divorce number two. It was during this time that I first attended the Smart Love seminar for singles and realized how hollow our relationship was. Divorce was inevitable.*

I knew that with the knowledge I gained through your seminar, my next relationship would be perfect. It started out right; we dated for two years and tried to do everything right. Now we've been married eighteen months, and I recognize I've still done everything wrong. First, we dated two years, but we were always in a crowd. We never had alone time to test ideas and thinking when others weren't around. We lived five hours apart, so we saw each other only on weekends. Even after marriage, we still live in two locations! You advise seeing each other during the week under normal circumstances. We have a marriage license but no marriage.

I've noticed that reality sets in sooner in each subsequent relationship because I've been down the road before. My husband and I are treading water. We have no quality time together. He dumps all issues that we need to settle on my shoulders. It's only now that we recognize how we should have spent our time before we married and that we should have waited to get married.

I'm sliding down a mountain, and I'm not sure I can save myself before I hit bottom again. I affirm everything you've written and said, even if it's too late for me. Just keep teaching what you're teaching!

Dear Disillusioned Wife: You've learned your lessons well, although in each case too late. Unfortunately, we are sometimes slow learners. I empathize with first-time divorcées, particularly if they were young and unlearned in the disciplines of marital life when they married. But the death of a second marriage signals a deeper problem. Either the people involved don't know how to select a partner or they need to solve some interpersonal problem. A third divorce signals major internal problems. In my estimation, your case involves all three.

No one but you can save your marriage or your sanity at this point. You need to put yourself in the hands of the best counselor in your area to unravel what's going wrong in your present relationship as well as to identify habits and traits in your personality that detract from marital harmony. The PREPARE-ENRICH marital inventory might help you identify areas that need work.

You can't wipe out the past, but you can make changes that will lead to a more productive future. It takes courage to admit you were part of the problem, to stop blaming others even when you are a victim, to stop nursing your hurts, and to work through complex issues. Rehashing your past poor choices and the consequences is useless at this point. There is no instant cure for the difficulties you face. But you can learn to live with the scars.

This next man's wedding did not produce a marriage.

Dear Nancy: *I write to you with a heavy heart and with tears in my eyes. I am twenty-three and from a good home. I had two years of college training to become a minister, and I dearly love the Lord. But I've made a big mistake.*

In a park one night, I met a girl, and we became friends. The next day I was with her again, and she told me she would come to my apartment. A few minutes after her arrival, she came on to me and told me that anything I started with her I had to finish. Then she seduced me; I'd been a virgin until then.

I moved from that city to another state. Six months later, I got a letter from this girl saying she was pregnant and that I had better come back and finish what I started. I was confused and hurt, since I didn't know or love her. But my pastor's wife advised me to accept responsibility for the child I had fathered. The girl wasn't a member of this church but had been studying and attending there. She also begged the pastor's wife to help her force me to marry her.

I moved back to the town where she lives, and one month later we were married. The baby was four months old at the time. Two days after the wedding, my mother-in-law came to live with us. Both she and my wife treated me terribly. I was out of work then, so I stayed home with the baby to cook and clean. (My mother was Jewish and taught me well.) But nothing pleased my wife. I love music, and in spare moments I would practice on a keyboard while she was at work. This angered her, and so she took the electric cords away. I've tried repeatedly to talk with her about our marriage, but she refuses to listen. She says she can do anything she wants because she supports me. We've had sex only seven times since we were married. I've left her and now live with my parents. I've ruined my opportunity to serve God as a pastor and am truly the prodigal son.

Dear Prodigal: You haven't ruined your opportunity to serve God. Granted, you've made some foolish choices—even when you tried to do the honorable thing. To marry a girl you had sex with one time, someone you had known only one month, was foolish indeed. This pastor's wife heavily influenced you. Her intentions may have been good, but her reasoning was faulty.

If your description of your wife's seduction is accurate, I question her emotional stability. Is it possible she was pregnant when she seduced you? Is it possible her desire to cover a previous indiscretion prompted her behavior, and you appeared to be a good candidate to parent her unborn child? In order to rule out such deceit, you need a doctor and a lawyer. Obtain the services of the best family lawyer in your area regarding the possibility of an annulment. An annulment might be possible on grounds of fraud or for some other reason. I would also have DNA testing done on the child to determine if you are the father. If you are, then you must accept responsibility for the emotional and financial support of the child. Before filing for divorce, get professional help to sort out all the complications of your difficult situation.

The battle to become emotionally whole is a beginning for the woman in the next letter.

Dear Nancy: *I'm a divorced woman with a seventeen-year-old daughter. Shortly after my divorce, I fell into a comfortable—but not exciting—relationship with a man I'd just met. He listened to all my heartaches, and I found having a male friend in whom I could confide so soothing to my troubled soul. In spite of my values and my resolve not to become sexually involved with him, I succumbed. Although he is a Christian, he doesn't share my specific religious beliefs, and for that reason I can never seriously consider marrying him. Five years have gone by, and there's no end in sight. I don't want to end it because he's such a comfortable person to be with, yet I want to get married again.*

Dear Troubled Soul: Any relationship that's comfortable but not exciting is a BTN (better than nothing). A BTN is an "OK" relationship with the wrong person. BTNs are only partially satisfying, but they drag on and on. They're safe, even if they aren't wonderful. People stay in them for the security they provide. However, BTNs take you out of circulation and consume time and energy that should be available for a lifelong relationship. This one may meet your short-term intimacy needs, but it's destroying your long-term goal of marriage.

BTNs are difficult to get out of because it's painful to think of ending a relationship that has gone on so long. In other words, you have stayed in this BTN because you haven't had what it takes to get out early enough. Although BTNs appear better than nothing, they are in reality worse than nothing. They chip away at your self-esteem. You must reinforce a love relationship with positive messages. But you'll have difficulty feeling good about yourself while you're spending time with a person who doesn't contribute to your self-esteem. The fact that you stay in a BTN says that your self-esteem is already in trouble. Whenever you're in a relationship that eats away at your feelings of worth, it becomes critical to fix it or end it.

If a partner isn't suitable, even though parts of the relationship may be great, it is much better to get out when you first realize the problem. That moment may come on your first date or months later. But to allow it to drag on for five years when you already know you won't marry this man is nothing less than foolish and risky business. You might be tempted to give in to the "comfortableness" of it all and later end up with serious regrets or with another divorce.

I can also surmise that your spiritual life has been faltering. God has clearly defined rules for conduct after divorce. Sex outside of marriage is a sin against God. He asks His children to confine sexual intercourse to marriage. The biblical injunction is simple, clear, and straightforward, and it's not archaic. God didn't make His laws to see how good we are at jumping through hoops or scoring points. He gave them to us for our benefit. If we follow them, we'll live longer, happier, and more fulfilling lives, and we'll prosper. This is true even though His laws may not make sense to us now.

Once you make the choice to end this relationship and come into harmony with God's plan for your life, you can enjoy that richer and more prosperous spiritual life. You need to end this BTN you are currently in *now*. If you need help on how to tackle this sticky issue, read "Ending It" in my book *Smart Love* (see appendix).

A pastor writes after a traumatic situation occurred in his home.

Dear Nancy: *I am the pastor of a large church. My wife has left me for another man—our best friend, a backslider whom I helped come back to the Lord. My wife says she has prayed about the matter, and God approves her actions. She feels that divorce will be better for the kids, that she needs to do her own thing, and that she never loved me. She says the church won't discipline her for her actions. I still love her, and I am afraid for our children who are eleven and sixteen and who live with her. I went to counseling, but found it too contrary to the teachings of Scripture. Please comment on my situation.*

Dear Hurting Pastor: Death is often easier than this type of situation, because it will never be over. People who have lost a loved one to death can begin to put the pieces of life together again after an initial period of suffering. They can put away reminders of the past. They don't have to keep dealing with them. That will not be true for you, because when children are involved, divorce is never over.

Here's some advice that may help: Don't rush to a divorce court! Many people become so devastated by a situation that they act too soon. I know it won't be easy, but I highly recommend that you sit back and let her make the moves. If she files for divorce, accept her action, but make no more moves than absolutely necessary to protect yourself. Sometimes these hot affairs burn themselves out just as rapidly as they began. While waiting to see if this might happen, read James Dobson's book *Love Must Be Tough* to learn how to respond to her during this difficult time. He offers specific advice on how to salvage your self-worth during the process of trying to win a spouse back.

The pastor's saga continues.

Dear Nancy: *Things have deteriorated. My wife has taken our children out of Christian school and put them in public school. This is contrary to her upbringing and what she has told others she would do. I have stopped all contact with her, and this has made it difficult to communicate with my children. I read Dr. Dobson's book* Love Must Be Tough *as well as other books on marriage, communication, divorce, and reconciliation. I think I understand my feelings, yet I still don't know how this affair happened under my nose. Friends knew about it and told her that she was playing with fire, but nothing helped. Now she and her lover both work in the same office and live in the same apartment complex.*

Church administration has informed me that I may be put on administrative leave and lose the church I am pastoring because my home is in such chaos. Yet I've also been offered a pastorate. My wife has filed for divorce. Your support means very much to me, and I long for the day when things are back to a degree of normalcy.

Dear Pastor: My heart hurts all over again as I hear what you're going through. I think you're wise to stop all contact with your wife, and this certainly is what Dobson recommends in *Love Must Be Tough.*

Satan is working hard to destroy the church by crippling our most effective pastors through their marriages. The stresses on a pastoral marriage are higher than those most marriages face for several reasons. Church members expect so much from the shepherd of the flock. Pastoral families live in a fish bowl, with the congregation watching every move. And the pastor is always on call, and unless he guards his time carefully, he can neglect his marriage and his children. Could it be that you were so busy tending the flock that you missed obvious clues?

Take courage, my friend. If your marriage ends, you really need to slow things down and take time to heal before forming a new romantic relationship. You are a handsome, talented pastor with a charismatic personality. Single women will flock to your church, hoping they might be lucky enough to catch your eye. You won't have to look for them; they'll just appear.

When you're ready to form a new relationship, take your time in building a solid future. Make certain that you are entirely healed from the hurt of the past before you marry again. And you will marry someday, I feel sure of that! But you can't combine burying the past and building for the future. It takes nearly two years at a minimum to get over a divorce and two years to build a solid new relationship. This means four years at a minimum to heal and build for the future. It's better that you take that time now than end up in a poor, unstable relationship.

The rest of the story: This pastor didn't lose his pastorate after all. In time, he did marry a lovely, supportive woman. Today they are working for the Lord, and he has put the past behind him.

Oh, how many women feel the same as the next writer.

Dear Nancy: *All I ever wanted since I was a little girl was to meet a great guy, get married, be a wife and mother, and have a perfect marriage. When I* *accepted my husband's proposal, I thought we would never fight. I was so in love. Now we've been married five years, and we have one child, three years old. And now I know that my expectations were unrealistic—we fight constantly. It's gotten so bad that I am nearly at the end of my rope. I think we still love each other down deep, but we just can't seem to have any positive experiences together. I've tried counseling with our pastor, and we've gotten nowhere. We've both mentioned divorce, and now it seems like we talk about divorce nearly every day. What should I do?*

Dear At the End of Your Rope: You are one of those who feel that it is wrong to argue, disagree, engage in conflict, or fight in a marriage. But couples who say they've never had a fight either are deluding themselves or are entirely out of touch with their emotions. Those who refuse to acknowledge the need to fight suffer from displaced anger, which produces hostility, emotional instability, depression, and a long list of other health problems. And their marriages lack depth and intimacy.

In today's world, many consider occasional fighting a sign of a healthy, fulfilling relationship. It shows warmth and caring—*provided the combatants know how to fight right!* Fighting is risky. Learning how to fight fair might be the most important communication skill you ever learn. When two people who really care about one another fight, they need not be destructive. Their fights can be highly constructive experiences. They mean that the combatants care about each other so much that they'll negotiate and deal with a problem until they find a mutually satisfying solution. Couples who withdraw do not care about one another enough to risk upsetting the status quo.

So, fighting is OK—even for a Christian couple. The measure of fighting's acceptability for a Christian couple boils down to the methods and style used during the fight and the result. To find out how to fight right, read chapter five, "Coping With Conflict," in my book *Smart Listening for Couples.*

Get your mind off your husband's flaws and focus on the good in your relationship.

In the next letter, a shattered husband seeks counsel.

Dear Nancy: *My wife of eleven years left me for another man. I waited around, went into counseling, and prayed that she'd change her mind and come back. But it didn't happen. She's taken the kids away, and I get to see them only on weekends. The divorce will be final this month, and I feel like I am going* *down for the third time. My life is shattered. My emotions are raw. I'm barely coping at work. I come home to an empty apartment and get more depressed. My friends are all married and busy with their own families. I'm an emotional wreck and think I may be close to a breakdown.*

Dear Emotional Wreck: No one can escape the emotional crisis that comes with divorce. But things may not be as bad as you think they are. Four stages follow divorce. Let's take a brief look at each stage to see where you might be.

The first stage is *denial.* Early in the process, you experience shock. To protect yourself, you say, "She'll come back—I just know she will" or "When she comes back, I'll make her so happy she'll wish she'd never left." This is denial of the reality of what has happened.

When in denial, some people move, stop going to church, or refuse to see friends. Others feverishly throw themselves into work. Some get involved immediately in superficial relationships. Some pour excess energy into everything they attempt. Some people become overly "happy"—they laugh too much, feel too "good"—all in an attempt to forget or deny their real feelings. In time, most people move beyond this level, but it is a real problem when a person stays here.

The second stage is *feelings of worthlessness.* Anyone who has lived through the nightmare of divorce knows this cycle well. Feelings of total failure dominate. In *Growing in Remarriage,* Jim Smoke says that 75 percent of those in his divorce-recovery seminars have suffered having their spouse leave for someone or something else. The remaining 25 percent left their marriage due to abuse, perversion, drugs, or some other difficult situation that they felt they could not survive. In both cases, feelings of rejection are the primary result.

After massive doses of rejection and a failed marriage, self-worth hits an all-time low, and good judgment is clouded for a time. It takes people months and possibly years to regain the self-confidence and emotional stability they once had. Until they do, they operate from a plane of weakness and vulnerability rather than from one of strength and self-assurance.

Stage three is *total emotional turmoil.* This stage includes intense grief and anger. Feelings that have been bottled up and held beneath the surface break through, and the divorced person feels totally overwhelmed. Sometimes he or she will lash out uncontrollably at those around him and will often cry at inappropriate times over insignificant things.

This is where you are. You're at the stage where you need to grieve the loss of your dreams, values, beliefs, and marriage partner. You need to grieve the loss of your children, home, church, friends, possessions, finances, and the support of people you once depended on. Allow yourself to face this loss and grieve so that you can let go of this dead relationship. Grieve it now so that you don't go into intense rage, which can result in depression. Don't allow yourself to be consumed by these feelings of overwhelming bitterness and vindictiveness due to the unfairness of it all.

The fourth and final stage is *letting go*. You can't reach this stage in a couple of months. It is a complicated stage and involves forgiveness of others as well as forgiveness of yourself. From this stage, a person can emerge whole and free to love again.

Working through all this takes time—a minimum of two years and perhaps closer to four. When you get to the letting-go phase, the toughest part of the divorce journey is over. This is when you will grow the most and can best lay a good foundation for a new life. Don't rush your trip through these stages. And be certain that you don't remarry quickly in an effort to sidestep the stages. That won't work. You may be able to delay the stages, but to be whole again, you must still go through them.

This next divorcée has worked through the stages and moved on.

Dear Nancy: *I've been divorced two years now, I've launched my children, and I feel I'm over the major trauma of the experience. I feel I've gotten my act together. I work full time, have a busy social life, am active at my church, and basically enjoy my life. I haven't had a date in a year now. This doesn't bother me, but it really seems to bother my family and friends. They're always encouraging me to do more dating. Yes, from time to time I wish I had a partner to share my life with, but finding one isn't that easy. Do I have to start dating again in order to find happiness? Who's right— them or me?*

Dear Dateless: Family and friends often encourage divorced people to date to get their mind off their problems. They think this will ease the pain. What it really does is retard personal growth. Divorcées simply must find out who they are as individuals and heal again before re-entering the dating scene. And it takes two to four years for this to happen.

During this period of singleness, the newly divorced person must bring closure to the previous marriage. Divorce is more a process than an event.

No one can open and close these doors overnight, regardless of what the courts or others say.

Jim Smoke, author of *Growing in Remarriage,* talks about three categories of divorcées: The Forever Bitter and Battered, The Quickly Rescued and Remarried, and The Growing and Guarded. The first two are self-destructive. The third group is the only one moving toward health and responsibility. From the description you gave of your life, this is where I would place you.

Dating before your self-worth is intact again only short-circuits your personal growth. When you begin dating, you direct energy toward establishing a new relationship, and you automatically decrease the time and energy spent on improving yourself. The new relationship steals your focus and siphons away the energy you need to make your journey toward wholeness. It's definitely more exciting to spend time on a new relationship than to work alone on your self-worth. But if you jump into new relationships too soon, you'll pay a heavy price later on because your personal growth will be stunted. If you hope to marry again and have a happy, long-term relationship, you must first complete the journey toward wholeness.

You're on the right track. Keep on doing the right thing!

A lonely man meets a new Miss Right.

Dear Nancy: *The Miss Right I married turned out to be nothing more than Miss Wrong. Somehow, we survived eleven years of marriage and two children before she took off. Four months later, I feel that I'm through the worst of the trauma. And now I think I've found the real Miss Right. We've been dating pretty steadily for the past couple months. My divorce will be final soon, even though the custody of the children remains unsettled. What can I do to make sure I don't make some of the same stupid mistakes I made last time when I thought I'd found Miss Right? I want to be smarter this time around.*

Dear Wants to Be Smarter: Number one: If you want to be smarter this time around, *you won't date until the divorce is final!* Until the divorce is final, you're still married, and there is always the chance for reconciliation until you sign the final decree. Many "almost divorced" people have been shocked by their spouse's announcement that he or she wants to try again. Getting emotionally involved with someone during this period could be damaging even to a remote possibility of reconciliation, as well as hurtful to the person you are dating. Married people don't date. And yes, until the final divorce decree is signed, you are still married.

Number two: You are not yet emotionally ready to date. Dating during the separation period, when you are waiting for the divorce to become final, entails little more than "mutual commiseration." This sharing of loneliness and hurt binds a couple together, making them think they're in love. You won't be able to see clearly until some time has passed. You'll need to be extremely careful when dating during the two to four years following your divorce. The exhilaration of finding a new partner brings on surges of romantic affection that can sweep even the most levelheaded people off their emotional feet. Both of you need time to develop an unhurried relationship that's not dominated by periods of physical excitement and high-flying emotions. When the glands heat up, the brain melts down. You shouldn't make any decision about the permanency of a relationship during these two to four years of post-divorce adjustment—*and certainly not before the divorce is final!*

Number three: Dating at this point in your life isn't fair to the person you're dating. One couple began dating shortly after the man separated from his wife. The new couple's friendship blossomed quickly into a romance. Custody and property settlements repeatedly necessitated the postponement of the court date for the finalization of the man's divorce. Suddenly, without warning, his wife wanted to reconcile. Then he had a difficult dilemma on his hands. He knew that reconciliation would be preferable for all involved, but he was truly in love with his new girlfriend. He had to put his feeling for her on hold while he and his wife attempted to reconcile. The girlfriend suffered tremendous pain. As Christians, we each must take seriously our responsibility not to hurt others.

Next to the rule specifying two years of dating prior to marriage, the strongest advice I give to the about-to-be-divorced is not to begin dating too soon after a divorce—and certainly not before the divorce is final!

Read on to discover how to deal with a new dating relationship when children are involved.

Dear Nancy: *I'm divorced and have two young children, five and seven. I've not had much opportunity to date until recently, when a guy from work started asking me out. I haven't gone out with him yet because I just don't know how to* *handle the issue with my kids. What do I say to my children about Mommy dating again? How do kids react when Mommy does date? I want to conduct myself in the best possible way when dating and don't want to do anything that will add to the hurt my kids have already experienced. What, if anything, should I tell them?*

Dear Dating Mommy: It's difficult to predict in advance a child's reaction when a parent begins dating after a divorce. Much depends on the personality of the child, how much trauma the child has been through, and how much healing time there's been. Some children are relieved, welcoming the fact that Mommy has a "boyfriend." Others may resent losing Mommy's attention. Some children are even rude to a parent's date. Others are more passive and internalize what they think about their parent's date life. They may sulk, pout, or develop behavior problems.

You need open communication with your children at this time—but let your children remain children; don't make them become confidants in your developing love life. This is especially true as your children enter the teen years. Often teens feel threatened when a parent is dating alongside them. Teens feel that dating is their privilege, not their parent's. When two generations dress up and present themselves appealingly to the opposite sex, dating can develop into a type of competition.

Sometimes, though, children even attempt to become matchmakers. This can become embarrassing, especially if they should ask if your date is going to be their daddy. Children who do this are attempting to meet their needs; you shouldn't punish or ridicule them. If this happens with one of your children, you should definitely talk with them about their feelings and help them to feel loved and secure before you begin dating.

The attention you are getting from this fellow will be good for your self-worth. Life may take on a new meaning. But don't let a new relationship take you away from your children too often. In other words, be smart in all your decisions!

Check out the dating guidelines I give in my answer to the following correspondent.

Dear Nancy: *Since my divorce, I've been in several dating relationships that have gone nowhere. Now, for the first time, I'm in a relationship with a woman who I think is compatible with me and would make a good mother for my two* *boys. So far, I've left the boys with a sitter, and they haven't met my new friend, Melody. She's anxious to meet them. Yet I hold back. At what point should I introduce a girlfriend to my children? I need some guidelines, because my children have been through enough in their young lives.*

Dear Guideline Seeker: There are many theories about the answer to your question. In my opinion, parents should generally avoid involving their children in their dating lives until they're "engaged to be engaged"—in other words, until the couple have dated for several months to a year and are beginning to talk about the possibility of marriage in the future.

Children need permanence, stability, in their lives, and children of divorce have already suffered through the dissolution of their family. They've already lost one parent for most of the time. You'd be asking too much of your children were you to have them become emotionally involved in a succession of girlfriends. Should you and Melody break up, your children, who will have grown to love her, will lose a friend as well and will suffer from the breakup. Additionally, keeping your children separate from your dates will protect them from being used as pawns by someone who wants to capture your heart.

As time goes by and your relationship with Melody becomes more serious, you can include her in some family outings—but only as a friend. This should be the pattern until you're certain that she will become a permanent part of your life. Keep any displays of affection between you and Melody private. And don't discuss with your children the possibility of your marrying Melody until you and Melody are serious about it. When you do talk with your boys, do so privately, when Melody isn't there. Tell the boys you are thinking about marrying Melody. Ask them how they feel about it, but make it clear you are not asking for their permission. Tell them that you'll consider carefully all they have to say and then you'll prayerfully make the decision.

In my response to the next letter, read how to deal with children who don't like a new dating partner.

Dear Nancy: *I'm in what I consider a good relationship after a prolonged divorce. I took my time in introducing my children to Herb, my new partner, just as you advise. But they've taken a definite dislike to him. I'm devastated. Herb is truly a good person—and good to me—and he'd make a wonderful* *father to the children. I feel like I'm facing a death sentence. Do I really have to choose between what my kids want and what I want? What will happen to my family should I go ahead and marry Herb when my kids say in advance they don't like him?*

Dear Devastated Mom: This is a tough call. When your children's attitude toward a dating partner is negative, the first thing you need to do is to slow down. You'll need to think carefully through the consequences of bucking negative attitudes in all the days to come. If you disregard your children's feelings today, they may think you are siding with a stranger against them. Respectfully listen to your children, letting them know you'll consider their feelings. Especially at first, talk to them one-on-one rather than as a group. This will help them each to form their own conclusions rather than to be influenced by the opinions that others in the family express.

Convey as respectfully as you can that you want them to be able to express their feelings, but that in the end you will make your own decisions about what is best for the family. By all means, avoid implying that you'll do what you want regardless of what they want. In a few years, your children will be choosing mates. You don't want this same attitude coming back to haunt you then.

Just remember that becoming the stepparent to a child of divorce is not as easy as it looks. The new stepparent may feel like he can rescue your lonely children and heal their hurts. But the children may feel like the new parent is an intruder.

Next, we'll look at some of the complications divorce causes.

Dear Nancy: *I'm a woman in her early forties who has never married. My husband-to-be and I have been going together for about seven months. We're planning to have a small but very nice wedding in the chapel of our church. Everything is going smoothly, except for one thing. My mother doesn't know about the upcoming wedding yet because my fiancé has only recently been divorced. No one in our family has ever been divorced, and my mother is sure to be prejudiced against him because he is divorced. I don't feel his past has anything to do with our future together. The past is finished. We've been very honest with each other. The divorce wasn't his fault. Divorce is so common now that it would be silly for me to reject this man just because he's been married before. But how do I handle my mother?*

Dear Bride-to-Be: You think that marriage involving a divorced person is the same as the marriage of two people who've never been married before. It's not! Certainly, no one need feel like a second-class citizen because of a divorce. But being divorced does change things. A second marriage is far more complicated than a first marriage. Let's look at some of the complicating factors.

First, people view second marriages differently than they do first marriages. The church as well as society smiles approvingly on first marriages and supports and celebrates them with enthusiasm and anticipation. They often greet a second marriage with less enthusiasm, although at first this may not be obvious. Friends and relatives often assume a wait-and-see attitude. A first marriage for both partners almost always includes a bridal shower. If both have been married before, only about one in three are given a bridal shower. Such attitudes are symbolic of the way friends and society support a first marriage as opposed to succeeding marriages.

Second, as in your mother's case, there is often a strong likelihood of opposition from relatives when a member of the family marries someone who has been divorced. Your family will likely view your upcoming marriage with mingled hope and fear, whether or not you think those fears justified. And your fiancé's family can't help but make comparisons between you and his former partner. Even though you feel all that is in the past, the fact that there was a previous marriage will affect everyone's thinking about your future.

Third, a divorced person is less tolerant of difficulties the second time around. This is reflected in the fact that second marriages have a higher divorce rate than first marriages. Today, there is less stigma to divorce, so when serious problems arise, those who have divorced before are more likely to again choose divorce as a solution, and they do so at least two years sooner than the first time around.

Divorced persons may also have been hurt so badly from the trauma that they try to compensate by rebounding rapidly into a new love experience. This may be the most important item for you to examine, since you've been dating only seven months. Divorced people tend to remarry quickly after a divorce, with shorter engagements.

Please contemplate how much your fiancé has learned from his marriage failure. Does he feel blameless and say that it was all his ex-wife's fault? If so, he's likely not a good prospect for marriage. Those who have failed once should learn from experience and pinpoint areas in themselves that demand improvement. It is possible to learn through bitter experiences how to make a better choice the second time around. Ask yourself as well as him: What have you learned that might have helped the first marriage succeed and that will make your marriage better?

Most important of all, remember that when you marry, you are not marrying just one person but your fiancé's family as well—and he, yours. There's a strong possibility that your family may not welcome him. Never stand in the way of family relationships. If your marriage results in an open war between your family and him, it may be that you'll never be able to visit your parents with your new husband. It could produce a lifetime of misunderstanding, hurt, and anger. Move ahead slowly.

Slowing down a relationship frequently makes sense no matter what the age.

Dear Nancy: *My husband passed away last year after thirty-six years of marriage. Ours was a happy marriage, and I miss him terribly. I still get teary-eyed at times and occasionally break down, but it is happening less frequently. I'm gradually adjusting to single life after almost a year of struggling. I never thought I'd be dating at age sixty, but a widower from next door has been asking me out. This is developing into an almost regular relationship. It's escalating so fast that it's scaring me. Any advice for a sixty-year-old woman who is thinking of trying it all over again?*

Dear Widow: Yes. Slow the relationship down! You simply can't build a new love relationship and bury the dead simultaneously. Bury your husband first. Make sure you move through all the stages of grief before you proceed. Breaking down only on occasion means that you have moved through some of the stages of grief, but you still need to face a stage or two. On average, people work through the stages of grief in two to seven years. But those who are attempting to build a new love relationship while also attempting to work through grief will eventually run into major problems. You may have the potential for becoming a great marriage partner, but you must first overcome your grief at the death of your husband.

Attend a grief seminar. Then slowly and surely take your time in building this developing relationship. Start with friendship and move on up through the stages of dating (see part two of *Smart Love—A Field Guide for Single Adults*). Progress through the stages, taking two full years—even if you are sixty years old. It's better to spend quality years together now than to rush into marriage and regret it the rest of your life!

An eager-to-marry man asks about connecting with an older woman.

Dear Nancy: *My wife abandoned me and our three children (ages eight, ten, and twelve) a couple of years ago. It's been rough, but we've survived. I know I can't be both mom and dad to the kids, but we're doing pretty well.*

I've prayed sincerely that God would bring into my life a woman who could be both a wife to me and a mother to my kids. Now I think I've met that woman. She too has been married before and is five years older than me. This makes her two children (ages thirteen and fifteen) a little older than mine. We've been dating for over a year now. Our kids seem to get along fine, and we just don't see any major problems ahead. If we wait the full two years you recommend, what do you think our chances are for making it with our age differences and all?

Dear Future Stepparent: The problem you face isn't that your girlfriend is five years older than you are. It's stepparenting. Some people say that stepparenting is five times more difficult than any other kind of parenting! The major problem is that stepfamilies tend to be less cohesive than primary families. The most confused, angry, bitter, and uncooperative families I encounter are those who are trying to blend "his kids" and "her kids." And when one marries someone with children, it's a package deal. The children come with the parent.

Your intended will have the more difficult task, because it is more difficult to be a stepmother than a stepfather. And stepdaughters have more trouble adjusting in stepfamilies than do stepsons. Obviously, then, your intended is going to have to work harder than you at developing cohesive relationships. Is she prepared to do this?

Stepparenting the eight- and ten-year-olds will likely be only moderately challenging. Children between the ages of twelve and eighteen present the biggest challenge. Since three of the five you'll be blending are in this age category, you need to be prepared for some major struggles.

Should you decide to put these two families together permanently, the most important thing for you and your wife to remember is to present a united front. This means you must discuss your expectations for the children and be sure they coincide. Once agreed, both of you should discuss matters with the children so that they clearly understand that both parents are part of the permanent "team."

Although you and your intended may already have discussed a lot of this, you can still expect opposition from the children after you marry. During the first few years after remarriage, children tend to recognize only the natural parent's right to discipline. They will test and retest the limits set by their stepparent. This fulfills their need to explore the limits of any new relationship. The sooner stepparents make their presence felt and show the children that they are there to stay, the sooner the children will accept the reality that their former family is gone and accept the new parent.

Be patient during this adjustment process. Most authorities agree that it takes two to three years for the average child to work through the stages of recovery after the loss of a parent, and some say as many as seven years. Do take advantage of family counseling both prior to and after the wedding. Read a book or two about stepparenting, and attend a stepparenting class. Such efforts will pay off in the end.

The next letter talks about rebuilding a broken relationship. This is a hard thing to do, but it can be done.

Dear Nancy: *I was a successful pastor who left the ministry when my wife decided she didn't want to be married anymore and we separated. I found another very good job and tried to keep my life as normal as possible even though I suffered three great losses: my beloved profession, my marriage, and my children. Now my wife wants to reconcile. I love her and want our marriage to work. I also miss my former ministerial work. I'm very unsure of what to do.*

Dear Unsure Pastor: Since you didn't divorce and are only separated, the opportunity for reconciliation exists. You say you still love her. But marriages today take a lot more than just "love" to make them work. Before you rush into each other's arms, step back and look at the whole picture.

Have the two of you addressed and clarified the issues that caused the separation in the first place? Are the issues that drove you apart related to your ministry? Are her needs being met? Are you home enough to satisfy her? Are you communicating? Does she feel that the congregation gets more of you than she and the children do? Many pastors' wives resent the fact that their husbands are on call 24/7 for everyone but them. If you haven't resolved these issues, there isn't a chance that your marriage will work the second time around.

Prior to reconciliation, obtain qualified third-party intervention to address each issue and make certain you have solved them. I suggest that while you are going through this marriage counseling, you begin dating each other all over again. While dating, attempt to re-establish communication, eye contact, and light, nonsexual touching. At no time should you proceed further than step nine of the pair-bonding process (see chapter two of *Smart Listening*).

Above all, do not attempt intercourse (yes, even though you are still married) until you have both determined that the relationship will work. Sex now would blur your perception and distort your judgment. What you are trying to do is to backfill the steps you skipped or missed the first time you went through the pair-bonding steps. As you take the time now to build each level solidly, what you should do about your future will unfold right before your eyes.

I also recommend that you take PREPARE-ENRICH, a marital inventory designed to assist in determining which areas in a relationship need growth and the strengths that will enable you to move in a positive direction. Willingness to work on a marriage through counseling is always a positive sign, but I'm still concerned about your future. You gave up a lot when you left the ministry. You can still re-enter the ministry if you feel the call of God and can find a pastorate. First, however, you must stabilize your marriage. This may take some time.

Attempting reconciliation is like going through major surgery. When the surgery is over, you remain in intensive care. Your condition is stabilized, but for a time, you continue to need round-the-clock care. Eventually you recover enough to move to a general nursing floor, and as time goes by, you heal totally. The scars remain, but the pain recedes, and you are released from nursing care. Even then, you must guard your relationship carefully, even to the point of taking inventory once a month to stay on top of things.

Move slowly and prayerfully into the rebuilding phase. What you are learning now about rebuilding a relationship could teach you more about ministering to families in your congregation than you could learn in a lifetime at a seminary.

*   *   *   *   *

It is a serious matter for a committed Christian to seek a divorce outside of a biblical reason. We learn some of life's most important lessons when we work through marital difficulties instead of attempting to escape them. Many people can bear witness to this fact through miracle stories they can tell about how God honored their efforts to persevere under desperate circumstances. Granted, sometimes the marriage bond is damaged beyond human willingness and ability to restore it. But a caution is in order here. Be very careful not to ignore God's ability and desire to work in your life. He can do anything, but we have to be willing to let Him work out His will for us in His time. Jesus clearly outlined the conditions under which divorce and remarriage are justifiable in Matthew 19:9. People have interpreted this verse in many ways, but I, along with others, accept it at face value.

A word of caution to anyone considering divorce: Since we have all been born with a bent toward sin and find ourselves pitifully weak when facing the enemy, we often become masters at rationalization. We can deceive even ourselves. We say, "God doesn't want me to be unhappy"; "I prayed and prayed about this, and I feel God wants me to divorce"; "God can forgive a divorce just as He forgives all other sin." So, instead of gaining the blessing that can be ours when we work through difficulties, we rationalize that divorce is the utopia God wants us to pursue. We choose that option while ignoring the still, small voice as well as the biblical admonition against divorce.

In situations where divorce and remarriage are biblically justified, each should proceed humbly but without undue guilt. May none of us be guilty of condemning others—especially when we have only a partial picture of the situation. On the other hand, neither should we pretend God has said what He has not said. As Charles Swindoll, the author and great preacher, stated in his book *Strike the Original Match,* "There is something much worse than living with a mate in disharmony. It's living with God in disobedience."

CHAPTER SEVEN

Hot Potatoes—"Please Help Me Solve This Problem"

Have you ever wondered, "What on earth can I do about anything important? I'm just one person in a fast-moving, impersonal world." Even though you are only one person, you're not so insignificant as to have no influence. You can make a unique and important contribution within your circle of friends, because the happiness of your family will have a direct bearing on the families of friends as well as on the eventual happiness your own children will experience within their families. Someone has estimated that every family directly influences twelve other families a year. If this ratio holds true and parents made their influence more positive, they could change the world!

Many Christians struggle with the questions this chapter contains. We begin with a question about financial chaos.

Financial disorganization can cause chaos. Read on.

Dear Nancy: *I'm seven years into a marriage that is a financial disaster. I'm working full time, and we just can't get ahead. Our bills are driving me crazy. My husband says he wants to pay the bills, but he rarely remembers to pay things on time. We had a car repossessed a couple years ago; we're constantly overdrawn at the bank; and we have credit-card debt up to our eyeballs.*

I'm at the point where I can barely sleep at nights. I wasn't raised this way, and I'm not used to living like this. Before I married my husband, I knew he wasn't careful with money. I thought he'd become more responsible after we got married and had children. Big mistake!

I'm so ashamed. I can't take many more calls from creditors. Is there anything we can do to change the way we're living?

Dear Ashamed: You are just one of many couples burdened by uncontrolled debt. Much of this happens because no one has taught young couples how to handle money. Today's philosophy seems to be "Spend and spend, and if you don't have the cash, charge it. If you want it, get it, because you deserve it." People seem to have abandoned the concept of saving in order to buy.

Contrary to the direction society is going, God wants His people to live debt free. The blessings that come with living debt free go far beyond financial freedom. How we handle our money spills over into the spiritual and marital areas of life as well. No one who is financially burdened can be spiritually free. And debt and financial bondage have far-reaching effects on a marriage.

How do you get out of debt? Here are nine steps Crown Financial Ministries developed to help couples get out of the debt trap:

1. *Pray.* Transfer ownership of all your possessions to God. Then ask Him for guidance and wisdom in all matters pertaining to how you handle what belongs to Him.

2. *Give to God first.* Tithing must be your first commitment—give ten percent of your income to the Lord before you allocate the rest of your money. Without faithfully fulfilling this commitment, all other efforts will fail.

3. *Establish a written budget.* A balanced budget is the primary tool in any family's plan for managing money. List all of your obligations. Start with all the debts you owe. Include credit-card debt, all payments, and any loans you have. Monthly bills, such as the electric or gas bill, aren't considered debt until you're late on a payment, but add these other items to your budget as well. It will take a month or so to write down all of your expenses and realize where your money is going. Keep a log of everything you spend—write down everything, even a soda from McDonald's and ice cream from Dairy Queen. Then evaluate this list at the end of the month. What can you eliminate?

4. *List your assets.* Write down everything you own. Is there anything you currently own that you could sell and apply the money toward debt reduction? Consider items of value that you may not use or need any more.

5. *Work out a payback plan with your creditors.* Most creditors are more than willing to work with people who honestly want to repay them. Make

sure that every creditor gets something, but stay within the guidelines of your budget. Decide which debts to pay off first. You should base your decision on two factors: the size of the debts and the interest rate charged. In most cases, it is wise to pay off the smallest debts first. You'll be encouraged as they're eliminated, and you'll also be freeing up money to apply against the other debts. Consider also what rate of interest you're paying on each debt. Try to pay off those debts that involve high rates of interest before you pay off those that charge less.

6. *Consider earning additional income.* Whether we earn a lot or a little, we tend to spend more than we make. Could your husband or you earn additional money without harming your relationship with the Lord or with your family?

7. *Accumulate no new debt!* The only way to accumulate no new debt is to pay for all your purchases with cash, a check, or a debit card at the time of purchase. Put away or destroy all credit cards until you're out of debt. Once out of debt, either never use a credit card again or charge only what you can pay off within thirty days. Credit cards aren't evil, just dangerous!

8. *Consider making a radical change in your lifestyle.* More and more people are lowering their expenses to get out of debt by selling their homes and moving to smaller ones or even moving in with other family members temporarily until they get on their feet again. You can sell relatively new automobiles for cash and purchase cheaper used cars.

9. *Don't give up!* From the very beginning, you'll think of a hundred reasons why you should delay getting started or quit along the way. Don't yield to this temptation. Follow through so that you can experience what it's like to live debt free. God wants us to live debt free so that we can serve Him to the utmost of our abilities and resources. When we're in debt, we're bound to our creditors and are not free to serve God to the utmost. Proverbs 22:7 says, "Just as the rich rule the poor, so the borrower is servant to the lender" *(The Living Bible).* You can become debt free and stay that way if you have the desire and the discipline; you'll no longer be enslaved to your lenders.

I also highly recommend that you call Crown Financial Ministries (see appendix) and get yourself into one of their small-group studies, where you'll learn how to do everything I've just recommended plus much more. It's a life-changing experience.

This next relationship is in big trouble.

Dear Nancy: *After thirty-five years of marriage, I learned my husband has accumulated massive gambling debts. We've always had different views on financial matters. I was raised in a family in which debt was abhorred, credit cards avoided, and bills paid on time. He was raised by an alcoholic father who rarely worked. After his father and mother divorced, his mother lived on welfare. Although my husband has always earned enough to support us, we've been forced to live frugally.*

Now I've learned that he has diverted funds and maxed out every credit card to support his gambling habit. We're more than eighty thousand dollars in debt and in danger of losing our home and everything we own as well as facing bankruptcy. Our whole marriage revolves around lies and deceit. I realize the wedding vows state "for richer or poorer," but we don't have enough years left to pay off eighty thousand dollars of debt. I don't want to divorce the man, but I do need more than a miracle to be able to trust him again and to handle the bankruptcy.

Dear Needs More Than a Miracle: God does His best work when we realize our helplessness and surrender ourselves totally to His leading. Let's try this approach and see how He'll work in your seemingly hopeless situation.

Let's outline a plan of action. First, don't pray for eighty thousand dollars to clear up that debt; instead, pray for a willingness to obey God's leading in all matters. Express your willingness to learn the lessons you need to learn through this devastating experience and your willingness to make necessary adjustments.

Second, read Larry Burkett's book *Debt-Free Living* from cover to cover. (Keep a box of Kleenex handy, because you will likely shed a few bitter tears over your ignorance regarding financial matters.)

Third, call Crown Financial Ministries in Gainesville, Georgia, and ask them to recommend an experienced Christian financial counselor in your area.

Fourth, call and meet with this financial counselor. This person will both pray for you and outline a plan of action that fits biblical guidelines.

Fifth, insist that your husband join Gamblers Anonymous (see appendix). Should he resist, you must stand firm. Regardless of his promises to reform or never gamble again, inform him that if he wishes to have a marriage, he must attend GA faithfully to deal with his addiction. Should he deny that he has an addiction or refuse to attend GA, you'll have to seek a temporary separation until he agrees to face the addiction.

Sixth, and perhaps most important, locate the nearest Gamanon meeting. You'll find help and hope there for yourself.

Points to remember:

DO talk to someone who understands gambling addiction.

DO learn the facts about gambling addiction.

DO learn about yourself—your needs, desires, reactions, and behavior patterns.

DO maintain a healthy and consistent atmosphere in your home as much as possible.

DO take care of your needs and let your husband take care of his needs.

DO share your knowledge with others.

DO be committed to your own growth, health, and life goals. Be constructively selfish.

DON'T preach and lecture your husband about his addiction.

DON'T make excuses for him.

DON'T rescue him. Let him clear up his own mistakes and assume responsibility for the consequences of his gambling behavior.

DON'T make threats that you won't carry out.

DON'T believe you are the cause of your husband's addictive behavior.

DON'T suffer for your husband.

DON'T try to protect him from gambling situations.

DON'T make an issue over his choice of treatment.

DON'T expect immediate, full recovery.

You are facing your darkest hour right now. I know you can't see it, but there is a rainbow over the dark clouds that hover over you. You aren't the first woman to face life with an addict or with massive gambling debts. Remember this is his shame, not yours. Don't keep his addiction a secret from your family.

The story continues: Ten years passed after this woman first contacted me. She and her husband read *Debt-Free Living*. Then they cut up their many credit cards and tearfully put themselves into the hands of a Christian financial counselor. They describe those years as shameful and painful, but also as a time of growing. The husband sought treatment for his addiction. Together they read books, watched videos, and attended seminars on financial management. God blessed this couple during that time beyond anything they thought possible. They headed into their retirement years with the surplus they needed to survive in today's economy. However, the wife then discovered that her husband was gambling again. She wrote:

Dear Nancy: *Remember me? My husband had a gambling addiction. Now I've just learned that he's at it again, although he vehemently denies it. We are in our retirement years now. My mother has just passed away and left me with a sizeable inheritance. Everything is at risk. I'm devastated all over again and feel I can't face another day of his lies. Most of the time our life is good, but this last episode has scared me spitless. What now?*

Dear Scared: A frog was playing on the lily pads one day when a scorpion begged for a ride across the pond. "No way," said the frog. "If I give you a ride, you'll sting me."

The scorpion promised he wouldn't sting the frog. "If I do," he reasoned, "we'll both die."

This made sense to the frog, so he agreed to take the scorpion across the pond. The scorpion hopped on the frog's back, and with powerful strokes of his hind legs, the frog headed across the pond. Then, as he approached the halfway point, the scorpion stung him.

"Why did you do that?" the frog croaked as he sank under the water.

"Because it's my nature to sting," the scorpion responded.

Just as it's the scorpion's nature to sting, so it's the nature of addicts to repeat the behavior to which they are addicted. You have no time to lose. Contact a lawyer to see what course you can pursue to protect your future.

Now for a question about organizing one's home.

Dear Nancy: *I am convinced that marriage needs constant care and cultivation. But I'm like so many other women today who work outside the home. I don't have the luxury and security of making my home into what I'd like it to be. My husband wants his shirts ironed to perfection and gourmet meals prepared on time, and he expects me to find time to pay the bills and plan our budget. And to top things off, I feel like I'm neglecting my children. What's a "superwoman" to do?*

Dear Superwoman: If you've sorted your "needs" from your "wants" list and absolutely must work in order to survive, you need help organizing your time. Getting a home "decent and in order" has to do with establishing good habits rather than offering excuses as to why you can't get it together at home.

If you've lost control of your time, you're malfunctioning. The bottom line here is that you need to seek ways of improving your homemaking skills so that you, as well as your family, can be happier.

You can learn the skills you need to master the household and family responsibilities that now overwhelm you. It takes determination, but you can do it—not overnight, but step by step. I've outlined such a plan for women just like you in my book *Get Organized—Seven Secrets to Sanity for Stressed Women* (see appendix). You can put these seven secrets to work in your life. Once you begin to achieve orderly living, the rewards—both direct and indirect—outnumber the disadvantages. The atmosphere in your home will change—you will notice a new spirit of cooperation. This will result in fewer hours of housework and more time for leisure and family.

Does your home smile at you at the end of the day when you return? It should. And that's exactly what a picked-up, uncluttered home can do for anyone entering it. After a long, hard day at work, it is discouraging to enter a home that is in total disarray. It is difficult to begin preparing the evening meal before you've cleaned up the kitchen. By the time you do that, you're already one task behind and you've barely entered the door!

Spend fifteen to twenty minutes every morning picking up in the bathroom, bedroom, and kitchen. This will improve how you feel about yourself all day. But the most remarkable change will occur when you walk in the door at night because the order and beauty of your home truly welcomes you.

As you plan, organize, and get your life under control again, know that you are also providing the best possible role model for your children. Rather than allowing them to grow up in confusion and disorganization, you're training them for orderly living while also giving them a greater measure of confidence to succeed in their own marriages and life choices. Best of all, you will have a feeling of success and achievement.

This next mom also wants to get organized.

Dear Nancy: *My whole life is a disorganized mess. I need to get it straightened out, starting with my relationship with God. My budget is in chaos. And the raising of my children and my relationship with my husband is all upside down. The days come and go and the mountain is so high that I can't handle it, so I do nothing at all, and it continues to pile up. I am depressed, anxious, and helpless. I start a new job on Monday, and I can't find my nursing license or my* *children's birth certificates. My goal is to become debt free, to manage a workable budget, and to unclutter my life. The task is so massive—where and how do I begin?*

Dear Disorganized Mom: You say your whole life is a mess and needs straightening up—your relationship with God, your budget, parenting, and marriage. You can't tackle all your life problems at one time. Here's our plan. We begin with what we have today. Open your Bible and read a few verses—may I suggest you begin with 1 Corinthians 14:40. Ask God to help you put order and decency in your life. Then tackle one room today, putting away all visible clutter. Don't try to tackle your entire house, or you'll make a bigger mess and get discouraged.

Next I recommend you read my book *Get Organized*, focusing especially on chapter 6, "How to Sort Through the Clutter." I give step-by-step instructions on how to get your home decent and in order. Follow my plan for six weeks, getting one room per week under control. You'll find that the clutter and disorganization soon become part of your past. Once you can see over the visible clutter, you'll gain control in other areas of your life.

The second book I recommend is Larry Burkett's book *Debt-Free Living* (see appendix). When Harry and I first read that book, we wept all the way through it as we realized how, through our ignorance, we had wasted money and resources. We became very serious about our finances, and within a relatively short time, we paid off every debt, including our home mortgage, and began living debt free. We cut up all our credit cards—we keep the pieces in a jar as a reminder never to go back to that style of living. What freedom we experienced!

After you get these two areas of your life under control, read my book *Highly Effective Marriage* (see appendix). You and your husband will benefit from putting the principles outlined there to work in your relationship. You'll find that when you get your home, your finances, and your relationship with God under control, many of the other problems you're dealing with will automatically melt away.

Now, go, take on the day!

How do you feel about unwed mothers and baby showers? Read on.

Dear Nancy: *I offered to help with a baby shower for an unwed mother at our church. The invitations were prepared and handed out at church to all the ladies. Last night I got a call from one of the women. She said she just couldn't* *see her way clear to go to a baby shower for an unwed mother. She went on and on about how we celebrate these things. The church has a policy against holding baby showers in their fellowship hall for mothers who aren't married. Does this make sense? They provide many services for the dregs of society who come into their Community Services center, but they can't hold a shower for one of their own who made a mistake? Now I find that others feel the same way this woman does—that we shouldn't celebrate the birth of a child whose mother isn't married and who won't have a dad. How do you feel about this? I can see both sides to this issue.*

Dear Baby Shower Sponsor: I've always thought that as a church we need to be forgiving and treat an unwed mother with all the love and kindness we can muster. I still feel that way. What did Jesus say to the woman caught in adultery? "Go, and sin no more." Simple. Clear. Direct. Jesus could accept her back into His good graces the minute she asked for forgiveness. We can and should also do this as a church.

However, this doesn't mean that we should celebrate an unwed woman's pregnancy with a fancy baby shower. It doesn't mean that we should honor her with a baby shower as we honor other young mothers in the church who are married and have a husband and will provide the type of family God recommends for His children. When we honor an unwed mother with a baby shower, we are celebrating the fact that she's about to become a mother, bring a baby into the world, and establish a family without a husband and father. In many cases, we're going to have to support her—as we do thousands of others like her—through the paying of taxes.

When we honor her in such a way, we'll have to invite her young friends. How will this look to them? If a woman can receive honor and have the birth of her illegitimate baby celebrated when she isn't married, then this must not be such a bad thing after all. The church certainly doesn't frown on it. After all, they're celebrating this event through a shower. And rather than anyone learning a lesson from the situation, we've minimized the tragedy of it. In my estimation, making this an "event" encourages the birth of babies to unwed mothers.

So, what's the answer to this dilemma? The tragedy of unwed mothers will be with us until the Lord returns. How do we as a church respond in a loving, kind, and forgiving manner to a young girl who has erred? Not in a hateful manner that will ignore this life-changing event that she's experiencing. I believe that one of the sisters in the church, perhaps a deaconess, should evaluate this girl's needs. If her family has disowned her and left her without a place to live or if she needs counseling, the church should rise to the occasion in a private way and help just as they would through Community Services for anyone who is down and out.

As the baby's birth approaches, the woman's needs should be evaluated once again. Should she need a layette or baby things to get her on her feet, the deaconesses can provide these things for her privately, as gifts from a church who loves her, cares about her future, and forgives her just as Christ has forgiven her. But providing for her in this manner is much different from celebrating the birth of her child as you would that of an infant who has two parents and a stable future.

There may be exceptions to the general suggestion I've given. Each situation needs to be evaluated on its own merit and exceptions made when the most loving gesture might be to give a shower for an unwed mother. But once the precedent has been set, it will be more difficult not to follow it for every unwed mother.

A mixed-up girl wants to know how to live with the consequences of her behavior.

Dear Nancy: *I am twenty years old and in a terrible mess. Four years ago I started having sex with a guy I was dating. I got pregnant and had an abortion. After the abortion, I stopped seeing this guy because he didn't treat me well. It was difficult because I still had feelings for him. I began praying that God would send me the right man to date and decided I would not be sexually active again until I married.*

Then I met another guy, and one thing led to another and we began sleeping together. I was shocked when I found out I was pregnant again. We discussed at length what I should do. I was still in school, scared, and neither of us was financially able to support a child. I couldn't tell my parents. After much discussion, I had another abortion. I felt terrible but also felt it was my only choice. I didn't want any pressure from my church, family, or friends about this situation. Most of all, I didn't want to disappoint my parents.

After my second abortion, the nurse gave me birth-control pills. But neither my boyfriend nor I thought they would work, so I didn't use them. We began having sex again. I asked him to use condoms, but he didn't do it, and we went ahead without precautions. Now I think I'm pregnant for the third time. I'm in agony. I think I should keep this baby because I'm almost finished with school and am better able to support a child then when I was pregnant before. I know

I've disobeyed God and I'm living with the consequences of my behavior. This last guy who got me pregnant is nice, and my mother likes him, but I don't know if I want to marry him. I'm a slow learner but I'm trying. What next?

Dear Slow Learner: You are a slow learner indeed! You said you had read my books. If so, where did you come up with the idea that birth-control pills don't work? When used as directed, they are the most effective contraceptive known (outside of total abstinence). When taken as prescribed, without omitting a single dose, there should be no more than one unplanned pregnancy per year in one thousand users.

I plead with young adults to practice abstinence until they're married. But if they're going to proceed with premarital sex in spite of all the evidence I present against it, they should be responsible. In other words, they should use measures to prevent pregnancy and sexually transmitted diseases. *This means both he and she should use contraception.* Unmarried sex calls for *double protection.* Male contraception consists of condoms. Females can use vaginal jellies or foams, an IUD, a diaphragm, or the pill. All of these should be used under a physician's guidance.

When you take time to double protect, your desires may cool down and become easier to control. It gives you time to think. It isn't very romantic, but neither is parenthood.

Now, let's deal with the issue of abortion. Abortion is the tragic aftermath of human failure. Abortion is not the problem. It is only an attempt to find a solution. The problem is the misguided, misinformed, wanton use of sexuality that resulted in the unwanted pregnancy. The time to think about the abortion issue is before one finds oneself in need of one.

Once a woman finds herself trapped in a pregnancy that she can't cope with or assume responsibility for, it becomes difficult to make a sane decision. Women who abort a child often go through a grief process that only compounds the grief they already feel. This is doubly true in your case because you've had not one but two abortions already.

The issue of abortion is a moral one and very complicated. In a spirit of love and forgiveness, I would like to offer some things for you to think about. Sincerely go before the God of the universe and ask for forgiveness for your sins. First John 1:9 offers encouragement: "If we confess our sins, he is faithful and just and will forgive us our sins *and purify us from all unrighteousness*" (NIV, emphasis supplied). Note the last six words, which many people forget. Not only will Christ forgive our sins, but He will also *purify* us. What a promise! I encourage you to do a serious study in the New Testament, searching for similar texts that speak of forgiveness. Write them in a notebook. Paraphrase each verse by expressing how each applies to your dilemma. Review these texts whenever you feel overwhelmed by guilt.

When experiencing periods of anger, grief, and guilt, it is healthy to express such feelings to God in prayer. Denying emotions doesn't make them go away, and it often compounds the problem. You may have a combination of pain and guilt from past hurts. If so, you may also need professional Christian counseling.

You need to forgive yourself as well as those who may have influenced you to have the abortions. You may need to express pain individually to those involved or by writing letters to them. This may be an extremely difficult task, but it may help you overcome negative feelings.

While you are healing, remember that God's love for you is unchanging and that He still has a plan for your life. Your past sins didn't forfeit His compassion and love for you. Instead of dwelling on the past or what might have been, get involved in giving of yourself to others. Your counselor can help you select an activity or two that will help you get your mind off yourself. Serving others will help you get over negative thinking about yourself. You can also help yourself by contacting post-abortion support groups. Check the appendix for this information.

Many Bible characters also committed grievous sins. God not only forgave them but also used them in extraordinary ways. Moses, David, and Paul were all responsible for the death of others. In Paul's case, God not only forgave him but also made him into a new person and totally removed his guilt (see 2 Corinthians 5:17).

Remember that healing takes time. It might be a long while before you feel completely free of guilt and grief. Even though you may not always *feel* forgiven, once you have asked for forgiveness, you *are* forgiven and never need ask again.

Now to the issue of whether you should marry your current boyfriend: You shouldn't marry this guy just because your mother has positive feelings toward him. With your history, you shouldn't even think about marriage to *anyone* for two years or longer. You need to get over the trauma of the past and you need to heal before you marry. Right now, you would be offering yourself to this man as a broken, traumatized person.

And please don't get married to "give the baby a name." Babies always get names, whether or not their parents marry. May I suggest the possibility of adoption? It's a valid alternative to abortion or a "shotgun wedding" or single parenting. You should give it careful consideration. Although it is very difficult, it is often in the best interest of both the baby and the mother. But you must come to this conclusion without pressure from others.

The fact that, today, 95 percent of unwed mothers choose to parent their own babies doesn't mean that this is a wise choice. It simply does not work well for the unwed mother to live with her parents, nor should the child have two mothers. Once the baby is born, you will form your own family and should live as a family—not with another family. Yet you will likely be unable to do so for financial reasons. Carefully think through finances, housing, and all the other details and complications of single parenting before making your final choice.

Let me encourage you to make an informed decision by contacting an adoption agency. Look for a Christian agency. Find out how much information the agency is willing to share with you about the adoptive parents. Ask whether the agency will allow you to care for your child during your hospital stay. Acquaint yourself with all the legal steps involved in adoption. Check also whether the agency will allow you to send a memento—such as a letter or an article of clothing—with the new parents to assure the child that he or she was loved and not just rejected. Be aware of the agency's stand and laws about opening closed records in medical emergencies. Ask about putting a letter in your file stating your position should your child search for you sometime in the future. (See the appendix for more information on adopting.)

One final suggestion: *no dating for two years!* Take the next two years to look deep inside yourself and find out who you are and who you want to become. Since you are a slow learner and continually fall into the sexual traps Satan sets for you, you are not ready for a relationship of any kind. Maybe you think that if you don't have a man in your life, you don't have a life. Even worse, maybe you believe that you can't hold on to a man's affection without engaging in sex.

Hopefully, in two years you'll have the maturity to handle a dating relationship and make mature decisions rather than hasty ones. Even then, choose a partner to whom you become accountable for your thoughts and behavior. (See *Smart Love* for more information on this.) And to make certain you don't become sexually involved, a third party must always be present when you're dating. This is drastic, but necessary in your case.

When it comes to sex, is anything we do OK? Is it possible to sin when pleasuring one another even though married?

Dear Nancy: *What's your opinion regarding oral sex? I personally believe that Satan has a counterfeit for everything God has given. Could oral sex be Satan's counterfeit? I need a straight answer.*

Dear Curious: Satan has counterfeits for the good gifts God has given us. I believe pornography is more likely the counterfeit for the beautiful sex act He's given to us. Oral sex has been exploited and glorified by the porn industry as well as by the homosexual and lesbian communities in their search for the ultimate sexual experience. This exploitation might well be termed a counterfeit when used in a selfish, exploitive manner. There is also the possibility that some people could become so focused on oral sex that they can't think of or respond to anything else.

When engaging in oral sex, most couples will include it in a portion of their love play rather than as a substitute for intercourse, unless there is a medical condition that prevents them from having intercourse. A word of caution: Both husband and wife should desire it. Neither should attempt to force the other into any unwanted sex experience. Love never demands its own way. Both should be free to do whatever they both enjoy behind closed doors.

The next questioner obviously feels like a "dirty old man" when performing certain sexual acts.

Dear Nancy: *My wife frequently desires oral sex and is very willing to perform it on me. Although I have engaged in this, I feel very guilty. Isn't oral sex unhealthy? Doesn't it spread disease? Is oral sex a sin?*

Dear Feeling Guilty: The issue of oral sex always has been and always will be a controversial one. And before deciding to engage in it, you should know the facts.

The virus known as herpes simplex III is sometimes present in male and female urogenital tracts. Its presence there causes no health problems, but when it is transferred to other parts of the body, it can cause infection. In most people, the most serious consequences will be a sore similar to a cold sore in the mouth or oral cavity. There is no known cure for this infection. It must run its course; eventually, the sores heal on their own. Discomfort is the major problem.

Oral sex can introduce this virus to the oral cavity and possibly beyond. This virus is not a major health problem; there is no death risk to adults. (It is common practice for obstetricians nowadays to check the vagina for this virus prior to delivery. If the virus is found, the doctor will elect for a Cesarean section because the virus can cause blindness and even death in a newborn. The danger to newborns has no connection with oral sex.)

Some people argue the genitals are dirty because they're found in the area where wastes are eliminated from the body. However, people's mouths harbor more germs than do their genitals when the genitals have been washed, and urine is sterile unless there's an infection in the urinary tract. So, if someone is objecting to oral sex because "it's dirty," that person had better give up kissing too! Let's get back to reality. What's the chance of a totally monogamous couple—neither of whom is engaging in sex with anyone else—getting the herpes virus? Nil. End of conversation.

A couple should decide on whether to include oral sex on the basis of whether it is genuinely pleasurable and agreeable to both parties. When both enjoy it, agree about it, and haven't been having sex outside of marriage for at least the past fifteen years, it is an acceptable practice. No "Thus saith the Lord" in Scripture nor statement in inspired writings says anything about oral sex specifically, much less that it's a sin. The Bible forbids persons of the same sex engaging in sex. Since homosexuals lack the "equipment" to satisfy their sexual desires, they frequently practice oral sex. But the sin there is that they are the same sex.

Since God hasn't made a pronouncement, neither shall I. You should commit yourself to God and not violate your conscience. You should be comfortable with all the sexual practices you try. This is between you, your mate, and God, and no one else. I believe that in their sexual experience, a couple should feel free to do whatever they both enjoy that moves them into a full expression of their mutual love.

Does God hold us to a rigid right or wrong when it comes to sex?

Dear Nancy: *I've read what you have to say about oral sex. I'm curious. Do the same guidelines apply to anal sex?*

Dear Curious: Anal sex presents a problem different from that presented by oral sex. The colon of every healthy human contains the bacteria *Escherichia coli,* commonly known as E. coli. These bacteria are present to aid in the final breakdown of fecal material before elimination. In a healthy individual, the colonies of E. coli cause no problem, and, in fact, their absence would cause problems. However, when transferred to other parts of the body, E. coli bacteria can cause serious infections. Through anal sex, the penis can spread these bacteria, enabling them to travel up the urinary tract to the bladder and/or kidneys. They can also enter the reproductive organs, causing infection in the uterus, fallopian tubes, ovaries, or any site along the way.

The bacteria can also enter the urinary tract of the male and travel to his bladder and/or kidneys. Or they may enter his reproductive system: the seminal vesicles, prostate gland, and/or testicles. The resulting infection can be serious and difficult to cure. If the couple engages in oral sex following anal sex, they may expose more systems of the body to possible infection. In addition, anal sex damages the tissues of the rectum.

Now, you have the facts. You and your partner will have to decide for yourselves whether you wish to engage in anal sex and risk infection.

Does everything and anything go in the bedroom? Or are there limits to sexual freedom?

Dear Nancy: *My husband lived a fairly colorful life before we married, and he enjoys anal sex. I abhor it, although I've engaged in it several times just to please him. Is there any substantial evidence that anal sex is harmful?*

Dear Worried Wife: The one exception to the "anything goes when both partners enjoy it" rule is anal sex. And doubly so when your husband has had a "colorful" past. Anal sex poses the danger of HIV infection when any couple has not had an exclusive relationship. Let me give you some basic facts about this. Anal sex is the most efficient sexual means of HIV transmission. It's also an easy way to spread hepatitis and all other STDs. The rectal mucous membranes seem to have more receptors to bind to HIV, and the tissue is more easily torn or broken, leading to easier transmission of HIV and STDs.

In heterosexual anal sex, the female is at higher risk because while the male is exposed to any disease organisms present only through the head of the penis, the female is exposed through the entire lining of the rectum. Additionally, the female retains any infected secretions within her body, while the male is exposed only during the actual sex act. Furthermore, the rectum lining is thin and fragile and is not made to handle thrusting. In fact, it's made to absorb the water in feces. Also, when thrusting takes place in the rectum, small breaks or tears can occur, allowing infected semen directly into the bloodstream of the recipient. This may also start autoimmune problems.

Another infection commonly transmitted through anal sex is HPV—condyloma, or genital warts. These condyloma, or genital warts, can be very uncomfortable. One study at a university health center showed that 46 percent of sexually active coeds were infected with HPV, which is associated with the development of anal cancers. A man may not even be aware that he has a wart until his partner develops an abnormality. A man may ignore a small growth or may not want to admit that he has one, and it is difficult for his partner to know that he has an infection. The HPV infection can be passed from one person to the other regardless of whether or not the warts are visible. Some warts on men can be treated easily, but others need repeated treatment. Sometimes the use of a laser or surgery may be necessary.

Anal sex is different from other sex practices due to the risks involved and the fact that your husband had a "colorful" past. It poses too many risks.

A worried man wrote the following:

Dear Nancy: *Leviticus 15:19-23 says a menstruating woman is unclean. It says that she should be "put apart" for seven days, and whoever touches her shall be unclean until that night. What are your views about having sex while a woman is menstruating?*

Dear Worried About Menstruation: The verses mentioned do call a menstruating woman "unclean." But these are ceremonial laws, which no longer apply. In addition, sanitary conditions have vastly improved since Bible times. Women can bathe daily now. Methods of caring for the issue of blood differ greatly now from when people were camping on a desert where water was scarce.

The potential disadvantage of sex during a woman's menstruation is possible infection through her reproductive organs. But if you're worried about infection, you'd probably be better off not to kiss your wife, because the mouth contains more germs than do clean genitals! Furthermore, some authorities go so far as to recommend sex and orgasm for the female during menstruation. The contractions accompanying orgasm help reduce the discomfort and pain associated with menstruation. Outside of being a little messy, there are few known disadvantages. But remember, all sexual experiences should be those both husband and wife desire. Neither should force the other to do anything he or she doesn't want to do. Love doesn't force.

Many Christians have concerns regarding masturbation. Read on.

Dear Nancy: *I am a forty-five- year-old male, married, with two children. I've been masturbating since I was ten years old. When I married, I continued this practice in addition to married sex. As I age, I find that masturbating is my preference. Sex is OK, but it is so much work, and pleasuring myself is much easier and faster and my orgasms are more intense. I've read some material that leads me to believe that masturbating can harm me physically and emotionally. Last month my wife caught me in the act. She was horrified. She thinks masturbating is a sin. I don't see a problem with it. What do you think? I'm confused.*

Dear Confused: The subject of masturbation stirs up a good bit of controversy among God's saints. The Bible doesn't mention masturbation. The story told in Genesis 38:2-10 of Onan spilling his seed on the ground doesn't refer to masturbation. According to the custom of the country, it was Onan's duty to marry his widowed sister-in-law, Tamar. He refused and spilled his semen on the ground to keep from producing offspring for his brother. According to Scripture, what he did was wicked. He refused to do his duty, acted rashly, and because of his sin, died without leaving an heir. But this incident didn't involve masturbation. Onan used what we would term "withdrawal" to keep from impregnating Tamar.

To help us understand what masturbation is, let's first clarify what it is not: It is not a child's examination of his or her own genitals. It is as natural for young children to examine their genitals as it is for them to examine their fingers and toes. Masturbation is not something husbands and wives do for each other during lovemaking. People have used the term *mutual masturbation* to refer to a couple stimulating each other sexually, usually to the point of orgasm. This is a misnomer because masturbation is an act of self-stimulation. Nor is masturbation the nocturnal emissions commonly called "wet dreams" that most young men experience after puberty. A nocturnal emission is an involuntary release of seminal fluid after this fluid has accumulated in the seminal vesicles.

What then is masturbation? It is stimulation of one's own genitals, usually to the point of sexual climax. It is a sexual activity that involves only one person. The drive toward masturbation usually reaches maximum intensity between the ages of three and six years of age, subsides and reappears at age eleven or twelve, when it increases in intensity once again.

Before 1950, people thought masturbation caused insanity, deafness, blindness, epilepsy, baldness, weight loss, weakness, and sterility. Children who were caught "in the act" were often beaten and warned that they would go to hell because of it. And most authorities reported only the ill effects of masturbation. There are still, within the ranks of conservative Christendom, those who consider it be one of the most vile and sinful vices one can practice. However, current society as a whole has come to decry the idea that masturbation might have the slightest influence on mind, body, or morals. The majority of professionals in medicine, social services, and the field of psychology actually encourage it. However, little investigation has been done to determine the safety of this practice that some now recommend so freely.

It is highly unlikely that a single or even an occasional act of masturbation would lead to insanity, deafness, blindness, epilepsy, or any of the other illnesses listed any more than would intercourse in marriage have deleterious effects on a married couple. However, many who masturbate do so several times daily or weekly—many more times than a couple engages in sexual intercourse, at least after the first few months of marriage.

Over the years, bits and pieces of research have reported some ill effects. Most of this research reports only the opinions of the authors. In 1978, the medical journal *Patient Care* suggested that if boys or girls complained of genital problems or lower abdominal pain, they should be questioned about masturbation.[1] An Australian report suggested that anxiety resulting from masturbation and guilt associated with it plays a major role in frigidity and impotence later in life.[2] Other research found that in 120 persons ages 22 to 38, blood pressure levels increased in all cases when they were masturbating. The researchers commented on the apparent stress that resulted in the discharge of epinephrine and norepinephrine from all adrenergic nerve endings in the body and brain. Laboratory tests found an increased level of both hormones after masturbation.[3] And another journal reported the rupture of a berry aneurysm with sub-arachnoid hemorrhage during masturbation.[4]

Again, the frequency with which a person masturbates likely plays a part determining whether an illness or other malady results. Certainly, any behavior, including masturbation, that people engaged in continuously, repetitively, and compulsively, would have pathological effects. And masturbation engaged in while viewing pornographic material or while fantasizing about someone other than a spouse would not qualify as marital faithfulness. Pornography and masturbation go hand in hand. The use of such materials to stimulate erotic fantasies flies in the face of all that the Bible says sex can and should be.

God's ideal for the ultimate of sexual expression for husband and wife is that of mutuality. According to Genesis 2:18, 21-24, men and women were created for companionship and to establish a permanent commitment to each other in love. The physical union of their bodies was meaningful within the setting of permanency and love. Scripture indicates that a person is not just a body that can be detached from the totality of his or her being, to function only for pleasure, for sexual satisfaction. People can't separate their personal value system from their bodies. Doing so would dehumanize the body, mar one's self-image, and carve permanent scars on the soul. A lone act of sex without love and permanent commitment is spiritually, morally, and emotionally degrading.

Now, where do you see yourself fitting into the big picture? It's your body, your marriage, your sexuality, and your future. You have to make the final decision. Remember, God won't leave you to struggle alone. He promises, "No temptation has seized you except what is common to man. And God is faithful; he will not let you be tempted beyond what you can bear. But when you are tempted, he will also provide a way out so that you can stand up under it" (1 Corinthians 10:13).

Is this mother worrying over nothing? Or is something really wrong?

Dear Nancy: *My husband and I have been married six years and have a little girl who is two and a half years old. I am a nurse who works three nights a week. My mother cares for Chelsea while I work. She insisted I ask you about her concern for Chelsea's welfare. Mom says that when my husband picks Chelsea up, she will claw to get away from him. She says that Chelsea acts as if she is scared of him. She claims that Chelsea prefers to go to anyone but her daddy and that she will run to Nana crying, "No! No! No!"*

I've never seen this behavior in my daughter when she is around her daddy. I allow Chelsea to go with him, and she never acts that way. Although my husband had a strict and physically abusive father, he has never shown any abusive behavior toward Chelsea. I do remember one time when he tried to kiss her and she cried, "No!" He kissed her anyway, and she screamed, "Owie!" He walked off, and that was the end of it.

My husband is a recovering alcoholic and went to Alcoholics Anonymous meetings when we first married. He doesn't attend now. I want to protect my daughter and do what is right. Do you see anything I don't see that indicates he could be a child molester?

Dear Wants to Protect Daughter: With no more facts than you present here, I see no evidence of child abuse. It is only natural for a two-year-old child not to want to leave her mommy or her grandmother with whom she spends a lot of time. But I suggest that you get as clear a picture as possible from your husband as to what is actually happening.

You say that you have checked your daughter for any bruises, rashes, or other evidence of physical or sexual abuse and found nothing. There are certain other signs that indicate a need to get further information. Here are some of the major ones:

- Inappropriate sex play with dolls or toys, drawing naked bodies, speaking or acting seductively, or sexual aggression.
- Behavioral changes at home or school, such as withdrawal or rebelliousness; your feeling that "something is not quite right."
- Sleep disturbances, nightmares, bed-wetting, or fear of the dark.
- Regression to infantile behavior, excessive crying, thumb sucking, or withdrawal into fantasy.
- Clinging behavior or fear of being left alone.
- Depression.
- Lack of appetite or overeating.
- Psychosomatic illnesses.
- Body or skin irritation, pain or injury.
- Torn or stained underclothing.
- Aggressive or disruptive behavior.
- Running away.
- Failing in school.

The profile of a family in which sexual child abuse might be a problem would most likely show a combination of the following characteristics:

- There is a stepfather or live-in boyfriend.
- One of the parent figures was molested as a child or lived in a home where a sibling was molested.

- The family is isolated, doesn't have a network of friends or family, and the family members appear to be "loners."
- There is poor communication in the family, especially between spouses.
- There is little if any intimacy between the mother and father.
- The family is very religious and attends a fundamentalist church. The religion emphasizes a strong patriarchal system in which the father's word is law.
- The family does not go outside itself to meet any of its needs.

If at any point there is a sudden change in your daughter's behavior, you'll want to check it out. (See appendix for more suggestions.)

How should you respond when you think sexual abuse may be occurring but you have no proof?

Dear Nancy: *I am a pastor confronted with a problem that I don't know how to handle. In our church, we have an active Pathfinder program. One of the Pathfinder girls told a friend that the male Pathfinder director has been molesting her. This friend told her mother, and the mother has come to me. The girl who made the charges is a little on the wild side and may not be telling the truth.*

What complicates this even more is that the Pathfinder director and his wife have just bought and moved into a large home with a garage. They're planning to remodel the garage and turn it into the Pathfinder building, and we've allocated church funds to make this possible. If the funds are withdrawn, everyone will have to know why, and the whole thing could blow up in our faces. This man has been director of the club for three years. To my knowledge, there have been no other incidents or allegations against him. He is well liked and respected in the community. I feel helpless and ill equipped to handle this one.

Dear Ill-Equipped Pastor: It is never easy to process charges of sexual misconduct within the church. Here are some broad guidelines that will assist you:

1. Take a respected female church leader with you to visit the girl in question. (I suggest a female because the girl may be intimidated if two men do the interviewing. You will likely need to go to a private place so that the girl can talk without distraction.) Interview the girl directly to establish whether the allegations are plausible. Let her tell you about the sexual abuse. Don't attempt to interrogate her or to lead her in what she says. Children

often want to talk about the experience to relieve the burden of keeping it a secret. Encourage the girl to express her feelings.

2. Remain calm and nonjudgmental. It is very important that you not express negative feelings toward what you hear or about any person involved.

3. Let the girl know you believe her story.

4. If the allegations are not frivolous and appear sound, go directly to the offender. Unless he resigns as director of the Pathfinder club, you must suspend him until further notice, regardless of his protests of innocence.

5. As the pastor of both of these individuals, you should send each a loving letter expressing concern and spiritual support on behalf of the church. When the conduct is against a child, as in this case, the letter should advise the alleged offender that he is to have no more contact with children within the church setting until further notice.

6. The alleged offender must be supervised at all church functions. He must be accountable for his whereabouts and behavior at all church functions to some church elder that you or the board of elders selects.

7. Document all your visits, letters, and other communications with each party.

8. Most states require that when a minor child is involved, you must report the incident to child protective services or law enforcement within a specified period. Legal counsel can tell you what that period is.

9. Under certain circumstances, you may need to disclose facts to your church membership. Seek advice from conference administration and, if necessary, legal counsel before disclosing any information outside of the parties involved. You shouldn't make any disclosure unless you have concrete information regarding known facts. Your purpose then is to inform parents so that they may protect their children and/or enhance the congregation's healing process.

10. If at any stage you determine that the church may be exposed to legal action, consult with your conference administration.

Since on the average, child molesters abuse about 360 children before they're caught and stopped, responsible leaders must take allegations seriously and do all they can to protect the innocent. Your first responsibility is to discover whether the accusation is true. This responsibility supersedes any responsibility you may feel to protect the reputation of the Pathfinder director. Hurt feelings are inevitable, but to arrive at factual truth as quickly as possible is essential.

Just as soon as you have *any evidence* that the allegations are true, you should *immediately* report them to child protective services (see appendix). In many states, failure to do so could lead to felony charges. While it may be true that the director's move to a new home will provide adequate space for the club to meet, it is just as plausible that the move was motivated essentially to provide greater access to potential victims. Act now!

A shocking secret revealed in the next letter is confusing a father and mother.

Dear Nancy: *My wonderful and successful twenty-eight-year-old son dropped a bombshell on our family last week. He told us he is leaving his beautiful wife and two small children for a man he has been "in love with" for several years. We've tried to talk some sense into him, but he says he always knew he was gay but he didn't know what to do about it. His father and I are so shocked that we don't know what to do or say. His wife is devastated. We are very confused about what attitude we should have toward him. Did we do something to cause this? How can we support him in what obviously is a deeply ingrained attraction to members of his own sex?*

Dear Shocked: Your letter is touching. I can only imagine the pain you are currently suffering. You weren't aware of your son's identity crisis, but even when parents are aware, they don't know what to do about it. There is even more pain—for both parents and child—when the child has grown up in a Christian home. Both you and your son are likely suffering from intense guilt.

Some authorities have associated homosexuality with a son's poor relationship with his father, difficulty in separating from his mother, and a lack of feeling masculine. Other issues contribute to homosexuality. A major one is early sexual abuse; some 30 percent of homosexuals say they were abused as children. All the causes of homosexuality remain unclear.

The homosexual believes he has always been "different from others" and been misunderstood by others. Did you do something to cause this? Who knows. Can you rectify it now? No. Will it help to fall into major depression and whip yourself until the Lord returns? No. The best thing you can do for yourselves and for him is to get yourself into a support group for the parents of homosexuals (see appendix). Such a group will provide an outlet for your pent-up emotions and give you the emotional support you need while you are adjusting to his chosen lifestyle.

Please note: There is *no evidence* to support the idea that there is a "homosexual gene," that it is genetic or unchangeable. Contrary to popular opinion, homosexuality is not inherited, nor are homosexuals "born that way." *And it is possible to change.* I know people who have changed their sexual orientation, and many more homosexuals than I know have successfully modified their behavior, identity, and what turns them on sexually. Exodus International (see appendix) is doing an outstanding job of helping those who want help.

You can't force your son to get help. And you can't change him yourself. Your task during this difficult time is to get support, get educated about homosexuality, and stay on your knees. And, as difficult as it might be, you must maintain your relationship with him as well as with his wife and your grandchildren. Should he ever wish to "come home," he'll need that relationship. And his wife and children need you now as they never have before. Be strong.

Putting It All Together

I've discovered that if left to their own instincts, families will take the route of least resistance. Left to their own inclinations, husbands and wives will join ranks with the one out of every two families that ends up in divorce court instead of working through their problems. I've also discovered that in order to live successfully as a family, we must check with the Master Architect of the family, who has left us in His Word a blueprint for family living.

When we're armed with His Word, we can work through the problems that arise rather than running from them. The continuance of family ties just *must* come to mean more to us than splitting them because of personal unhappiness or some inconvenience we are temporarily enduring. While we may face trials, outbursts, sharp words, injustices, unmet needs, and frustrated feelings, we must come to recognize that building a successful family—what I call a highly effective family—is a *career*, a lifelong project.

The challenge for you today, then, is to follow God's leading so closely that others will see God's power at work in your life and in your family. Friends and neighbors will begin asking questions about the secrets of your success, and they'll listen to your response. When people see something that works in the lives of others, they stop, take notice, and ask questions.

Yes, the changes that occur in your family can have a profound effect on others. Yet home can be the most difficult place on earth to practice something new! But it's there—where things may seem the most hopeless, where others seem to work against you, and where you are the most tired and face the most trials—that you must begin to improve things. Every family member, of course, plays a vital role in the interplay of a successful family. But since I have access to no one but you, and you can control no one else's behavior but your own, you must do what you can to enrich your home. You have a tremendous power to make your home approximate more closely God's idea of what a family should be.

You can find a better way of living if you're willing to open the door to change. No matter how shattering your family problems may be at present, you can have hope. Even if you are teetering on the brink of separation, divorce, despair, or despondency, you can discover healing. You can put into effect methods of stabilizing your life so that you will be strong enough to withstand the stresses of everyday living. You can do this even if you're the only one in your family committed to trying!

This may seem a bit idealistic to you. You may be countering, "But you don't know what I've got to deal with at home!" I may not be aware of your specific circumstances, but one thing I can tell you: Other families have dealt with similar problems. And no one said it would be easy! There are no instant cures, no magic potions that will solve everything overnight. But if you follow God's plan for your life, you will learn how to act toward family members in such a way that you will elicit a more positive response from them. And if you have a good relationship now, it will get even better.

Because I deal with families all day every day, I see much heartache. I see hurt beyond the wildest imagination. But I also see healing. And miracles! What lies ahead, then, is up to you. You can stay where you are, or you can look up. You can say, "Lord, I can't" or "Lord, I will." God and you can make those changes happen.

---

1. See *Patient Care,* October 15, 1978, 105.

2. *Australian Family Physician* (May 1976), 5:529–533.

3. *Indian Journal of Physiology and Pharmacology* 20 (October-December 1976), 4:226–230.

4. *Japanese Journal of Legal Medicine* (January 1972), 26:42–45.

Appendix

Chapter 1: When Holy Wedlock Becomes Unholy Deadlock

Organizations, hotlines, and Web sites

Al-Anon/Alateen World Service Office
1600 Corporate Landing Parkway
Virginia Beach, VA 23454-5617
Telephone: 1-888-4AL-ANON
(1-888-425-2666)
Web site: <http://www.alanon.alateen.org>

La Hacienda Treatment Center
2100 Kramer Road, Suite 200
Austin, TX 78727
Telephone: 512-835-1994
Email: <info@lahcsolutions>
   This is a superior treatment center for alcoholism and other chemical dependencies.

Binding the Wounds Seminar
Ron and Nancy Rockey
Telephone: 888-940-0062
Email: <rockeys@itsfixable.com>
Web site: <http://www.itsfixable.com>

The Binding the Wounds seminar helps people overcome life-long, agonizing, destructive behaviors and offers tools for repairing broken relationships. The Connecting seminar, designed to follow Binding the Wounds, offers participants a prescription for recovery from wounds received during childhood, providing hope for a positive future.

Cognitive Behavior Therapy (CBT)
Web site:
<http://www.cognitivetherapy.com/basics.html>
   Dozens of controlled clinical trials have established the effectiveness of CBT as the preferred treatment for most emotional, behavioral, and relationship problems.

National Association of Cognitive-Behavioral Therapists
P.O. Box 2195
Weirton, WV 26062
Telephone: 800-853-1135

Web site: <http://www.nacbt.org>

Contact information for CBT therapists in your area.

Other Christian counselors

New Life Ministries (Christian Counseling Center)
P.O. Box 866997
Plano, TX 75086
Telephone: 800-639-5433

Call or write to locate a New Life clinic in your area.

Focus on the Family
Colorado Springs, CO 80995
Telephone: 800-A-FAMILY (232-6459)
Web site: <http://www.family.org>

Ask for counseling referral. Focus on the Family offers expert advice on financial planning, retirement, health service opportunities, spiritual growth, inspiration, and humor.

Christian Association for Psychological Studies (CAPS)
Randolph K. Sanders., Ph.D., Executive Director
CAPS International
P.O. Box 310400
New Braunfels, TX 78131-0400
Telephone: 830-629-2277
Fax: 830-629-2342
Email: <capsintl@compuvision.net>

This is a referral service of counselors.

Fuller Psychological and Family Services
The Psychological Center
180 North Oakland Avenue
Pasadena, CA 91101

Telephone: 626-584-5555

Counselors are available by appointment.

Biola Counseling Center
The Biola Professional Building
12625 La Mirada Boulevard, Suite 202
La Mirada, CA 90638
Telephone: 714-903-4800

Counselors are available by appointment.

Co-dependency

Web site:
<http://www.adventistrecoverynetwork.org>

Co-Dependents Anonymous, Inc.
P.O. Box 33577
Phoenix, AZ 85067-3577
Telephone: 602-277-7991
Web site: <http://www.coda.org/newcom.html>

The Bridge Fellowship
1745 Logsdon Road
Bowling Green, KY 42101
Telephone: 877-866-8661
Web site: <http://www.thebridgetorecovery.com>

The Bridge is a residential facility specializing in short- and long-term programs that jump-start people's recovery from negative behavior patterns that sabotage their lives and relationships. Other specialties include working with self-esteem issues and "clean addictions," such as work, sex, and food.

Marriage seminars

Highly Effective Marriage Seminar
Telephone: 559-325-2006
Web site: <http://www.heartnhome.com>

This dynamic, ten-hour seminar deals with

critical issues within the marriage relationship. This seminar is also available on audio CDs and as a fee-based online seminar. Order through <http://www.heartnhome.com>.

Clearinghouse for marriage courses
Web site: <http://www.smartmarriages.com>

Books
Dobson, James C. *Love Must Be Tough*. Waco: Word Books, 1983.
Harley, Willard F., Jr. *His Needs, Her Needs: Building An Affair-Proof Marriage*. Grand Rapids: Fleming H. Revell, 1986.
McGraw, Phillip. *Relationship Rescue*. New York: Hyperion, 2000.
Van Pelt, Nancy. *Get Organized—Seven Secrets to Sanity for Stressed Women*. Hagerstown, Md.: Review and Herald Publishing Association, 1998.
Van Pelt, Nancy. *Highly Effective Marriage*. Hagerstown, Md.: Review and Herald Publishing Association, 2000.
Van Pelt, Nancy. *Smart Listening for Couples*. Grand Rapids: Baker Book House Co., 2003.

CDs and videotapes
Van Pelt, Nancy. *Highly Effective Marriage Seminar*. Five audio CDs obtainable from Web site <http://www.heartnhome.com>.
Van Pelt, Nancy. *His Needs/Her Needs* and *Why Can't My Partner Understand What I Say?* CDs and VHS tapes obtainable from Web site <http://www.heartnhome.com>.
Van Pelt, Nancy. *Love, Sex, and Lasting Relationships*. Audio CD and VHS tapes obtainable from Web site <http://www.heartnhome.com>.

Chapter 2: Strangers in the Night
Erectile dysfunction
American Foundation for Urologic Disease
1000 Corporate Boulevard, Suite 410
Linthicum, MD 21090
Telephone: 410-689-3990 or 800-828-7866
Web site: <http://www.afud.org>
Provides free information and treatment options.

Impotence Information Center
Telephone: 800-843-4315
Provides free literature.

Impotence Institute of America & Impotence Anonymous
Telephone: 800-669-1603

Sexual Function Advisory Council of the American Foundation for Urologic Disease
Web site: <http://www.impotence.org>
This Web site lists services where people can obtain accurate, unbiased information provided confidentially.

Other erectile dysfunction Web sites: <http://www.menstuff.org/issues/byissue/erectile.html>; <http://www.healthcentral.com/bcp/main.asp?=408&brand=9&page=newsdetail&id=513356>

Premature ejaculation
Premature ejaculation information Web sites: <http://www.sexhealthinplainenglish.com/men_articles/premature_ejaculation/premature_ejaculation_1.htm>; <http://ejaculation.all-sexualhealth.com/>

Sexual addictions
Exodus International
P.O. Box 540119
Orlando, FL 32854
Telephone: 888-264-0877 or 407-599-6872
Web site: <http://www.exodus-international.org>

Sex Addicts Anonymous (S.A.A.)
ISO of SAA
P.O. Box 70949
Houston, TX 77270
Telephone: 800-477-8191
Email: <info@saa-recovery.org>
Web site: <http://www.saa-recovery.org>

Sexaholics Anonymous International Central
   Office
P.O. Box 3565
Brentwood, TN 37024
Telephone: 615- 370-6062 or toll free 866-424-8777
Email: <saico@sa.org>
Web site: <http://www.sca-recovery.org>

Sexual Compulsives Anonymous
P.O. Box 1585
New York, NY 10011
Telephone: 800-977-HEAL (international +1 212-606-3778)
Email: <anon7901@anon.twwells.com>
   A twelve-step fellowship designed to help people stop acting out addictive sexual behavior.

Sex and Love Addicts Anonymous
Fellowship-Wide Services
P.O. Box 338
Norwood, MA 02062-0338
Telephone: 781-255-8825

Fax: 781-255-9190
Email: <slaafws@slaafws.org>
Web site: <http://www.slaafws.org>
Sex Offenders Anonymous (SOANON)
Van Nuys, CA 91409
Telephone: 818-244-6331

Codependents of Sexual Addictions (COSA)
Web site: <http://www.cosa-recovery.org>
   Deals with issues of codependency with sex and relationship addicts.

Recovering Couples Anonymous (RCA)
Web site:
<http://www.recovering-couples.org>
   Help for rebuilding trust and intimacy.

S-ANON International Family Groups
Web site: <http://www.sanon.org>
   Deals with issues of codependency with sex addicts.

The Augustine Fellowship of Sex and Love
   Addicts Anonymous (SLAA)
Web site: <http://www.slaafws.org>
   Deals with issues of obsessive and compulsive sexuality, fantasy, love, and relationships.

Books
Allender, Dan B. *The Wounded Heart—Hope for Adult Victims of Childhood Sexual Abuse*. Colorado Springs: Navpress, 1990.
LaHaye, Tim and Beverly. *The Act of Marriage*. Grand Rapids: Zondervan Publishing House, 1976.
Nedley, Neil. *Depression: The Way Out*. Ardmore: Nedley Publishing, 2001.

Penner, Clifford and Joyce. *The Gift of Sex: A Christian Guide to Sexual Fulfillment.* Waco: Word Books, 1981.

Phillips, Bob. *What to Do Until the Psychiatrist Comes.* Eugene: Harvest House Publishers, 1995.

Van Pelt, Nancy. *Highly Effective Marriage.* Hagerstown, Md.: Review and Herald Publishing Association, 2000. Part 6: "Good Sex Doesn't Just Happen."

Van Pelt, Nancy. *Smart Listening for Couples.* Grand Rapids, Mich.: Baker Book House, 2003. Chapter 7: "Sexually Speaking: Strangers in the Night."

Chapter 3: Smart Advice for Singles Under Pressure

Organizations, hotlines, and Web sites

Al-Anon/Alateen World Service Office
1600 Corporate Landing Parkway
Virginia Beach, VA 23454-5617
Telephone: 888-425-2666
Web site: <http://www.alanon.alateen.org>

Life Innovations, Inc.
PREPARE/ENRICH
P.O. Box 190
Minneapolis, MN 55440-0190
Telephone: 800-331-1661

PREPARE (Premarital Personal and Relationship Evaluation) is an inventory of a couple's compatibility. It predicts with 86 percent accuracy which couples will divorce and with 78 percent accuracy which couples will stay happily married. PREPARE-MC is a test for new marriages that will include stepchildren. PREPARE-CC is a test for cohabiting couples. ENRICH is a test for married couples and those cohabiting, with children of their own. And MATE is a test for couples over the age of 50.

Christian dating services

Adventist Contact
P.O. Box 5419
Takoma Park, MD 20913-0419
Telephone: 301-589-4440
Web site: <http://www.Adventistoptions.com>

Adventist Date
Telephone: +420 605 277 447 (Europe)
Email: <service@adventistdate.org>
Web site: <http://www.adventistdate.org>

An international dating service for Seventh-day Adventists based upon a detailed compatibility test.

Adventist Match.com
800 Steeles Avenue West, Suite B10-253
Thornhill, Ontario, L4J 7G2, Canada

Ebony Choice Adventist Singles
P.O. Box 2747 Nonparell
Sutherlin, OR 97479

Discover
15550 Burnt Store Road #153
Punta Gorda, FL 33955

Discover
PMB #150-PUR
14536 West Center Road
Omaha, NE 68144

Online Christian dating services

<http://www.Adventistsingles.org>

<http://www.Christian911.com>
<http://Christianoptions.com>
<http://ChristianSinglesDating.com>
<http://www.eHarmony.com>
<http://www.ShiningStarSingles.com>
<http://www.ShiningStar.net>
<http://www.Lifepartners.org>
<http://www.Adventistdate.org> (an international dating service)

Books
Cannon, Carol. *Never Good Enough.* Nampa, Idaho: Pacific Press® Publishing Association, 1993.
Van Pelt, Nancy. *Smart Love—A Field Guide for Single Adults.* Grand Rapids: Fleming H. Revell, 1997.

Chapter 4: Systems Gone Wrong
Organizations, hotlines, and Web sites
Adult Children of Alcoholics
P.O. Box 3216
Torrance, CA 90510
Telephone: 310-534-1815 (message only)
Email: <info@adultchildren.org>

Emotions Anonymous International Services
P.O. Box 4245
St. Paul, MN 55104
Telephone: 612-647-9712
Email: <info@EmotionsAnonymous.org>

Exodus International
P.O. Box 540119
Orlando, FL 32854
Telephone: 888-264-0877 or 407-599-6872
Web site: <http://www.exodus-international.org>
    Offers group support for parents of

homosexuals and/or lesbians.

Gambling
Gamblers Anonymous
P.O. Box 17173
Los Angeles, CA 90017
Telephone: 213-386-8789
Email <isomain@gamblersanonymous.org>
Web site: <http://www.gamblersanonymous.org>

Internet accountability
Covenant Eyes
7321 North Shiawassee, Suite B
Corunna, MI 48817
Telephone: 877-479-1119
Email: <info@covenanteyes.com>
Web site: <http://www.covenanteyes.com>

For sexually abused males
Menweb
Web site:
<http://www.menweb.org/sexabupg.htm>
    A Web site for male survivors of childhood sexual abuse. It offers information, articles, and books.

For physical abuse
Childhelp National Headquarters
15757 North 78th Street
Scottsdale, AZ 85260
Telephone: 800-433-4453 (national child-abuse hotline) or 480-922-8212
Web site: <http://www.childhelpusa.org>

National Domestic Violence/Abuse Hotline
P.O. Box 161810
Austin, TX 78716
Telephone: 800-799-7233 or

800-787-3224 TTY
Web site: <http://www.ndvh.org>
Trained volunteers are ready to connect.

On the Wings of a Dove
Web site: <http://www.overcomingviolence.org>
   A worldwide campaign on overcoming violence against women and children.

Polly's Place Ministries
P.O. Box 19471
Spokane, WA 99219
Telephone: 509-624-6333
Email: <retreatcenter@ppmin.org>
Web site: <http://www.ppmin.org>
   A place where abused women and children can experience safety and protection.

Women in Renewal, Inc.
P.O. Box 72
Berrien Center, MI 49102
Telephone: 616-687-9822
Web site: <http:www.womeninrenewal.org>
   A nonprofit organization dedicated to restoring wholeness and well being to families affected by domestic violence.

Rape and incest
Rape, Abuse, and Incest National Network
   (RAINN)
635-B Pennsylvania Avenue Southeast
Washington, DC 20003
Telephone: 800-656-HOPE (4673) or
   202-544-1034
Email: <RAINNmail@aol.com>
Web site: <http://www.rainn.org>
   A system that links callers to the nearest rape crisis center automatically. All calls are confidential, and callers may remain anonymous if they wish.

Books

Allender, Dan B. *The Wounded Heart—Hope for Adult Victims of Childhood Sexual Abuse.* Colorado Springs: Navpress, 1990.

Carter, David. *Torn Asunder.* Chicago: Moody Press, 1992.

Groom, Nancy. *From Bondage to Bonding.* Colorado Springs: Focus on the Family, 1996.

Hall, Laurie. *An Affair of the Mind.* Colorado Springs: Focus on the Family, 1996.

Hunter, Mick. *Abused Boys.* New York: Fawcett Columbine, 1990.

Lew, Mike. *Victims No Longer.* New York: Nevraumont, 1988.

Means, Marsha. *Living With Your Husband's Secret Wars.* Grand Rapids: Fleming H. Revell, 1999.

Vermilyea, Elizabeth. *Growing Beyond Survival: A Toolkit for Managing Traumatic Stress.* Baltimore, Md.: Sidran Institute Press, 2000.

Willingham, Russell. *Breaking Free.* Downers Grove: InterVarsity Press, 1999.

Chapter 5: Raising Sane Kids in an Insane World
Organizations, hotlines, and Web sites
Childhelp USA National Child Abuse Hotline
Telephone: 800-422-4453
Web site: <http://www.childhelpusa.org>

For single parents
Focus on the Family

Telephone: 800-A-FAMILY (800-232-6459)
Web sites: <http://www.family.org>;
<http://www.focusonyourchild.com>

Focus on the Family offers a complimentary special-edition magazine just for single parents. Parents of children under twelve can sign up for the Focus on Your Child membership program to receive age-customized advice in discipline, education, relationships, and more.

Web sites
<http://www.solosingles.com/ssparent>;
<http://www.singleparentcentral.com>;
<http://www.ParentsWithoutPartners.org>;
<http://www.ParentsWorld.com>

Home-school curriculums
K12 Home-School Curriculum
Web site: <http://www.k12.com/homeschool/pricing.html>

Provides pricing and enrollment information.

Switched-On Schoolhouse
P.O. Box 4201
Carlsbad, CA 92018-4201
Telephone: 888-967-3764
Web site: <http://www.discountchristian.com/alphaomega/homeschool.html>

Christian homeschool curriculum on CD-ROM that holds a student's interest.

The Sycamore Tree
2179 Meyer Place
Costa Mesa, CA 92627
Telephone: 714-668-1343
Web site: <http://www.sycamoretree.com>

Email: <info@sycamoretree.com>

Complete accredited homeschool program for children K-12.

Silver State Adventist School
Telephone: 755-322-0714
Web site:
<http://silverstate.org/highschool.htm>

An innovative approach to secondary education, allowing students to take classes online.

Residential-care facilities
Advent Home Youth Services
900 CR 950
Calhoun, TN 37309-5150
Telephone: 423-336-5052
Email:
<adventhome@adventhomeonline.com>

Advent Home is a licensed child-care facility providing residential care, counseling, remedial and accelerated schooling, group therapy, character development, parent training, and placement for twelve- to sixteen-year-old boys with ADHD.

Miracle Meadows School
Rt. 1, Box 289-B
Salem, WV 26426
Telephone: 304-782-3628
Email: <mms@iolinc.net>

This is a school for boys and girls seven to seventeen who are experiencing defiance, dishonesty (lying and stealing), school failure, trouble with the law, alcohol and drug abuse, aggressive and violent behavior, spiritual disinterest, poor social skills, or other harmful behaviors.

Project PATCH Ranch
13455 Southeast 97th
Clackamas, OR 97015
Telephone: 503-653-8086
Web site: <http://www.projectpatch.org>
This is a faith-based residential treatment center that specializes in children with challenges of thinking errors, anger management, authority issues, peer relationships, issues of abandonment or loss, or history of sexual abuse and who have potential for successful treatment.

Solid Rock Ranch
14677 You Bet Road
Grass Valley, CA 95945
Telephone: 530-272-2221
A Christian residential home and school for teenage boys with ADD, ADHD, or ODD.

Provo Canyon School
Campuses in Orem and Provo, Utah
Telephone: 800-848-9819

A self-help organization
TOUGHLOVE International
P.O. Box 1069
Doylestown, PA 18901
Telephone: 215-348-7090
Web sites: <http://www.toughlove.org> (provides general information);
<http://www.toughlove.org/HTML/crisis.htm> (provides crisis assessment)
A self-help organization that provides families with ongoing education and active support, empowering parents and young people to accept responsibility for their actions. They deal with drug and alcohol abuse, family violence, teen pregnancy, suicide, family dissolution, school dropouts, and runaways.

Parenting for stay-at-home moms
Web site: <http://www.lhj.com/lhj/category.jhtml?categoryid=/templatedata/lhj/category/data/WorkAndFamily_StayAtHomeMoms.xml>

Books
Dobson, James. *Bringing Up Boys*. Wheaton, Ill.: Tyndale House, 2001.
Dobson, James. *Hide or Seek*. Grand Rapids: Fleming H. Revell, 1974.
Jensen, Peter. *Making the System Work for Your Child With ADHD*. New York: Guilford Press, 2004.
Magid, Ken, and Carole A. McKelvey. *High Risk—Children Without a Conscience*. New York: Bantam Books, 1989. (Addresses the issues of day care and character-disturbed children)
McKenzie, Robin. *Setting Limits: How to Raise Responsible, Independent Children by Providing Clear Boundaries*. Roseville, Calif.: Prima Publishing, 1998.
Moore, Raymond. *Better Late Than Early*. New York: E. P. Dutton, 1989.
Moore, Raymond. *School Can Wait*. Provo: Brigham Young University Press, 1989.
Van Pelt, Nancy. *Smart Love—Straight Talk to Young Adults About Dating, Love, and Sex*. Clovis, Calif.: Young Life Specialties, 2003.
Van Pelt, Nancy. *Smart Love Sexual Values Discussion Guide for Parents and Teachers*. (Obtainable on the Web site <http://www.heartnhome.com>)

Van Pelt, Nancy. *The Compleat Parent.* Hagerstown, Md.: Review and Herald Publishing Association, 1985 (revised).
Van Pelt, Nancy. *Train Up a Child: A Guide to Successful Parenting.* Hagerstown, Md.: Review and Herald Publishing Association, 1984.
Wiggin, Eric. *The Gift of Grandparenting.* Colorado Springs: Focus on the Family, 2001.

Cassettes
Van Pelt, Nancy. *The Art of Making Sabbath Special*—an audio CD obtainable on the Web site <http://www.heartnhome.com>.
Van Pelt Nancy. *The Compleat Parent*—audio CDs obtainable on the Web site <http://www.heartnhome.com>.
Van Pelt, Nancy. *Seven Stupid Things Parents Do to Mess Up Their Kids*—audio CD and VHS tape obtainable on the Web site <http://www.heartnhome.com>.

Chapter 6: When Your Spouse Says Goodbye
Books
Dobson, Dr. James. *Love Must Be Tough.* Waco: Word Books, 1983.
Phillips, Bob. *What to Do Until the Psychiatrist Comes.* Eugene: Harvest House Publishers, 1995.
Van Pelt, Nancy. *Highly Effective Marriage.* Hagerstown, Md.: Review and Herald Publishing Association, 2000.
Van Pelt, Nancy. *Smart Listening for Couples.* Grand Rapids: Baker Book House Co., 2003.
Van Pelt, Nancy. *Smart Love—A Field Guide for Single Adults.* Grand Rapids: Fleming H. Revell, 1997.

Chapter 7: Hot Potatoes—"Please Help Me Solve This Problem"
Adoption agencies
Adventist Adoption Agency
6040 Southeast Belmont Street
Portland, OR 97215
Telephone: 503-232-1211 or 503-232-2694

Adventist Adoption Agency (Michigan office)
125 College Avenue
P.O. Box C
Berrien Springs, MI 49103
Telephone: 616-471-2221

All God's Children International
3308 Northeast Peerless Place
Portland, OR 97232
Telephone: 800-214-6719
Fax: 503-282-2582
Email: <info@allgodschildren.org>
Web site: <http://www.allgodschildren.org>

Christian Adoption Services (North Carolina)
Telephone: 704-847-0038
Web site: <http://www.christianadopt.org>
Provides help with adoption.

Mandala Adoption Services
6601 Turkey Farm Road
Chapel Hill, NC 27514
Telephone: 800-295-3191
Fax: 919-942-0248
Email:<mandalaadmin@earthlink.net>
Web site: <http://www.mandalaadoption.org>

Christian World Adoption
Telephone: 803-856-0305
Web site: <http://www.cwa.org>

Handles international adoptions from Russia, China, Bolivia, Mexico, and Guatemala.

Focus on the Family
Telephone: 800-A-FAMILY (800-232-6459)
Web sites: <http://www.family.org/pplace/topics/a0025300.cfm>; <http://www.family.org/pregnancy/benevolency/a0029843.cfm>

Focus on the Family offers help with adoption and several free booklets on adoption. This organization also offers several videos in both English and Spanish for those facing unplanned pregnancies.

For those considering abortion
Think About Abortion
Web site: <http://www.thinkaboutitonline.com>

A Web site that offers information, questions, and facts, challenging visitors to consider whether abortion is really a good choice.

For those needing support following an abortion
Post Abortion Support and Healing
Web site: <http://www.afterabortion.com>

Post Abortion Help and Healing
Web site: <http://www.seghea.com/cheryl/arch/page2.html>

Hope After Abortion
Web site: <http://www.hopeafterabortion.com>

Peace After Abortion
Web site: <http://www.peaceafterabortion.com>

Safe Haven

Web site: <http://www.postabortionpain.com>

Heaven's Healing Touch
Web site: <http://www.w-cpc.org/post-abortion/smith.html>

Focus on the Family
Web site: <http://www.family.org/pregnancy/hottopics/A0029709.cfm>

Offers help to those in a difficult pregnancy situation or for those suffering the aftermath of their abortion decision.

For child sexual abuse
National Center for Missing and Exploited Children
Telephone: 800-THE-LOST
Web site: <http://www.cybertipline.com>

To report child sexual exploitation, first call the police, then call the National Center for Missing and Exploited Children.

Child Abuse Hotline
Telephone: 800-792-5200

Child Find of America
Telephone: 800-426-5678 (for help in finding missing and abducted children); 800-292-9688 (for crisis mediation in parental abduction)

ChildHelp/IOF Foresters
Telephone: 800-4-A-CHILD
National child-abuse hotline.

Child Quest International
Telephone: 800-248-8020

For abducted, abused, and exploited children.

Children of the Night
Telephone: 800-564-2686

Covenant House Hotline
Telephone: 800-999-9999
Crisis line for youth, teens, and families.

Crisis Intervention Center
Telephone: 800-333-4444

Domestic Violence Hotline
Telephone: 800-562-6025

Help Now Hotline
Telephone: 800-435-7609

International Child Abuse Network
Telephone: 888-224-4226
National Adolescent Suicide Hotline
Telephone: 800-621-4000

National Domestic Violence/Abuse Hotline
Telephone: 800-799-7233

National Hotline for missing children
Telephone: 800-843-5678

National Youth Crisis Hotline
Telephone: 800-448-4663

New National Domestic Violence Hotline
Telephone: 800-799-SAFE

National Sexual Assault Hotline
Telephone: 800-656-4673

Childhelp USA National Child Abuse Hotline
Telephone: 800-422-4453

Teen Help Inc. Nationwide
Telephone: 800-637-0701
Town National Crisis Line
Telephone: 800-448-3000
Offers help in any type of personal crisis.

Help for victims of incest
Victims of Incest Can Emerge Survivors
  (VOICES) in Action
Telephone: 800-7-VOICE-8
An international organization that provides
assistance to victims of incest and child sexual
abuse.

Survivors of Incest Anonymous (SIA)
Web site: <http://www.siawso.org>
Provides healing and support from child-
hood sexual abuse.

Gambling
Gamblers Anonymous
P.O. Box 17173
Los Angeles, CA 90017
Telephone: 213-386-8789
Web site: <http://www.gamblersanonymous.org/
recovery.html>

For parents of homosexuals or lesbians
Exodus International
P.O. Box 540119
Orlando, FL 32854
Email: <info@exodus-international.org>
Web site: <http://www.exodus-international.org>

Web site: <www.someone-to-talk-to.net>

National Association for Research and
  Therapy of Homosexuality (NARTH)

16633 Ventura Boulevard, Suite 1340
Encino, CA 91436-1801
Telephone: 818-789-4440
Web site: <http://www.narth.com>

Provides understanding of the behavior patterns associated with homosexuality and of its treatment.

Parents and Friends of Ex-Gays (PFOX)
1401 1/2 King Street, Suite 2
Alexandria, VA 22314
Telephone: 703-739-8220
Email: pfox.exgays@usa.net
Web site: <http://www.pfox.org>

Where Grace Abounds
P.O. Box 18871
Denver, CO 80218
Telephone: 303-863-7757
Web site:<http://www.wheregraceabounds.org>
Email: <wga@aol.com>

This organization offers several video series that examine the spiritual, emotional, and psychological wounds that are often at the root of sexual difficulties. These videos also look at the scriptures that address homosex-uality and other issues.

For help with financial problems
Crown Financial Ministries
P.O. Box 100
Gainesville, GA 30503-0100
Telephone: 800-722-1976 (products and materials); 770-534-0100 (general information)
Web site: <http://www.crown.org>

Crown Financial Ministries offers resources and information. This organization has helped transform thousands of lives with God's financial principles.

Books
Burkett, Larry. *Debt-Free Living.* Chicago: Moody Publishers, 2001.
Dellinger, Annetta E. *Adopted and Loved Forever.* St. Louis: Concordia Publishing House, 1987. (This book is meant for children who have been adopted.)
Mazat, Alberta. *That Friday in Eden.* Nampa, Idaho: Pacific Press® Publishing Association, 1981.
Van Pelt, Nancy. *Get Organized—Seven Secrets to Sanity for Stressed Women.* Hagerstown, Md.: Review and Herald Publishing Association, 1998.
Van Pelt, Nancy. *Highly Effective Marriage.* Hagerstown, Md.: Review and Herald Publishing Association, 2000.

If you enjoyed this book, you'll enjoy these also:

Creating Love

Written by *Kay Kuzma,* speaker and director of Family Matters, a ministry for Christian parents, *Creating Love* goes beyond dealing with your children. It goes beyond getting along with your spouse. *Creating Love* offers help for relationships of all kinds. This fascinating book is filled with stories that demonstrate how any relationship can be improved—even your relationship with your co-worker, your roommate, your mother-in-law, or your fellow church member.

    0-8163-1382-2. Paperback.

    US$11.99, Can$17.99.

Belonging

Ron and Nancy Rockey. Based on biblical principles, *Belonging* will set readers on the road to unearthing the source of their personal traumas, which in turn will lead them to a deeper understanding of their own needs and God's ultimate healing. If you're ready to shed your "victim" label, read *Belonging* and start recovering what was taken from you . . . *today!*

    0-8163-1702-X. Paperback.

    US$12.99, Can$19.49.

Order from your ABC by calling **1-800-765-6955**, or get online and shop our virtual store at www.AdventistBookCenter.com.

- Read a chapter from your favorite book
- Order online
- Sign up for email notices on new products